Cyber Security on Azure

An IT Professional's Guide to Microsoft
Azure Security Center

Marshall Copeland

Apress®

Cyber Security on Azure: An IT Professional's Guide to Microsoft Azure Security Center

Marshall Copeland
Castle Rock, Colorado, USA

ISBN-13 (pbk): 978-1-4842-2739-8   ISBN-13 (electronic): 978-1-4842-2740-4
DOI 10.1007/978-1-4842-2740-4

Library of Congress Control Number: 2017947828

Cover image designed by Freepik

Managing Director: Welmoed Spahr
Editorial Director: Todd Green
Acquisitions Editor: Gwenan Spearing
Development Editor: Laura Berendson
Technical Reviewer: Newton Sheikh
Coordinating Editor: Nancy Chen
Copy Editor: Kim Wimpsett
Artist: SPi Global

Distributed to the book trade worldwide by Springer Science+Business Media New York, 233 Spring Street, 6th Floor, New York, NY 10013. Phone 1-800-SPRINGER, fax (201) 348-4505, e-mail orders-ny@springer-sbm.com, or visit www.springeronline.com. Apress Media, LLC is a California LLC and the sole member (owner) is Springer Science + Business Media Finance Inc (SSBM Finance Inc). SSBM Finance Inc is a **Delaware** corporation.

For information on translations, please e-mail rights@apress.com, or visit www.apress.com/rights-permissions.

Apress titles may be purchased in bulk for academic, corporate, or promotional use. eBook versions and licenses are also available for most titles. For more information, reference our Print and eBook Bulk Sales web page at www.apress.com/bulk-sales.

Any source code or other supplementary material referenced by the author in this book is available to readers on GitHub via the book's product page, located at www.apress.com/978-1-4842-2739-8. For more detailed information, please visit www.apress.com/source-code.

Printed on acid-free paper

To my beautiful wife Angela Copeland, 1,000 years and a day! Thank you, mentors and friends, Mark Russinovich, Keith Olinger, Anthony Puca, Julian Soh, Mark Ghazai, Charles Fox, Tara Larson, Steve Finney, Abel Cruz, Ben Callahan, and Darren Carlsen.

Contents at a Glance

About the Author xi

About the Technical Reviewer xiii

Acknowledgments xv

Introduction xvii

■Part I: All Businesses.. 1

■Chapter 1: Cybersecurity: How Security Vulnerabilities Affect Your Business 3

■Chapter 2: Azure Security Center Cost Model 33

■Part II: Cloud Security Operations 53

■Chapter 3: Getting Started with Azure Security Center 55

■Chapter 4: Azure Security Center Configuration 75

■Chapter 5: Azure Security Center Scenarios 105

■Chapter 6: Azure Security Center Extensions...................................... 131

■Appendix A: Troubleshooting and Cyber-Reference 165

■Appendix B: Know Your Enemy... 179

■Appendix C: Security Frameworks 195

Index... 203

Contents

About the Author xi

About the Technical Reviewer xiii

Acknowledgments xv

Introduction xvii

■Part I: All Business 1

■Chapter 1: Cybersecurity: How Security Vulnerabilities Affect Your Business 3

Executive Summary 4

Understanding Attackers' Motivation 8

Remain Current Through Security Facts 11

    Microsoft Security Intelligence Report 12

    Verizon 2017 Data Breach Investigations Report 14

    Verizon 2016 Data Breach Investigations Report 16

    IBM-Sponsored Ponemon Cost of Data Breach Study 20

    Other Annual Security Reports 22

Steps for a Secure Cloud 25

    Azure Cloud Networking, Encryption, Data Storage 26

    Identity Multifactor Authentication 26

    Software Is a Key Vulnerability 26

    OWASP Top Ten Project 26

    Finding Cloud Blind Spots to Improve Your Network Security Knowledge ... 27

    NVD Use with ITIL/Change Management Patching 28

    Security Responsibility Model 29

Summary 31

■**Chapter 2: Azure Security Center Cost Model** **33**

Shared Cost Model 34

License Cost of Security Center 37

Azure Cost of Data Storage 39

Quantitative Risk Assessments and Cost-Benefit Analysis 39

Other Considerations (Security Sensitive) 44

    Azure Active Directory 45

    Azure Support Plans 46

    Application Gateway 46

Enterprise Security Architecture 48

Ransomware Lessons Learned 50

Summary 52

■**Part II: Cloud Security Operations** **53**

■**Chapter 3: Getting Started with Azure Security Center** **55**

Cloud Security Challenges 56

Security Center Overview 57

Security Center Placement 58

    Preventing an Azure Infrastructure Breach 60

    Basic Review of Cybersecurity Practices 61

    Establishing or Improving a Cybersecurity Program 61

    Azure Virtual Networking Example 62

Select an Azure Subscription 64

    Navigating Microsoft Azure 71

Summary 73

■**Chapter 4: Azure Security Center Configuration** **75**

Azure Infrastructure Design 76

Azure Security Center Pricing Tier 83

Standard Tier Advantages 85

    Advanced Threat Detection 85

Anomaly Detection...86

Crash Analysis 86

Threat Intelligence..86

Behavioral Analysis...87

Using Security Center...96

Summary...104

Chapter 5: Azure Security Center Scenarios 105

Security Health Monitoring..106

Security Recommendations Procedures 109

Prevention Blade 117

Network Security Groups...119

Summary...130

Chapter 6: Azure Security Center Extensions................................ 131

Security Center Updates..131

Detection and Security Alerts..133

Recommendations 142

Next-Generation Firewalls...152

Vulnerability Assessment Integration 157

Summary...164

Appendix A: Troubleshooting and Cyber-Reference 165

Azure Security Center Diagnostics Troubleshooting.........................165

Cyber-Reference...174

What's in a Name...175

Glossary..175

Definitions 175

Security, Identity, and Cryptography 176

Attack Method 177

Appendix B: Know Your Enemy... 179

Professional Education...180

Security Risk Landscape 183

Understanding Cybersecurity Attack Details 188

Now to the Why and How Cyber-Attacks Are Achieved 189

Appendix C: Security Frameworks 195

Security Awareness Models 195

NIST 800-50 195

NIST 800-14 196

European Model 197

Summary 197

Analysis of Security Strategies and Frameworks 198

Zachman Framework 198

Sherwood Applied Business Security Architecture (SABSA) 199

The Open Group Architectural Framework (TOGAF) 200

Summary 200

Index 203

About the Author

Marshall Copeland is a security architect focusing on cloud cybersecurity services, multifactor authentication (MFA), cryptography, hybrid cloud network security, and federated services integration. Marshall obtained his master's of information assurance degree (MSIA) from Dakota State University and currently supports Fortune 50 companies with his security planning and deployment expertise. He previously worked at Microsoft Corporation and Level 3 Communications; he has been a security speaker at Microsoft Global Azure Bootcamp, Microsoft Management Summit, and Microsoft TechReady, and he regularly attends advanced cybersecurity training from industry-recognized professionals. Marshall is an active member in the Austin Texas, security community supporting organizations such as ISSA and OWASP, and he is the founder of AustinCyber.com, a site designed to help new IT and transitioning IT professionals prepare for security careers. Marshall cowrote *Microsoft Azure: Planning, Deploying, and Managing Your Data Center in the Cloud* and *Microsoft Office 365 Administration Inside Out.*

About the Technical Reviewer

Newton Sheikh is a consultant for cloud and distributed computing with a focus on Microsoft Azure. He is a .NET developer and a security expert for infrastructure services running on the cloud. Newton has been writing code on .NET and for the Web for five years. His interests are mathematics and algorithms.

Newton enjoys coding, designing, and architecturing solutions for the Web and the cloud. With a keen interest in game design, he has worked on multiple platforms, including XNA, Android, and iOS. He loves to try new, lightweight, and powerful game engines.

Most recently, he has taken up photography as a hobby and loves to carry his camera on his travels.

Acknowledgments

First, thank you to Gwenan Spearing, Laura Berendson, and Nancy Chen at Apress for their support in completing this book. Thank you to the fantastic technical editor, who made sure this book provides a good depth of technical detail and a greater level of accuracy.

Thank you to Microsoft Corporation and the Microsoft Azure team for creating a fantastic global cloud solution and to the Azure Security Center product team. Thank you to the companies that provide cybersecurity data resources such as the Microsoft Security Intelligence Report (released twice a year since 2006), National Vulnerability Database, Verizon Data Breach Investigations Report, IBM-sponsored Ponemon Cost of Data Breach Study, Cisco Annual Security Report, FireEye M-Trends 2017 Annual Security Report, and Georgia Tech Emerging Cyber Threats Report.

Introduction

Cybersecurity for a Cloud Infrastructure

Information technology (IT) is integrated into the fabric of a business, and without business there is no requirement for IT. In fact, there should not be IT processes without mirror business processes; the processes are interwoven to support the solid financial growth and sustainability of the business. The same is true for security beyond the traditional IT focus. Cybersecurity specifically pushes security beyond IT processes, procedures, governance, infrastructure design, and authentication. Cybersecurity protection, intrusion detection, intrusion prevention, and cyber-incident response all must also be integrated into the business fabric.

This book is a result of multiple customers of mine requesting guidance and best practices for cybersecurity as they move into the cloud. Security-focused businesses have invested in on-premises, layered security to protect their networks, systems, users, and customer data, and now as these businesses move into the cloud, they need to follow a hybrid, layered security approach. This book answers questions such as the following: What security options are available in the cloud for virtual networks, and how can they be audited? As you move virtual machines into cloud virtual subnets, how do you enable intrusion detection? Do you need to ask the board of directors for a budget increase to hire cybersecurity experts? IT has invested heavily in security standards for the business in a local datacenter; can you extend those standards and knowledge base to the cloud? The answer to each of these questions is a resounding yes, with Microsoft Azure Security Center.

This book was written for the following types of people:

- Chief information officers (CIOs) and chief information security officers (CISOs)

- IT subject-matter experts (SMEs)

- Cybersecurity teams

For CIOs/CISOs, the information in this book builds up trust when moving to the cloud, as follows:

- Trust in your team's ability to provide detection and protection against cyber-attacks in the cloud

- Trust that security risks are identified and reduced as business services are migrated to the cloud

- Trust that your customers' data is safe (sometimes safer) in the cloud than on the premises

This book also contains specific information about the total cost of Azure Security Center, cloud storage, and Azure subscriptions in comparison to other solutions. Other financial-related considerations discussed include time and materials for installation, updates, and intrusion detection when evaluating intrusion prevention services (IPSs) and intrusion detection services (IDSs) for use in a hybrid cloud solution from the cybersecurity market.

For IT SMEs, this book provides guided, step-by-step exercises for configuring and using Azure Security Center; it also provides examples of the types of cybersecurity attacks a particular feature is used to protect against. As an SME, you have deep knowledge of virtualization, networking, and infrastructure and can use the information in this book to ramp up quickly on cybersecurity in the cloud. In this book, you'll learn the boundaries of cybersecurity so you can extend cybersecurity requirements as part of your business and become integrated in the security business process.

For cybersecurity teams, this book improves your security posture by guiding you through the mitigation of cyber-risk as corporate "targets" move into the cloud. Besides helping you identify security issues, the book provides how-to steps to achieve best-in-class cloud security. This book also gives you new cybersecurity best practices for daily, weekly, and monthly processes to integrate with your other IT and security daily processes that are currently required to comply with National Institute of Standards and Technology (NIST) guidelines. This book guides cybersecurity team members to use cloud computing by addressing the shared responsibility model for cybersecurity that is required in order to maintain compliancy with PCI-DSS, ISO 27001/2, and other mandates.

Microsoft Azure Security Center, generally available in many Azure regions, offers security monitoring and management for a cloud infrastructure. Using Azure Security Center, you are able to do the following:

- Maintain a holistic view of the cloud resource's security state

- Control cloud security using business policies

- Review and use automated recommendations

- Monitor security configurations and take corrective action

- Deploy integrated security solutions

  - Trend Micro, Barracuda, F5

  - Cisco, Fortinet, Check Point

- Receive alerts based on real threats detected, not false positives, using advanced analytics such as machine learning and behavioral profiling stemming from global threat intelligence assets that span millions of daily security log events

You can stay current with Azure changes by subscribing to updates at `https://azure.microsoft.com/en-us/updates` and reading about the changes that affect your company. Stay up to speed with cybersecurity notifications, such as the WannaCry ransomware, at `https://www.dhs.gov/news/2017/05/12/dhs-statement-ongoing-ransomware-attacks`.

PART I

All Businesses

Cloud technology is truly innovative, offering increased speed to collaborate, communicate, and transform businesses. However, this pace of change also empowers a cyber-criminal's ability to put a business at economic, operational, and reputational risk. So, shouldn't you leverage cloud security services at the same rate of change? Microsoft Azure cloud services, and specifically Microsoft Azure Security Center, provide constant improvements so security architects can remain vigilant and up-to-date when moving their businesses to the cloud.

Part I of this book introduces C-level executives, subject-matter experts, and cybersecurity teams to Microsoft Azure Security Center. Part I also provides businesses with a cost model so they can understand the framework required to organize a security team, and it offers research and methods to evaluate Azure's economic value. The price of a security solution is only a small focus, though, with the bigger picture on identifying advantages of this agile cloud security solution.

CHAPTER 1

Cybersecurity: How Security Vulnerabilities Affect Your Business

Thought Leadership

A secure cloud is your goal, but a secure cloud is not the same as cloud security. When you are expanding your business into the cloud, you should use the information in this book to support your layered security approach to achieve a secure cloud within Microsoft Azure. This chapter benefits chief executive officers (CEOs), chief information officers (CIOs), and chief technical officers (CTOs) with its guidance for understanding the security risks that affect businesses as network teams adopt a hybrid cloud model. If you are a C-level executive, you need foundational security insight to understand a hacker's motivation with factual resources for insightful security data and not just scary statistics. You then need a process to put people into roles and to put roles into practice using a proven cloud security framework that leverages the addition of the secure cloud features found in Azure Security Center. As a CEO, if you are too busy to read all the chapters in this book, at least read this one; it has been crafted to enable your current security team to rapidly expand with the adoption of a defensive cloud security framework.

This chapter also provides chief information security officers (CISOs), security architects, and security analysts with a jump start into a secure cloud by leveraging the same guidance and then expanding with best practices and procedures to integrate with their current security processes. For a security team, the layered, on-premises security model expands into the cloud and requires you to fully understand your adversary's determination to breach your cloud infrastructure. You and your team must learn about the increased availability of attacking tools as services. Many of the current attack tools are leveraging automated deployment, often within minutes after a bitcoin purchase, and some come with a service level agreement (SLA) to be rebuilt if taken down by authorities.

Your business has a board of directors and CEO who provide the high-level requirements for the necessary security policy. After cloud security policies are written, they should be reviewed annually and updated to remain current as the business leveraging the cloud services changes. Security procedures should be created and updated to support the cloud security policies and then used to guide security teams with a "how-to" implementation process. These security procedures should be later reviewed and audited by third-party auditors to validate the security compliance of the company, and the security assessment findings are reported to the CEO and board of directors.

In this chapter, security terms and acronyms are defined in a business context. This chapter promotes the need for a common language for business leaders not only to hear but to understand recommendations from their security professionals. If you are a CEO, just reading a security definition

© Marshall Copeland 2017
M. Copeland, *Cyber Security on Azure*, DOI 10.1007/978-1-4842-2740-4_1

is not very helpful if you do not appreciate the financial impact to your business. If you are a security professional, presenting to business executives and using security acronyms they don't fully comprehend does not often promote agreement for the necessary security improvements. As a security professional, you need to present the security risks within the context of the potential financial impact to the business. In other words, to start and maintain a conversation, business teams and security teams are required to speak using a common language.

■ **Security Tip**   An *application vulnerability* is not an operating system (OS) vulnerability but a system flaw or weakness in an application. If the vulnerability (or *vuln*, as referred to in some documents) is discovered by an attacker, the exploit could lead to a compromised application. Application layer security flaws generally result from coding flaws in applications that are either shipped with or installed onto computational devices such as tables, laptops, and desktops.

Executive Summary

Many companies are migrating to the cloud, and they need to migrate securely. They have processes and procedures in place for their on-premises business, but when a business wants to lower or remove capital expenditures (*capex*) from a traditional on-premises datacenter, it can leverage the benefits of the Azure cloud operational expenditures (*opex*). This is not a discussion about the benefits of the cloud; this is a discussion using a common language to support securely migrating to the cloud and specifically creating a Microsoft Azure secure cloud. The fact is that applications are moving and services are moving, so security has to move at the same speed as the business.

Most companies create copious amounts of security data in the form of log files that are transformed into text, tables, and graphs. The information is delivered using many automated methods, so the reports are received on a regular basis and almost never have the intended security controls. There is a language of security as well as a language the business needs to properly consume the security data effectively. Business teams need to be presented with information that is effective for business decisions and, from a security standpoint, that focuses on the right business perspective. This is often presented by a CISO, who reports with key performance indicators (KPIs) and key risk indicators (KRIs). Gathering, evaluating, and presenting the correct information for the business KPIs and KRIs is often challenging.

■ **Security Tip**   *Key performance indicators* evaluate the success of an organization or business unit as the business continues to achieve business goals. *Key risk indicators* are metrics used by security teams to signal increasing or decreasing risk exposures in various business units as they affect the enterprise.

The CISO has the challenging task of building a long-lasting relationship with the business and with the business develop the right KPIs and KRIs after understanding what is important to organizations. One of the major security concerns is selecting information from a complex database and then sampling the data to display KPIs and KRIs that are well defined. The National Vulnerability Database (NVD) is a database of all known vulnerability types, and it provides the ability to search by keyword. Figure 1-1 shows vulnerability types such as code injection, cross-site forgery, input validation, and many others, tracking utilization over the years.

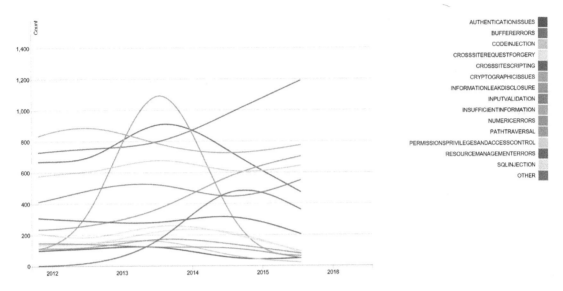

Figure 1-1. *U.S. National Vulnerability Database, view of vulnerability type change by year*

■ **Security Tip**   You can freely access the NVD database with all assets and visualizations at `https://nvd.nist.gov/`, and you can get specific visualization updates at `https://nvd.nist.gov/vuln/visualizations/cwe-over-time`.

The National Vulnerability Database is a product from the National Institution of Standards and Technology (NIST) and is a repository of standards-based vulnerabilities. The NIST project is sponsored by the Department of Homeland Security's National Cyber Security Division. The information in the database consists of security checklists, security-related software flaws, misconfigurations, product names, and impact metrics. All NIST publications are available in the public domain according to Title 17 of the United States Code, which means companies are able to use the data provided; however, an acknowledgment about the value of NVD is appreciated. You will learn about the NVD throughout this chapter.

Over the past few years many companies are increasing their number of security analysts and security architects for continuous improvement in their business security programs. Fortunately, several reports have been released from major corporations with worldwide data insight, including the Microsoft Security Intelligence Report (SIR), Verizon Data Breach Investigations Report (DBIR), IBM-sponsored Ponemon Cost of Data Breach Study, Cisco Annual Security Report, FireEye M-Trends 2017 Annual Security Report, and Georgia Tech Emerging Cyber Threats Report. As the data from these major reports is analyzed and their collective information correlated, customers have a desire to better protect their infrastructure in many different areas. The security focus is different for the type of business, location, and capability maturity level. The reports provide different information based on the respondents, location, and known historical information, and it is difficult for a single report to provide all the information necessary to understand the global view of cyber-breaches. However, common themes or areas of needed security focus are similar to past reports and for the next few years include recommendations for companies to invest security resources into many areas, including the following:

- Software development security

- Web site and application protection

- Endpoint threat detection and response

- Internet of Things (IoT) security

These attacks have continued over many years, and the trends to notice are the short amount of time in which a company's network is breached, often minutes or hours, and how long it takes before a breach is discovered, often weeks and months. In other words, you must improve security defenses and shorten the time to discovery and remediation of security breaches.

■ **Security Tip**   When attackers use a flaw in an application, they have the potential to exploit the application's vulnerability. *Cyber-crimes* target the confidentiality, integrity, or availability (the CIA triad) of resources via the application. The cyber-attacker also may gain access to manipulate other data points of the application and application users. Attackers typically rely on specific tools or methods to perform application vulnerability discovery and compromise.

Cyber-attacks are proliferating in each state, so the sharing of security information is critical to quickly identify new or morphed cyber-families of malware. Unfortunately, some attacks are reluctantly reported because of trust between customers and law enforcement. Figure 1-2 presents detailed data from the NVD of vulnerability totals over the years.

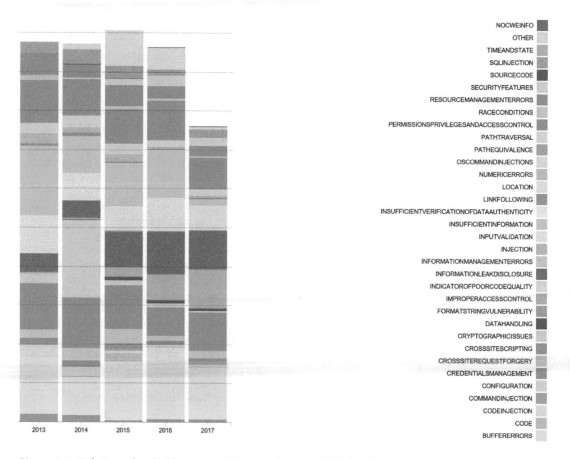

Figure 1-2. *Relative vulnerability type totals by year, from the NVD database*

Companies are losing intellectual property by the terabytes, petabytes, and exabytes yearly to cyber-crime, cyber-espionage, and cyber-terrorism. Future attacks may include a cyber-conflict beyond what was seen in the 2016 U.S. elections.

Security Tip The loss of data is not always the end goal of an attacker; sometimes changing source code and leaving it in place is the goal. As an example, during Operation Aurora in 2010, attackers were targeting technology companies including Google and modifying their source code repositories.

As a CEO, you need to create a cloud security discovery team to provide updates to you and other executives weekly as you prepare to migrate data, servers, and application services to Microsoft Azure. The world as well as private companies are built by digital technology, and we all need to improve security with best practices and continued due diligence through the following types of analysis:

- Intelligent security analytics
- Context-aware security analytics
- Big data security analytics

Also, as the CEO or CIO, you can provide clear objectives and a purpose for the cloud security discovery team using the following five cloud security best practices so your business can migrate to a secure cloud:

- Understand the Microsoft Azure share security model
- Secure cloud, code, and patch services
- Implement access management and governance
- Validate regulatory compliance and data protection
- Enable a business continuity and recovery model

These best practices are part of the journey to a secure cloud. Your business requires a framework for securing the expansion from your current IT services to the Azure cloud. The areas supported by a framework such as Azure are governance and security policy, cloud administrative management, identity systems and identity access management (IaM), threat awareness, and data protection. In addition, the process to move to a secure cloud for your business requires a team effort that is driven by the CEO, with momentum from the board of directors to change a mind-set of "This is the way we've always done it" by lowering the cost from operational expenses. For example, budgets can be reallocated from traditional three- or four-year hardware refresh cycles because the Azure cloud platform has a hardware refresh cycle about every two years. In addition, the monthly billing for infrastructure as a service (IaaS) or platform as a service (PaaS) workload services is included in your company's investment in Microsoft Azure, so the savings for your company continue to be delivered as business teams leverage Microsoft on a global scale.

Security Tip You can download the latest 2017 total cost of ownership document from https://azure.microsoft.com/en-us/resources/total-economic-impact-of-microsoft-azure-paas/.

Understanding Attackers' Motivation

Businesses have valuable assets, but one of the most difficult tasks is assessing the value of some business assets. To state the problem another way, what is the value of an asset and the cost to the business if it is compromised? Placing value on a business's physical asset is easy, but determining the cost of compromise is often difficult, especially if the business doesn't understand security impacts.

The loss of assets impacts the business directly and indirectly. The direct impact is the cost to keep, maintain, or replace the asset if it stolen or compromised. An example of a compromise is the possibility of a ransomware attack. In this instance, the cost of a security breach is often difficult to calculate because there is no single formula that includes the costs of potential fines, hours to remediate, and loss of business related to the damage done to the brand. Figure 1-3 shows an NVD visualization of security severity. The purpose for viewing data facts in this type of visualization is to put attention on the impact a security breach has based via severity (high, medium, low) over time.

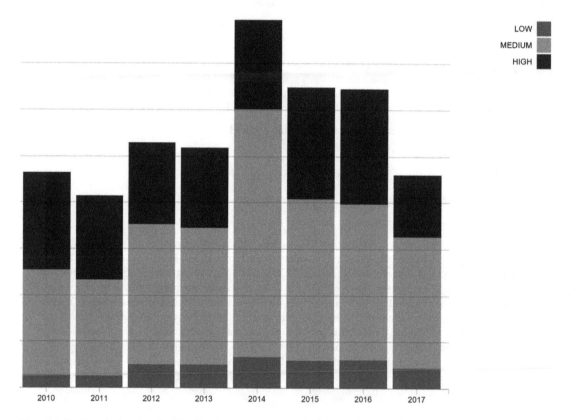

Figure 1-3. Graph showing the distribution of vulnerabilities by severity over time

This data breach visualization is a live version that is included as part of a larger project. However, for our purposes, this is the type of information from the database online tool that can be used in live presentations to your board of directors to gain insight into or amplify the overall effect of a security breach.

■ **Security Tip**   NIST updates the severity levels of threats at `https://nvd.nist.gov/vuln-metrics/` `visualizations/cvss-severity-distribution-over-time`. This type of data is similar to other projects like the one created by David McCandless, a London-based author, writer, and designer. You can access his project at `www.informationisbeautiful.net/`. You can find a friendly guideline for using the tool for education and internal meetings at `www.informationisbeautiful.net/licensing/`, and the security breach information provides current data at `www.informationisbeautiful.net/visualizations/worlds-biggest-data-breaches-hacks/`.

Editing the visualization with the appropriate data is helpful to remove all the noise and focus more on the type of business (such as legal, healthcare, web) and type of attack, leak, or hack.

The indirect impact to the business is hard to quantify because of the unknowns about how the asset's loss affects the business in totality. A business impact caused by security vulnerabilities requires a different perspective and introduces a different severity cost or penalty, if you will, based on the impact. Using a real-world example often helps executives gain insight into the unknown costs of security vulnerabilities.

The question most customers ask is, why would an attacker want to attack me? Some of the information is provided through a much longer report, the Verizon Data Breach Investigations Report (DBIR), discussed later in this chapter. However, Figure 1-4 provides motivations over a number of years.

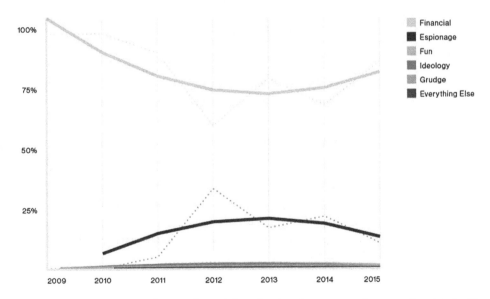

Figure 1-4. *Verizon DBIR showing financial motivation changes over the years. Reprinted with permission. Verizon 2016 Data Breach Investigations Report.*

The attacker or attacker nation is most likely after financial gain, as shown in Figure 1-4. However, your company may not be a financial institution. Money in bitcoins for attackers who use ransomware is a motivation for attacking small and medium-sized businesses. I recommend you read the Microsoft SIR and Verizon DBIR reports to understand the other motivations. If time does not allow you to read the reports from cover to cover, then the executive summaries of both are also informational.

The following example illustrates the difficulty in measuring the total dollar impact of an "unsecured" solution. This requires a greater and more impactful conversation regarding the need to include security due diligence and due care.

LARGE-SCREEN TELEVISION FOR LOCAL CORPORATE ADVERTISEMENT

Contoso Marketing Corporation has an internal marketing team that had funds available from their end-of-fiscal-year marketing budget, so they purchased several large-screen smart televisions to be used throughout the next year to promote local events that the company sponsors. The team wanted to drive awareness internally and gain support for internal employees to volunteer at these events. Additionally, the smart TVs would be used at an event to showcase Contoso Marketing Corporation's support for the community. Their "impromptu" business plan was to take the inexpensive smart TVs and connect them to a corporate guest wireless Wi-Fi network internally and to free local Wi-Fi networks near the downtown event sites. The Wi-Fi connection would allow them to download company-branded promotional videos of sponsored events.

To enable the marketing event to become a business-supported project, a corporate policy requires security analyses to be performed on any Internet-connected equipment. The Contoso Marketing Corporation security team evaluated the security risk to the business by connecting one of the smart TVs to the Internet guest Wi-Fi and performing security tests, including a security penetration test. The security team's report identified several vulnerabilities and required several thousand dollars of security measures to be purchased by Contoso Marketing Corporation before the security team would sign off on the business requirements stating the device had been secured as a company asset.

The CISO asked to meet with representatives from the internal marketing team to explain the security assessment findings, receive agreement on the cost of security, and move forward with supporting the use of the smart TV installations. The internal marketing team was astonished to read the report that said several thousand dollars in security assets were required, when the original plan was for a few hundred dollars for the purchase of smart TVs.

The CISO explained that the connectivity of a smart TV to the Internet would create a security risk to the company if the systems were compromised. The CISO explained the penetration testing on the test television set revealed a known backdoor enabled by the TV manufacturer. The company that created the software used an open source operating system and created a second default administrator account and password that could be used in the event of support and future updates to the smart TV software. This administration account was identified on Internet hacking blogs and was a known security vulnerability. To secure each smart TV from potential harm, a security firewall would be required to prevent a hacker from compromising the television.

The manager for the internal marketing team suggested that if one of the promotional events had a compromised television, they could simply replace it since the price point of each TV was very low. The CISO then asked, what is the cost to the company if the smart TV were compromised and the event-sponsored video were replaced with a video of pornography? What is the cost when the brand of the business is compromised and loss of business results in the compromise? What is the total financial impact from this single security vulnerability if a smart TV were compromised and used as part of a larger distributed denial-of-services (DDoS) attack on another business? If that business files a lawsuit against Contoso, what is the financial impact of that?

The result was that the smart TVs were returned, and the internal marketing team starting requesting a security team representative to attend planning events to gain security guidance at the beginning of a marketing plan rather than at the end.

This real-world example quickly brings into focus the financial impact of "brand" for many businesses with a security vulnerability impact that, if not remediated, may affect their customer base. The example did not involve loss of customer credit card information like the well-publicized attacks on several household names like Target and Home Depot. Companies such as these are investing in their current workforce by providing security training.

In the next section, you'll gain valuable insight through free reports from major professional security organizations. The individual reports vary but together complement the global security view and should be digested to gain clarity on potential impacts based on the type of business, attacker methods, and security countermeasures.

■ **Security Tip**   The breach examples of Target and Home Depot were publicized through September 2014 and can be found using a Bing or Google search. In these two examples, the data breach was caused by the same malware family. To learn more about the specific malware family, refer to Brian Krebs' blog at `http://krebsonsecurity.com/tag/target-data-breach/`.

Remain Current Through Security Facts

Security analysis is the key to remaining agile as the number and impact of security breaches continue to be announced publicly. You, as a security professional, must stay aware to show support for the boards of directors as they significantly increase their focus on cloud information security, hybrid network cybersecurity, and IT risk management. Your security team requires up-to-date resources that provide a global view of international cyber-armies, with in-depth information about their attack vectors, weaponized payloads, and industry-specific targeting.

Returning to a topic from the "Executive Summary" section, there are several key annual security publications that should be required reading. This list is not all that should be reviewed, but it's a good start for publications published yearly and biyearly. Infrastructure teams new to security should start with this list, reading the most current publication and then reading the reports from the previous three years. The value of reading the current publications is to understand current cyber-attacks. As you read the older publications, you'll notice the commonalities of the bad actors and families of malware. What is sometimes seen is the resurgence of previously successful attacks but with modifications and new signatures.

The following list is a starting point for cloud architects who are new to cybersecurity:

- Microsoft Security Intelligence Report (SIR)

- Verizon Data Breach Investigations Report (DBIR)

- IBM-sponsored Ponemon Cost of Data Breach Study

- Other security reports:

  - Cisco Annual Security Report

  - FireEye M-Trends 2017 Annual Security Report

  - Georgia Tech Emerging Cyber Threats Report

Microsoft Security Intelligence Report

You need to have good guidance on protecting your Microsoft Azure cloud subscription with solutions that include Azure Security Center, but an overall view of the cybersecurity landscape with attacks and weaponized payloads is required to "level set" your security researcher team. Many Microsoft customers are not aware of the SIR, and others have not realized the depth of information, understanding, and guidance provided by this free publication. (Microsoft does not allow the reuse of data graphs, which is why they do not appear in this section.)

Brash cyber-attacks continue with increased agility and newer sophisticated tool suites with what can only be interpreted as methodical methods. Some of these criminals are very organized and use cyber-tactics that indicate a complexity that provides evidence of state-sponsored attacks including cyber-espionage and cyber-terror. Some of the weakness in the security layering includes the data provided by end users on social media sites and many attackers using proven social engineering and zero-day vulnerabilities to break in to corporate networks.

While attackers access a network in order to gain considerable knowledge, stealing data, breaching privacy, or stealing money, once the breach is made public, the erosion of the business's trust by the public shopper begins.

For well-protected enterprises using many layers of security, attacks are incredibly expensive, costing them millions per incident. The greater damage to a company's brand is difficult to put into a dollar amount.

■ **Note** The SIR document uses the Common Vulnerability Scoring System (CVSS) as the Microsoft SIR standardized, platform-independent scoring system. It is used for rating IT vulnerabilities. The CVSS base metric assigns a numeric value between 0 and 10. Factors such as potential impact, access vectors, and ease of exploitation are included with the number rating. Bigger numbers represent a greater severity.

The information helps identify the many different types of attempts to exploit a security vulnerability. This illustrates the need to stay informed about vulnerabilities not just in the operating system but in all applications used on business systems. Additionally, you need to be aware of the use of exploit kits, which may have the ability to try different exploit methods rather than a single exploit type.

> *"The Angler kit (Axpergle) appears clearly to be targeted predominantly at wealthier countries and regions in Europe and the Americas, possibly because of a belief that computers in those areas have more valuable data to steal than in others."*

■ **Security Tip** An *exploit kit* is software written by hackers and sold to be used by other hackers. The kit is usually easy-to-use web-based software that makes it easy for attackers to target specific populations, countries, operating system versions, browsers, and more.

Reading through the report, you can see that thousands of such attacks were reported in 2015 and 2016. There are other annual security reports introduced in this chapter, and these two common threads appear in them:

- Hackers breached networks in minutes.

- It took IT security teams more than 100 days to discover a breach.

The Microsoft information comes from the many different operating systems that are being used in the world and that report data to online services. Information in the Microsoft SIR identifies the individual threat types by category, with Trojans being the most common.

As you read through the SIR information, you may notice the amount of data that is collected to help identify common themes of hackers and attack vectors. In addition to the global data provided in the SIR, the Microsoft IT team also includes data from internal systems, including Windows Defender, System Center Endpoint Protection (SCEP), Windows Event Forwarding (WEF), DirectAccess, forensics, and the manual submission of suspicious files. If you are asking how much data is analyzed, refer to the following quote:

> *Microsoft IT provides information technology services internally for Microsoft employees and resources. Microsoft IT manages more than 600,000 devices for more than 150,000 users across more than 100 countries and regions worldwide.*

One of the many reasons to read the Microsoft SIR is that the information is provided by a security team and includes best practices you can use as standards. For instance, according to the SIR, a security-compliant system requires the following: the computer must be connected to the Microsoft network, it must be running the latest version of the Defender or SCEP client, the anti-malware signatures must be no more than six days old, and real-time protection must be enabled.

Because attackers' techniques seem to be evolving at a faster pace than in past years and have become more sophisticated, the security layering approach needs to become smarter to provide valuable security guidance to large enterprises. If you ask IT directors, they most likely will tell you they need a full-fledged advanced threat protection solution that identifies attacks as fast as possible with wide-ranging intelligence, built-in actionable remediation, and less maintenance. Azure Security Center is clearly positioned as a cloud service (refer to Chapter 3), and the solution provides automated responses that in many applications remediate and then alert on the threat potential. The need to automate security alerts is a critical component because even professional developers can provide attackers with an unexpected advantage.

■ **Security Tip**   For example, many developers leverage public code repositories such as GitHub because they can use it without the need to build and support their own infrastructure repository. However, developers can accidentally publish digital credentials through "access tokens" on GitHub.

Accidentally publishing access tokens on public code sites is, unfortunately, common. Your cloud services can be compromised by attackers who search for and find these mistakes. Attackers have even created bots that have an algorithm that searches GitHub 24 hours per day for API keys.

Why It Is Important

The Microsoft Security Intelligence Report focuses on software vulnerabilities, software vulnerability exploits, malware, and unwanted software. Past reports and related resources are available for download at www.microsoft.com/sir. The Microsoft Security Intelligence Report has been released twice a year since 2006.

The Microsoft Security Intelligence Report used in this example focuses on the first and second quarters of 2016, with trend data for the last several quarters presented on a quarterly basis. The reports are updated each year with three different options to freely review and share them.

- SIR entire report

- SIR key findings

- SIR regional threats

"Each volume is based upon data collected from millions of computers all over the world, which not only provides valuable insights on the worldwide threat landscape, both at home and at work, but also provides detailed information about threat profiles faced by computer users in more than a hundred individual countries and regions."

Attackers can trick an end user, as an example of SIR data findings we can look at phishing, through a phishing e-mail, to install software that looks for the end user's cloud storage folder. The software replaces the user's cloud storage synchronization token with the attacker's cloud storage token, and then the attacker receives a copy of each file stored in the cloud folder. This type of attack is called a *man-in-the-middle attack*, but since it is for cloud storage, the company Imperva coined the phrase *man-in-the-cloud attack*.

■ **Security Tip**   To download a copy of the Imperva report, go to `https://www.imperva.com/docs/HII_Man_In_The_Cloud_Attacks.pdf`.

Where to Download

The free Microsoft Security Intelligent Report download page (`https://www.microsoft.com/security/sir/default.aspx`) provides the latest SIR report, key findings, and regional threats. Also, you have access to a link to all downloads of previous editions. You are required to enter company and personal information, so read about the sharing of data in the acceptable use policy before completing the form.

Verizon 2017 Data Breach Investigations Report

Verizon has released the Verizon DBIR report for the past ten years, and the 2017 edition was recently made available. The DBIR provides timely information needed to understand the things that threaten the security of your business.

The 2017 DBIR effectively exposes a worldview of cybersecurity with more than "40,000 incidents, including 1,935 confirmed data breaches." You can use this information as part of narratives and slides at any board of director meetings and executive briefings to tell the "security story" and help the business make clear connections between cybersecurity and business objectives. Figure 1-5 shows highlights of who is behind the breaches.

Who's behind the breaches?

75%
perpetrated by outsiders.

25%
involved internal actors.

18%
conducted by state-affiliated actors.

3%
featured multiple parties.

2%
involved partners.

51%
involved organized criminal groups.

Figure 1-5. Verizon 2017 DBIR executive summary of who is behind the breaches

In the 2017 report, you will see the latest data concerning the following:

- What business sector has the most impacting cybersecurity threats, with updated information on the mitigations of the threat

- Who was attacked and more importantly the entry point that needs to be reviewed in your own business

- What motivates the bad actors

In the "Executive Briefing" section, there is more data, as shown in Figure 1-6, that identifies the hacking, malware, and social engineering efforts to penetrate the layers of network security.

What tactics do they use?

62%
of breaches featured hacking.

51%
over half of breaches included malware.

81%
of hacking-related breaches leveraged either
stolen and/or weak passwords.

43%
were social attacks.

14%
Errors were causal events in 14% of breaches.
The same proportion involved privilege misuse.

8%
Physical actions were present in 8% of
breaches.

Figure 1-6. *Executive summary of tactics from the 2017 DBIR*

The Verizon 2017 Data Breach Investigations Report provides great insight into the attackers' motives, patterns, and attack methods. You can find a detailed discussion in Appendix B that leverages the visual information in the 2017 DBIR graphs. Please refer to the DBIR report updates to gain insight into the cybersecurity attackers' ability to compromise networks and exploit vulnerabilities.

■ **Security Tip**   You can download the 2017 DBIR at www.verizonenterprise.com/verizon-insights-lab/dbir.

Verizon 2016 Data Breach Investigations Report

The Verizon 2016 DBIR report features incidents in 82 countries and across numerous businesses and industries. The nine incident classification patterns identified from the 2014 report and the nine categories supporting most incident classes through 2017 indicate how attacks continue to gain profitable results.

There are no dramatic changes (from 2016-2017) in the information and data patterns when compared to past years' DBIR analysis reports. But if you read the reports every year, the research provides interesting data points to gain insight into hacker motivation, tools used, industry attack preferences, and cyber-attack focus. The 2016 report says this:

> *"This year's dataset is made up of over 100,000 incidents, of which 3,141 were confirmed data breaches. Of these, 64,199 incidents and 2,260 breaches comprise the finalized dataset that was used in the analysis and figures throughout the report."*

Each of the security reports provides cyber-attack insight; however, the different reporting organizations don't use the same formatting of data points. Figure 1-7 is from the 2016 DBIR report and provides a visual representation of the time taken to identify a security breach and remove it, known as *exfiltration*.

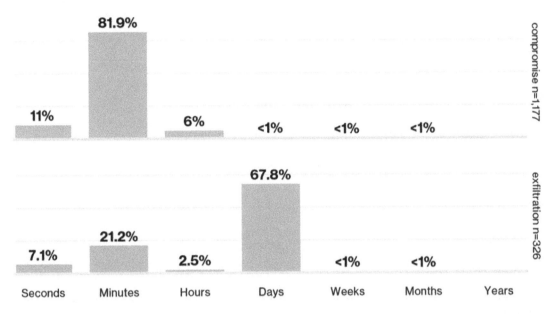

Figure 1-7. *Verizon DBIR time to compromise and exfiltration. Reprinted with permission. Verizon 2016 Data Breach Investigations Report.*

The Verizon DBIR uses a metric called the Vocabulary for Event Recording and Incident Sharing (VERIS). VERIS is a framework to record and share customer-reported security events and incidents that lead to breaches; VERIS can be used by any company using a predicable naming standard for repeatability. VERIS categorizes the data collection by cyber-action taken, the attack method (such as the relationship to a known malware family, if any), and the asset targeted. The overall DBIR process also captures the timeline, victim demographics, discovery method, impact data, and much more. Like with the other annual security reports, some of the important information is in the details; Figure 1-8 shows some exploit details.

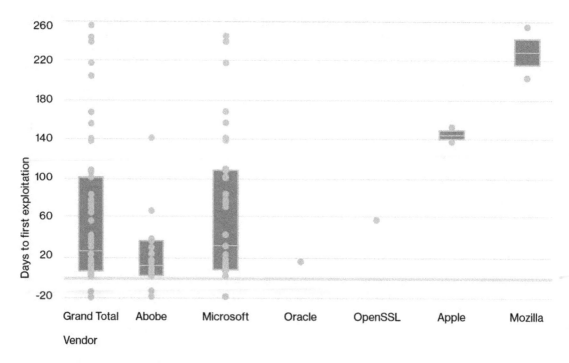

Figure 1-8. DBIR shows days to exploitation after publication. Reprinted with permission. Verizon 2016 Data Breach Investigations Report.

The box plot in Figure 1-8 is a view of the number of days that a exploit is quickly available, by hackers, after the public publication of the exploit is announced. If you interpret this data, you'll conclude that Adobe vulnerabilities are "weaponized" quickly, as are some of the Microsoft vulnerabilities. But others take more than 100 days. The Mozilla vulnerabilities take hackers much longer to have an exploit available after public disclosure.

The data collected also provides insight into "phishing" e-mail campaigns. Figure 1-9 provides data about how successful a weaponized e-mail was when it was identified.

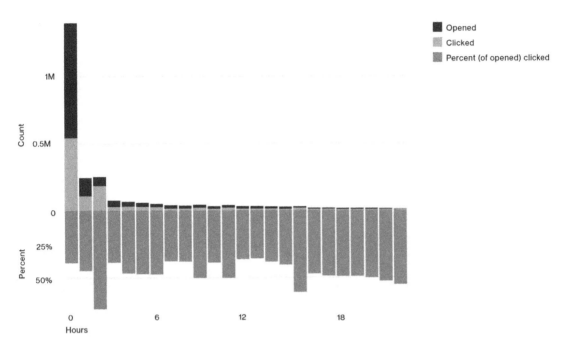

Figure 1-9. *DBIR report in hours of clicked on and opened phishing e-mail. Reprinted with permission. Verizon 2016 Data Breach Investigations Report.*

Many of the phishing e-mails sent were opened and not just deleted by the end user. The other important statistic shown here is that the e-mail attachment was clicked in a median time of 3 minutes 45 seconds after the e-mail was sent.

■ **Security Tip** *Spear-phishing attacks* are weaponized e-mail attachments targeted at a specific person or group of people, like a CEO, a CIO, accounting staff, or billing staff. Attackers get contact names from corporate executive web pages and corporate web sites with published organizational charts. Advanced persistent threat (APT) attacks, like Operation Aurora, used spear-phishing attacks to compromise systems. Read more about the Aurora attack by downloading a copy of the Sans.org white paper at https://files.sans.org/summit/euscada10/PDFs/29%20Pollet%20APT.pdf.

Why It Is Important

The Verizon Data Breach Investigations Report provides details that every security professional should read and use as a reference. You should use the data to educate users, executives, and other IT and security professionals, possibly through "lunch-and-learn" events.

One of the useful features in the DBIR is the at-a-glance information provided in a summarized view. Figure 1-10 shows an example of the at-a-glance topics, which are perfect for busy security professionals.

● At a glance	
Description	Use of stolen credentials and other hacking and malware actions targeting traditional username and password authentication are prevalent across numerous patterns.
Top patterns	Web App Attacks, POS Intrusions
Frequency	1,429 incidents with confirmed data disclosure.
Key findings	Static credentials continue to be targeted by several of the top hacking action varieties and malware functionalities.

63% of confirmed data breaches involved weak, default or stolen passwords.

Figure 1-10. DBIR using focused information at a glance to summarize topics. Reprinted with permission. Verizon 2016 Data Breach Investigations Report.

This at-a-glance view helps busy security teams understand the relevance of a security topic, such as a credential theft; these focused tables are used throughout the report for quick indexing of data.

Where to Download

To download this report, you will need to enter contact information and accept the usage rights, but the free report has a great deal of security insight. Since you are required to enter company and personal information, you should read about the sharing of data in the acceptable use policy before completing the form. You can find the download page at www.verizonenterprise.com/verizon-insights-lab/dbir/.

IBM-Sponsored Ponemon Cost of Data Breach Study

The 2016 Cost of Data Breach Study: Global Analysis is an excellent report full of information that could be included in a presentation for the CEO, CIO, or CISO. This report provides global evidence of the direct and indirect costs to companies that have experienced and reported data breaches. The reported data breach information is key because there are some (possibly many) breaches that are not reported because personally identifiable information (PII) data was not exposed. Many companies follow the payment card industry legal requirements about reporting breaches and do not publicly provide information that includes PII data. This is information such as who, when, how, and why.

The data provided in the global study encompasses the following:

- 383 companies in 12 countries

- $4 million in average total cost of data breach

- 29 percent increase in total cost of data breach since 2013

- $158 average cost per lost or stolen record

- 15 percent increase in per-capita cost since 2013

The dollar amounts used in the report are in U.S. dollars, and the overall message is that the cost of breaches is increasing and has a global impact on companies and countries. In the IBM-sponsored report, the data breaches need to fit a specific definition of compromised records. Figure 1-11 shows the number of breached records by country; in the United States, the number is 29,611, and these are only the breached records that were reported. The fact that the number was near 30,000 in 2016 is disturbing indeed.

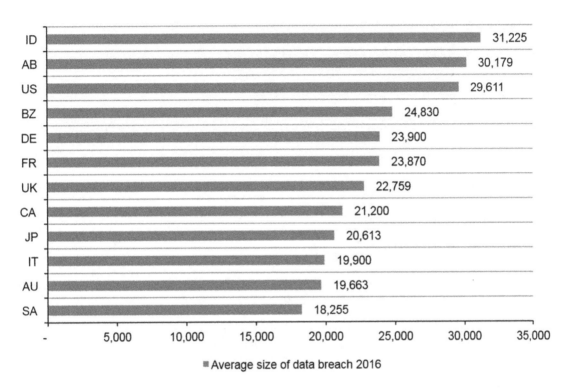

Figure 1-11. *Ponemon report for number of breached records by country. Reprinted with permission. Benchmark research sponsored by IBM. Independently conducted by Ponemon Institute LLC.*

The information provided in this report echoes other security data breach reports, and the fact that some industries had higher data breach costs than others across the globe should help those industries consider investing "differently" (solutions supporting Artificial Intelegence AI) in cybersecurity defense. Figure 1-12 shows the per-capita cost for sample industries such as healthcare, education, and financial organizations, which have substantially higher costs than the overall mean of $158 per lost or stolen record.

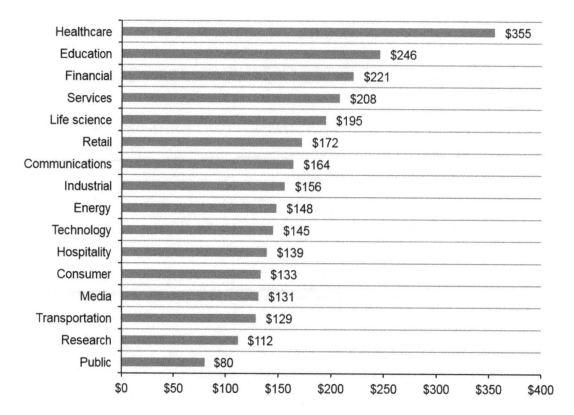

Figure 1-12. *Per-capita cost by industry classification. Reprinted with permission. Benchmark research sponsored by IBM. Independently conducted by Ponemon Institute LLC.*

Why It Is Important

Security analysts look for credible security information to help provide evidence of potential cyber-attacks based on industry, country, impact cost, and root cause. Reports like the one conducted by the Ponemon Institute are needed to gain a global view of the cybersecurity issues from both a global perspective and an industry outlook.

Where to Download

There are many reports provided by IBM that offer a great deal of insight for novice and seasoned security professionals. You are required to enter company and personal information, so read about the sharing of data in the acceptable use policy before completing the form. You can find the download page at https://www-03.ibm.com/security/data-breach/.

Other Annual Security Reports

Time is never an asset for the security "blue" team, and the same is true for cybersecurity. However, additional reports are available and should become incorporated in the daily conversations and weekly summarization for the CEO, CIO, and CISO. You do not want to simply reprint the many data points in these reports; you should review the reports discussed in this chapter specifically to "tell the story through a strong, simple narrative," as recommended by Jeffery Wheatman in his Gartner article "The Comprehensive Guide to Presenting Risk and Information Security to Your Board of Directors" from 2016 (Gartner ID: G00297818). This article and others are available if you sign up for a free subscription at Gartner.com. This article helps security analysts prepare information and reports that are concise, to-the-point, and attention-grabbing for a CISO, CIO, or board of director.

Cisco Annual Security Report

The 2017 Annual Cybersecurity Report from Cisco is updated every year and provides concise information about cyber-attackers such as who, why, when, and how. The divisions are similar to the processes identified by Certified Ethical Hacking (CEH) techniques or phases such as reconnaissance, weaponization, delivery, and installation. The information provides insight into certain corporations through defender behavior details. The information from Cisco is valuable, and without this report, it would be difficult to learn from the security expertise available at Cisco. You should read this report and make note of the data-gathering information to help defend against cyber-attackers.

Where to Download

You are required to enter company and personal information to download this report, so read about the sharing of data in the acceptable use policy before completing the form. You can find the download page at www.cisco.com/c/en/us/products/security/security-reports.html.

FireEye M-Trends 2017 Annual Security Report

The information in the FireEye M-Trends 2017 Annual Security Report is a continuation of the data that is provided when using FireEye's main product, the FireEye Malware Protection System. (Note that FireEye still uses the Mandiant name in the yearly report; FireEye acquired Mandiant in 2013.) The information in the report includes trends that define the landscape based on Mandiant's investigation of 2016 breaches and cyber-attacks. Here are the features in the report, according to FireEye:

> *Hundreds of intelligence analysts and malware experts worldwide*
> *Intelligence gathered from the world's most consequential breaches*
> *More than 14+ million virtual analyses per hours*
> *More than 9+ million endpoints deployed*
> *Hundreds of threat actor profiles*
> *Real-time detection across industries and regions*

This shows the global breadth of data in the Mandiant report, which is free to download.

Where to Download

You are required to enter company and personal information before downloading this report, so read about the sharing of data in the acceptable use policy before completing the form. You can find the download page at https://www.fireeye.com/current-threats/annual-threat-report/mtrends.html.

Georgia Tech Emerging Cyber Threats Report

The Institute for Information Security and Privacy (IISP) at Georgia Tech deserves recognition for compiling the data provided by the 11 cybersecurity facilities, labs, and centers across Georgia Tech and the Georgia Tech Research Institute. The 2017 Emerging Cyber Threats Report includes insight for future cyber-solutions from the faculty, students, and partners. In addition, the IISP should be considered for any cyber-security graduate studies, especially since the student team just "swept" the 2016 NSA Codebreaker Challenge contest, beating out 480 universities. This is not the only university that provides advanced degrees and the ability to learn from top cyber-security researchers, but it is one nationally recognized program to consider.

Where to Download

You are required to enter company and personal information to download this report, so read about the sharing of data in the acceptable use policy before completing the form. You can find the download page at http://iisp.gatech.edu/.

BRUTE-FORCE USING DICTIONARY ATTACK

Brute-force attacks can be more sophisticated than the name implies. A traditional *dictionary attack*, in its most simplistic form, is an automated script or set of scripting tools that will try to guess usernames and passwords from a "dictionary file." The actual file can be tuned and complied to cover words that are "probably" used by the owner of the account that is being attacked.

The tuning includes the ability to copy, parse, and combine the words on an end-user's blog postings or social web page, including family members' and business associates' web pages. By tuning a list of possible dictionary words that the victim has close association with as part of the algorithm, the attacker generates variations, search attacks, and rule-based attacks that include modification with numbers for letters.

Free programs such as THC-Hydra, Ophcrack, and John the Ripper have easily accomplished brute-forcing attempts with great success.

There are two types of attacks: active and passive (commonly referred to as online and offline). Online attacks typically have technical prevention policies as part of the identity account management (IaM) solution or web site. The policy in place limits the number of attacks to prevent a typical brute-force attack and lock out the account. Offline attacks take advantage of a password hash file. The attack is completed on systems that have local access and is limited by the computing power to compare known files from a rainbow table to the end user's password hash file. A cryptographic hash file is a mathematical algorithm that maps the arbitrary size (a password that uses random characters and numbers) to a fixed string size. The mathematical password hash file is designed to be a one-way function so it cannot be reverted to the password.

The weakness in a password created by a user is the password strength measured by the entropy strength. *Entropy* is the measure of a password's strength measured in digital bits of binary data. As an example, if a password has 15 bits of strength, then the number of attempts to exhaust all possibilities of the password is 2^{15}. This is not a difficult task if you consider the possibilities of password "guesses" per second using off-the-shelf hardware.

■ **Security Tip**   It has been demonstrated that using desktop servers with multiple graphics processing unit (GPU) cards can quickly crack passwords of low entropy. In 2012, Jeremi Gosney demonstrated a multicluster server that powers 25 AMD Radeon GPU cards cracking passwords at 350 billion per second. This is a distributed GPU password cracking process.

You can find a good article about passwords at `https://www.schneier.com/blog/archives/2013/06/a_really_good_a.html`.

Steps for a Secure Cloud

You need a solid, in-depth security strategy, one that uses the right tools and people to respond appropriately to threats today and in the future. This section covers the high-level steps needed to guide you and your security team to a secure cloud. The fundamental takeaway about cloud technology from Microsoft Azure services is the speed at which threats change. To keep up, you should expand on these steps and incorporate them into your company's best practices and guidelines as you move forward.

Your security framework needs to extend into the cloud. Federal and state government agencies are able to leverage the National Institutes of Standards and Technology (NIST) publications. Several public companies also leverage the free information from NIST provided for cloud computing, governance, and cybersecurity recommendations. I recommend reviewing the guides in Table 1-1.

Table 1-1. *Cybersecurity Publications*

Publication	Download URL
NIST Cloud Computing Reference Architecture Special Publication 500-292	`https://www.nist.gov/publications/nist-cloud-computing-reference-architecture`
Cybersecurity Framework	`https://www.nist.gov/programs-projects/cybersecurity-framework`
NIST Special Publication 800-53 Risk Management Framework	`https://nvd.nist.gov/800-53`
Shared Responsibility of Azure Cloud	`https://gallery.technet.microsoft.com/Shared-Responsibilities-81d0ff91`

NIST Cloud Computing Reference Architecture Special Publication 500-292 is a good starting place and should be required reading for anyone on a security team. In addition, there are Microsoft Azure–specific downloads that should be considered. The Cloud Platform Integration Framework from 2014 is a first attempt to help customers, organizations, partners, and integrators design and deploy cloud-targeted workloads. You can download it at `https://gallery.technet.microsoft.com/Cloud-Platform-Integration-d37ccd32`.

Chapter 2 discusses additional security frameworks. Finally, a Microsoft-supported free e-book is called *2016 Trends in Cybersecurity: A Quick Guide to the Most Importa nt Insights in Security.* You can download the e-book at `https://info.microsoft.com/SecurityIntelligenceReportDataInsights_Registration.html`.

Azure Cloud Networking, Encryption, Data Storage

Microsoft Azure virtual networks (*vnets*) extend your on-premises network into the Microsoft Azure cloud through IPsec-based site-to-site virtual private network (VPN) technology or a high-speed Azure ExpressRoute–dedicated wide area network (WAN) connection.

The Microsoft Azure networking white paper provides the infrastructure necessary to connect your virtual machines from one vnet to another, as well as to create a bridge between the cloud and your on-premises datacenter. You can download the document from `http://download.microsoft.com/download/C/A/3/CA3FC5C0-ECE0-4F87-BF4B-D74064A00846/AzureNetworkSecurity_v2_Oct2014.pdf`.

In addition, you can use Microsoft ExpressRoute as a private connection from your on-premises network to Microsoft Azure. Read more at `https://azure.microsoft.com/en-us/services/expressroute/`.

Identity Multifactor Authentication

One of the changes when moving into the cloud is the need for claims-based identity. Microsoft Azure provides support for open authentication solutions such as the following:

- OAuth 2.0

- OpenID

Enabling multifactor authentication is a best practice for both Azure cloud connectivity and on-premises directory services. Ensuring that user identification is supported for applications and cloud administration is a security best practice. Integration is often the first step for federation using Azure AD Connect. You can read about this at `https://www.microsoft.com/en-us/download/details.aspx?id=47594`.

You can learn more about claims-based identity in Azure at `https://www.microsoft.com/en-us/download/details.aspx?id=45909`.

Software Is a Key Vulnerability

Often the main reason for application security flaws is the pressure that application development teams have to get new software to market. This is not the only reason, of course, but this financial pressure forces many developers to overlook or disregard the security aspect of the software development life cycle (SDLC).

According to Gartner Security, the application layer currently contains 90% of all vulnerabilities.

OWASP Top Ten Project

While there are many different tools, utilities, and techniques for exploiting application vulnerabilities, the free Open Web Application Security Project (OWASP) Top Ten list is a list of common vulnerabilities when it comes to web and application development. The OWASP Top Ten list represents a global consensus for the most critical web application security flaws and contains thousands of recorded security flaws. The 2017 Top Ten list has been released but as "candidates." You can download the list from `https://github.com/OWASP/Top10/raw/master/2017/OWASP%20Top%2010%20-%202017%20RC1-English.pdf`.

The following are the top five security flaws on the 2017 list:

- Cross-site scripting

- SQL injection

- LDAP injection

- Cross-site request forgery

- Insecure cryptographic storage

Buffer overflows, insecure storage of sensitive data, improper cryptographic algorithms, hard-coded passwords, and backdoored applications are only a sample set of application layer flaw classes. Figure 1-13 shows the web site for the Top Ten list for 2017.

Figure 1-13. *OWASP Top Ten list to support web application security*

You should consider joining the OWASP by going to `https://www.owasp.org/index.php/Main_Page`.

Finding Cloud Blind Spots to Improve Your Network Security Knowledge

The white paper "Microsoft Azure Security Response in the Cloud" helps you to understand just how Microsoft investigates, manages, and responds to security incidents within Azure. You can download it at `https://gallery.technet.microsoft.com/Azure-Security-Response-in-dd18c678`.

Sometimes customers may not realize the Azure security response that Microsoft provides. The Azure security incident management program is a critical responsibility for Microsoft and represents an investment for any customer using Microsoft cloud services.

NVD Use with ITIL/Change Management Patching

As mentioned, the National Vulnerability Database is the U.S. government repository of standards-based vulnerability management data; the data is represented using the Security Content Automation Protocol (SCAP). SCAP is normally associated with the U.S. federal government as a method for using specific standards to enable automated vulnerability management. It is really a defined measurement and policy compliance evaluation of computers (and other applications) deployed in a business or agency to help maintain compliance.

Managing a hybrid environment includes applications and data in Microsoft Azure as well as in traditional datacenters. You can find best practices and support for this at https://msdn.microsoft.com/en-us/library/mt345523.aspx. With any large system, there must be some naming standards and definitions. The Common Platform Enumeration (CPE) dictionary is a structured naming scheme for information technology systems, software, and packages. Figure 1-14 shows the total number of products for major vendors.

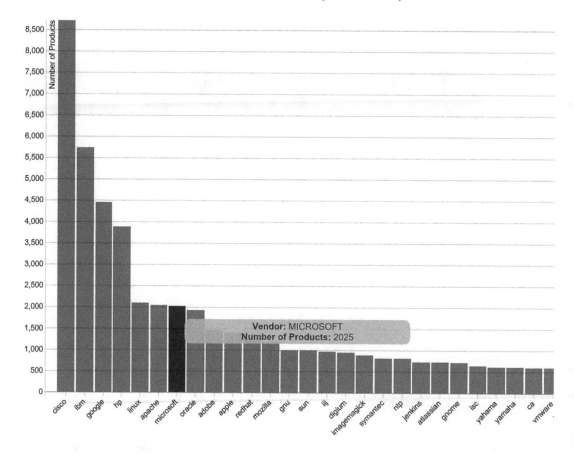

Figure 1-14. *Visualization of the total number of products for major vendors, with Microsoft highlighted. Source: https://nvd.nist.gov/.*

You need an understanding of the NVD system, which uses the CVSS, described earlier in the chapter. CVSS provides an open framework for communicating the characteristics and impacts of IT vulnerabilities. How the individual security vulnerabilities are categorized is by using a list of Common Vulnerabilities and Exposures (CVEs). The CVEs help to quantify the risk of vulnerabilities and are calculated from a set of algorithms based on metrics, including the complexity and availability of a remedy for the vulnerability. Figure 1-15 shows the CVE site.

Figure 1-15. *CVE web site to leverage a download list or continuous delivery of the CVE data*

CVE is the standard for information security vulnerability names, but downloading the database is not recommended for real-time information. Use the data feed options to gain access to the content as soon as it is updated.

■ **Security Tip** There are several discussion lists available on the NIST NVD web site. You can subscribe or update your subscription at `https://nvd.nist.gov/general/email-list`.

Security Responsibility Model

Customers have specific responsibilities to put security controls in place, and the Microsoft Azure service already has these controls in place for customers. For example, the security discovery must be clearly identified and methodically investigated to provide security needs for core capabilities based on the type of Azure cloud services your business may use. There are three types of services customers consider when migrating to the cloud: infrastructure as a service (IaaS), platform as a service (PaaS), and software as a service (SaaS). The security requirements are compared to traditional on-premises services including a traditional datacenter.

You compare traditional to cloud security and might call into question a description of on-premises private clouds identified by your cloud security team. It is a true statement that solutions such as the Microsoft Azure stack provide a private cloud solution on-site. However, some teams may confuse virtualization as a private cloud deployment. A highly virtualized environment is often not a private cloud.

■ **Security Tip** NIST has a short, three-page guide that defines the cloud provider services. The document can be used by your discovery team and downloaded at `http://dx.doi.org/10.6028/NIST.SP.800-145`.

A Microsoft Azure cloud specifically has met security certifications for regulatory compliance requirements and industry-specific requirements, beyond the short list here. You, as a Microsoft Azure customer, have access to independently verified cloud compliance offerings including the following:

- ISO 27001
- ISO 27018
- SOC 1, 2, 3 Type 2
- CSA STAR 1

More details are not included in this chapters executive summary, but later in this chapter and others additional information is provided for the specific features and controls of the individual management systems. Additionally, the industry-specific cloud compliance that have been verified include the following:

- HIPAA BAA
- PCI DSS Level 1
- FERPA
- CDSA

The security certifications required are expanded based on U.S. government requirements and are regional or country specific. If you don't know whether your business requires one of these compliance standards, you should invest in a security team member or contractor with experience in security audits to help identify your company requirements and to validate Azure security attestation.

■ **Security Tip**   *Attestation* is the compliance validation of the authenticity needed by the platform. For more information about Microsoft cloud security certification, refer to the Microsoft Trust Center at `http://microsoft.com/trustcenter`. For a complete list of compliance offerings, refer to `https://www.microsoft.com/en-us/trustcenter/compliance/complianceofferings`.

Out-of-compliance security may be attributed to the growth of *shadow IT*, which consists of agile IT systems such as cloud solutions created inside organizations that did not necessarily request business approval. When you consider that the Azure cloud solutions provide a worldwide datacenter at the cost of a credit card, shadow IT enables faster prototypes, sometimes referred to as *science projects*, that may become business critical or revenue generating. Solutions constructed by well-meaning teams almost always do not meet an organization's requirements for control, confidentiality, integrity, availability, and security. Shadow IT should be addressed quickly with an executive security policy and firm enforcement to prevent future security issues.

■ **Security Tip**   Shadow IT includes the transmission of data that is relied upon for business processes that the IT department did not develop and is not aware of. The uncontrolled flow of data transfer may cause your organization to fail to meet the security requirements of the Sarbanes-Oxley Act, Federal Information Security Management Act (FISMA), Health Insurance Portability and Accountability Act (HIPAA), Information Technology Infrastructure Library (ITIL), or Payment Card Industry Data Security Standard (PCI DSS).

Why It Is Important

The NVD provides the official Common Platform Enumeration dictionary and is a structured naming scheme for information technology systems, software, and packages. The name standard is based on generic syntax for Uniform Resource Identifiers (URIs). The CPE dictionary includes the following:

- Formal name format

- Method for checking names against a system

- Description format for binding text and tests to the name

The CPE dictionary hosted and maintained at NIST may be used by nongovernmental organizations on a voluntary basis and is not subject to copyright in the United States.

> *"NVD is the U.S. government repository of standards based vulnerability management data. This data enables automation of vulnerability management, security measurement, and compliance. NVD includes databases of security checklists, security-related software flaws, misconfigurations, product names, and impact metrics."*

■ **Security Tip**   A free utility from Microsoft for Windows is the Malicious Software Removal Tool. It checks your computer for specific, prevalent malicious software (including Blaster, Sasser, and Mydoom) and helps to remove the infection if it is found. Microsoft releases an updated version of this tool on the second Tuesday of each month. Refer to `https://www.microsoft.com/en-us/download/malicious-software-removal-tool-details.aspx` for more information.

Summary

This chapter introduced executives, managers, and leadership teams to the many details of how a business is impacted by security vulnerabilities. The focus began with an executive summary designed to make busy executives more aware; I gave some insight into how businesses are attacked through their security weaknesses. An attacker's motivation was shown through the metrics displaying the financial or tactical gain of adversaries.

Some companies are only beginning to build teams to review security analyst data and stay informed to maintain a stronger defense-in-depth strategy. Attackers have more sophisticated attacking solutions than ever before, which requires security leadership to comprehend weaknesses and prevent exploitation.

Chapter 2 discusses how to securely migrate to the Azure cloud, with specific needs to invest in security resources and expertise.

CHAPTER 2

■ ■ ■

Azure Security Center Cost Model

Financial Impact of Cloud Security

There is great value in using the Azure cloud infrastructure and security models in the form of a service that can reduce the cost of traditional on-premises life cycles. The cost of software—or in this case the cost of a cloud security service—is more than the licenses. Data storage, integration, and training are all considerations when selecting the right security solutions.

Security managers and teams often struggle to provide a cost justification for intrusion detection systems (IDSs) and intrusion prevention systems (IPSs). Azure cloud services are like a utility model for a ready network and servers, and Azure services also include security solutions in the cloud. However, just like the cloud infrastructure, security is a shared model. The security provided by the cloud and by the customer is not always easy to realize or to obtain an upper manager's approval to purchase.

In this chapter, you'll learn about the cost of Azure Security Center, including the following topics:

- Infrastructure as a service (IaaS), platform as a service (PaaS), software as a service (SaaS), traditional

- Shared security model

- License impact of Azure Security Center

- Azure cost of data storage

- Quantitative risk assessments and cost-benefit analysis (CBA)

There are additional costs that are often overlooked and underestimated, such as for the following:

- Azure Active Directory

- Microsoft Azure Premier plans

- Application gateways and firewalls

- Enterprise security architects (the cost of cybersecurity)

Some companies have specific financial- or business-compliant reasons for maintaining a small traditional datacenter on-site. One reason customers move to the cloud is to achieve the agility to build services quickly without the overhead cost to buy all the servers on day 1 of a new project and without the cost to maintain traditional datacenters when utilization is low. Traditional, on-site datacenters have a cost model including many areas that developers, managers, and administrative staff typically don't consider. However, the executives who approve policies for security operations, business continuity planning (BCP), and disaster recovery planning (DRP) are very aware of datacenter costs.

© Marshall Copeland 2017
M. Copeland, *Cyber Security on Azure*, DOI 10.1007/978-1-4842-2740-4_2

On-premises datacenters require real estate, fencing, security guards, security cameras, redundant power companies, backup generators, banks of batteries, air conditioners, air humidifiers, and racks on which to place network gear and servers. Most companies plan a five-year life cycle for infrastructure costs, so the yearly IT budget is used to replace hardware based on estimates of utilization for the revenue-generating software and assets. All the servers needed for the next calendar year are purchased at one time, but the cloud model allows companies to pay as they go.

Many companies can move all assets into the cloud over time, but others are slow to fully embrace the cloud's economic PaaS savings. Every company I work with has used a hybrid cloud infrastructure for an extended period. Some of my customers have stated they want to get out of the datacenter business, but the journey takes planning by IT and support from upper management. However, Azure can't automatically make applications security compliant. You need to fully understand the advantages and disadvantages of a cloud security model. There is a great deal of value you gain by leveraging the security components from the Azure cloud, and there are areas of security expertise you must continue to provide to keep your applications compliant and infrastructure secured.

Shared Cost Model

There are substantial challenges for IT security as you migrate to Microsoft Azure, including for the hybrid infrastructure model. The hybrid network is inclusive of the buildings, data closets, and datacenters you manage as well as the security requirements as the network extends into the Azure cloud, as shown in Figure 2-1. In a business using a traditional model, IT security resources are aligned with the locations in the existing buildings, such as the datacenter, and remote office buildings that include systems managed by IT. Applications, servers, and data outside the secure perimeter are beyond the local enterprise building and network.

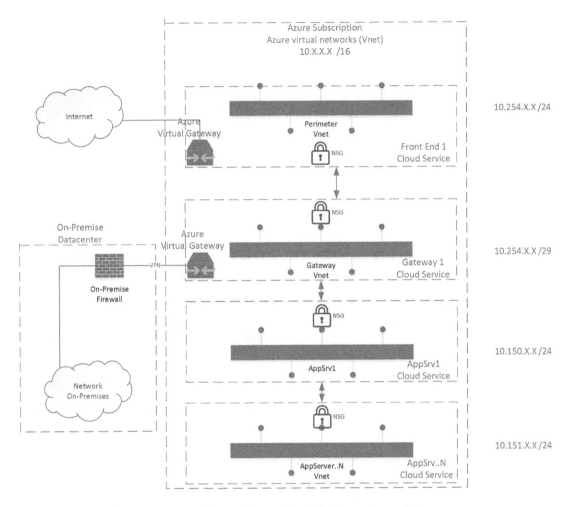

Figure 2-1. *Typical customer on-premises and Azure cloud hybrid security model*

The use of a cloud solution, like Microsoft Azure, introduces challenges to compliance, governance, and accountability with regard to being in control of network security. The solutions to the challenges include, at a minimum, supporting security with the flexible, dynamic resources from the cloud's elasticity. This dynamic global infrastructure is a partial reason your company is moving to the cloud in the first place.

In this book, you will learn how to gain the flexibility to enable, configure, and operate Azure Security Center. A side benefit of using Azure Security Center is the on-the-job training of staff members who can leverage the security best practices provided by Azure Security Center. You may often hear the term *shared responsibility* but may not have a clear understanding of what a cloud provider supports versus what your company, IT staff, and security team still need to maintain. The shared security responsibility is between the customer, which is you, and the cloud service provider (CSP), which is Microsoft Azure. The advantage of expanding the network infrastructure is that you get the benefits of the different cloud models (IaaS, PaaS, and SaaS) when compared to a traditional IT datacenter model, as shown in Figure 2-2.

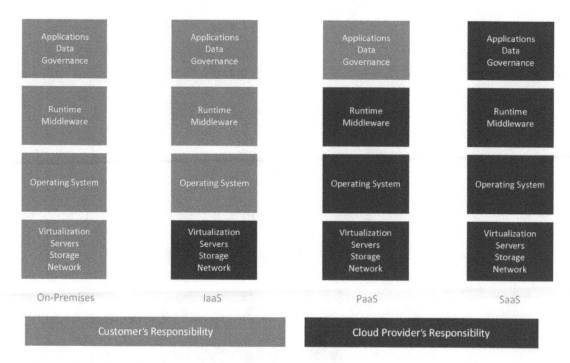

Figure 2-2. *Azure cloud provider model for IaaS, PaaS, SaaS*

In this book you'll learn about the shared model of security requirements and where there are security "gaps" that must be addressed. The topic of shared security vulnerabilities often reaches the security team after the business decision to migrate applications to the cloud is made. As security is "top of mind" to every CIO and CEO, the initial cloud conversations are increasingly including the network security team to prepare for the necessary additions of security.

I've worked with many customers and have provided clarity around this topic by allowing as much time as needed for Q&A when I talk to them. In Figure 2-3, the areas of responsibility can be interpreted as areas of security "risk" your company is responsible for understanding and maintaining.

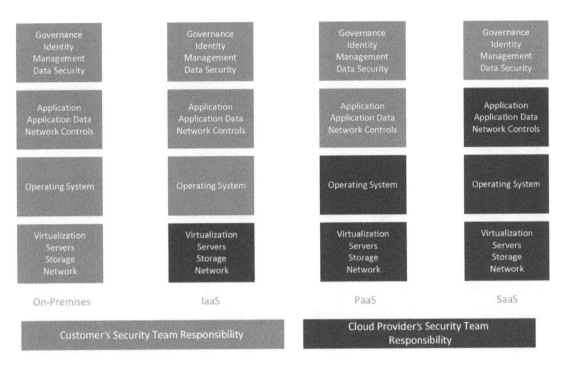

Figure 2-3. *Network security model*

Azure Security Center could be categorized as a cloud security solution from the cloud provider, Microsoft Azure, that supports security requirements for its IaaS and PaaS infrastructure. A cloud security solution would also be used in any SaaS solution that is provided by the cloud provider or built as a SaaS offering by your company. We'll concentrate on Security Center for the IaaS and PaaS models for now.

License Cost of Security Center

Changes in cloud computing occur often, so you should review the most current pricing for Security Center and Azure storage rates so you can provide a very close estimate the most accurate cost analysis before you submit a proposal to upper management.

■ **Security Tip** You can find current pricing for Security Center at https://azure.microsoft.com/en-us/ pricing/details/security-center/.

Two pricing models are available for Azure Security Center: a free tier and a standard tier. As you review the cost comparisons, the decision should not be between these two options, but the cost should be between the standard tier and another IDS or IPS. Table 2-1 lists the security features provided by Security Center.

Table 2-1. *Azure Security Center Tier Pricing Details*

Standard Tier	Free Tier	Security Feature
✓	✓	Security policy, assessment, and recommendations
✓	✓	Connected partner solutions
✓		Advanced threat detection
✓		Threat intelligence
✓		Behavioral analysis
✓		Crash analysis
✓		Anomaly detection
500MB/day/node	No cap	Daily data ingested per node
$15/node/month	Free	Price

The standard tier's pricing trial period has changed from 90 days to 60 days as of this writing. If you change the pricing tier in the Policy view of Azure Security Center, as explained in Chapter 5, the charges per month begin automatically. The automatic billing increase is important to consider both for the long term and when planning to test Azure Security Center. You can view the amount of time remaining on your free trial by opening the Security Center blade, selecting the Security Policy table, and selecting the Pricing tier, as shown in Figure 2-4.

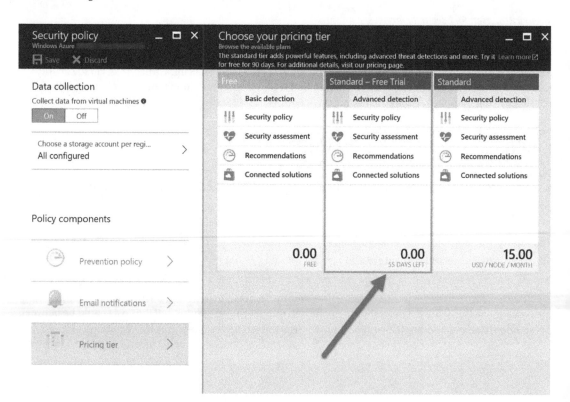

Figure 2-4. *Security Center standard tier days left in the trial period*

The term *node* is generally considered to mean each virtual machine (VM). However, as more security features are enabled, other Azure services, such as Azure cloud services and SQL databases, are considered nodes. One additional consideration is related to the free tier of Azure Security Center concerning the service level agreement (SLA). The SLA does not cover the free tier, so this may be another consideration for selecting the standard tier pricing.

■ **Note**   You can find the SLA for Azure Security Center at `https://azure.microsoft.com/en-us/support/legal/sla/security-center/v1_0/`.

Azure Cost of Data Storage

Microsoft Azure has four types of storage: blobs, files, disks, and queues. The different types of storage options are important for the total infrastructure costs. However, for Azure Security Center, the price of blob storage is included in the cost model when considering the purchase of Azure Security Center. You are not going to see an exact cost from the cloud infrastructure analysis here; the discussion will just make you aware of the additional costs of the overall solution.

The prices of block blob storage are based on the redundancy level of the storage type. This example is used for Azure Security Center storage, and you do not need to consider cool or hot storage because the storage used initially is hot storage. Table 2-2 shows the pricing for block blob storage.

Table 2-2. Azure Blob Storage Considerations for Security Center

	Locally Redundant (LRS)	Globally Redundant (GRS)	Read-Access (RA-GRS)
First 100TB/MTH	$0.024	$0.048	$0.061
Next 900TB/MTH	$0.023	$0.046	$0.058
Next 4,000TB/MTH	$0.022	$0.044	$0.046

You have to consider the cost for cloud storage when determining the overall cost of Azure Security Center. However, a potentially larger cost, specifically for cloud storage considerations, is for long-term storage to use with BI Analytics. The amount of data collected and the length of time to keep the data for data mining both need to be considered.

Finally, one additional cost consideration is that the local on-premises data collected from traditional security information and event management (SEIM) devices uses Azure cloud storage. The number of log files you have can increase the overall cost; however, the automatic analysis of the costs is often included with Azure Operations Manager Suite and not necessarily Security Center.

Quantitative Risk Assessments and Cost-Benefit Analysis

Often the question isn't can you afford Azure Security Center or any other security solution, the real question is how do you provide upper management with the information to show how much Azure Security Center can help your business?

Risk assessments are not something the IT staff is directly responsible for; they are often monetary values of a solution provided by the chief information security officer (CISO). Walking step-by-step through a risk assessment is a great opportunity for you to learn the definitions of the formulas and then apply the value of business assets to your own assessment.

There are two distinct categories of risk assessments.

- Quantitative risk assessments assign a dollar value to all elements of the assessment.

- Qualitative risk assessments use value terminology for high, medium, and low.

Both assessments consider the likeliness of a cyber-attack occurring and the overall cost of that impact. To begin, you need to understand the quantitative risk assessments starting with the individual elements.

- *Asset value (AV), in U.S. dollars*: This can be considered in a number of different ways, such as the amount of cost to create the asset or how much it would cost to replace the asset. The asset value is the amount of value the business places on the asset.

- *Exposure factor (EF), in percentage (%)*: This percentage represents the impact compared to the overall business at 100 percent.

- *Single loss expectancy (SLE), in U.S. dollars*: This is the loss in U.S. dollars if the loss, because of a security breach, occurred one time.

- *Annualized rate of occurrence (ARO)*: This is expressed as a number using the # symbol. If the occurrence happens once a year, then it is an annual occurrence. If the security threat happens once in every ten years, it would be 1/10 or one-tenth.

- *Annualized loss expectancy (ALE), in U.S. dollars*: On an annual basis, what can the business expect as a loss total?

- *Cost-benefit analysis (CBA), in U.S. dollars*: The CBA is the cost of placing controls into the overall security processes to reduce security risk.

Now that you understand the elements used in quantitative risk assessments, you need to understand the formula used. Then you'll see a scenario that helps justify the cost of security controls.

The following is one formula used in security cost justification:

```
Single Loss Expectancy = Asset Value × Exposure Factor
SLE in $ = AV in $ × EF in %
SLE = AV × EF
```

The following is another formula to use in cost justification:

```
Annualized Loss Expectancy = Single Loss Expectancy × Annualized Rate of Occurrence
ALE in $ = SLE in $ × ARO as a number
ALE = SLE × ARO
```

The cost benefit is also calculated to identify the value of enabling a security solution, as shown here:

```
Cost-Benefit Analysis = (Annualized Loss Expectancy1 - Annualized Loss Expectancy2) -
Annualized Cost of Mitigation
CBA in $ = (ALE1 - ALE2) - Annualized Cost of Mitigation
```

These are the formulas used in a security quantitative risk assessment and often where the senior leadership's eyes start to "glaze over."

These calculations are often put into an Excel spreadsheet to make slight changes and recalculate the numbers quickly. The Excel spreadsheet is used to support the subjective value of a specific business asset. The owner of the asset may place a larger or smaller value on the asset in support of the overall business. There are likely many different security exposure calculations that should be completed. There is not a single exposure factor and a single security mitigation number. This process should be completed for many if not all security risks that could expose the business to vulnerabilities, as discussed in Chapter 1. You need to understand the quantitative risk assessment process using the following steps necessary to calculate the risk mitigation:

1. Determine the asset value. Several factors contribute to the AV.

2. Determine the exposure factor. This is the impact if the security breach occurs.

3. Calculate the singe loss expectancy. Use this equation: $AV \times EF = SLE$.

4. Determine the annual rate of occurrence. How often can you expect this type of security event or vulnerability to occur?

5. Calculate the annualized loss expectancy (this is the ALE1) before you look at any mitigating controls.

6. Identify the mitigation controls. This is used to reduce the annualized loss expectancy.

7. Calculate the ALE, taking into consideration the mitigation controls (this is the ALE2).

8. Calculate the cost-benefit analysis. Does the price justify the security controls?

Figure 2-5 shows a visual representation of the steps used in the example exercises.

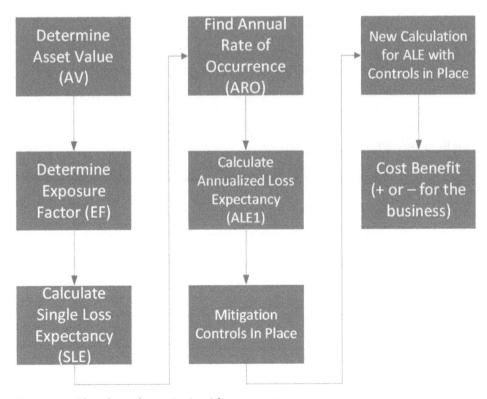

Figure 2-5. *Flow chart of quantitative risk assessment*

You can use these eight steps to validate the cost of Security Center compared to the cost of a data breach from a cyber-attack. It is difficult, however, to measure all types of security incidents, so you should walk through the quantitative assessment with a single, focused attack. The following sidebar describes the real-world risk of ransomware, one of the current threats worldwide that was discussed in Chapter 1. This example uses the formulas that are often used by CISOs to create a security risk cost-benefit analysis, and it's an example I use when I walk customers through the process, using specific examples of their data. This example is typical of some business models leveraging the cloud platform today.

RANSOMEWARE QUANTITATIVE RISK ASSESSMENT

Contoso Stock Photos has created a business that provides photographers across the United States with the infrastructure to upload their stock photo images into Azure VMs in an IaaS deployment model. The photos are distributed for purchasing through the Contoso Stock Photos web site, which is running on these highly customized OS virtual machine and back-end SQL databases, with each available in four Azure regions in the United States. Currently, there are 300,000 photos available each calendar year, and each photo generates $5 in revenue. The Contoso IT team has estimated the stock photos could be subject to a ransomware compromise once each year, with the compromise being contained to only one of the four Azure regions.

1. Determine the asset value, which is equal to the value of each photo multiplied by the number of photos.

   AV = $5.00 × 300,000 | AV = $1,500,000

   Here you are not considering the cost of creating the web sites and customizing the servers or the resources needed to create the infrastructure. Specifically, the Contoso IT team does not consider the Azure SLA requirements of two servers per region to guarantee uptime. The AV calculated is only the value of the photographer's photo as an asset.

2. The exposure factor is 25 percent. You know this because there are four VMs in four Azure regions, and the Contoso IT team stated that only one of the four servers is likely to be compromised.

3. Calculate the single loss expectancy using the AV multiplied by the exposure factor.

   $1,500,000 × 0.25 = $375,000

4. The annualized rate of occurrence is once a year. You know this because the Contoso IT team provided this information based on the calculations of photographers who upload photos, and the DevOps team has input validation on the web site along with other security features.

5. To calculate the first annualized loss expectancy (ALE1) per security breach, you multiply the asset value by the annual rate of occurrence.

   SLE × ARO = ALE

   $375,000 × 1 = $375,000

   ALE = $375,000

The cost to the businesses is very high, with an ALE1 of $375,000. As you learned in Chapter 1, most small businesses do not recover from a ransomware attack without cybersecurity mitigation in place. Now you need to work with the Contoso IT team to identify ways to mitigate the risk exposure. What can the Azure architect team design to help reduce the risk of a ransomware compromise?

The Contoso IT team members have reviewed their Azure deployment plan and stated they would like to distribute the infrastructure to two additional servers in each of the four regions. This provides an increase in Azure spend by increasing the total number of servers to eight. They also recommend enabling Azure Security Center as an enhanced threat detection system and Azure Backup to reduce the annual likelihood of a successful ransomware attack to once every three years.

6. You can now consider the mitigation factors the Contoso IT team has recommended using the same formulas. The AV is the same ($1,500), but the security mitigation factors change the ALE.

   EF = 1 of 8 servers, or 12.5 percent

   SLE = $1,500,000 × .125 = $187,000

   ARO is 1 every 3 years = 0.33

   So, the updated ALE is calculated like so:

   ALE = SLE × ARO

   $187,000 × 0.33 = $61,875

   ALE2 = $61,875.00

Overall, the security mitigation of increasing the number of servers has reduced the risk of a ransomware breach to $61,875. Now, the CBA must be calculated to justify the purchase of Azure Security Center. Said another way, does increasing the number of servers and the cost of protecting all the servers justify purchasing Azure Security Center?

The Contoso IT team members reviewed the available Azure VM sizing and have determined their budget will increase annually to $90,000; this amount over 12 months is $7,500 per month for four more customized VMs. This increase in budget allows Contoso Stock Photos to leverage the Azure SLA with two servers in each region. The cost of Azure Security Center per node (retail USD) is $15 per server, which includes 500MB of data. The cost of Azure Backup (retail USD) is $10 plus the storage cost.

■ **Note** The cost of data storage for Security Center is 500MB per VM, and the cost for Azure Backup is $0.05/GB (retail USD). Locally redundant storage (LRS) as of this printing is $0.024 for 100TB/month.

Azure Security Center (standard tier) = $15/node/month for each server

Azure Backup = $10/node/month for each server

$90,000 + ((15 × 8) × 12) + ((10 ×8) × 12)

$90,000 + 1440 + 960

$92,400 (cost of security controls)

7. The increase in the Contoso IT budget for the additional Azure VM spend is $90,000 annually, and the cost of mitigation is $2,400 (retail USD). The annual cost of mitigation is $92,400. This is the annual spend for the new VM budget + Azure Security Center + Azure Backup. Now you need to answer this question: is the cost of Azure Security Center worth the savings to the business in preparation of (at least) one ransomware attack?

$$CBA = (ALE1 - ALE2) - \text{Annual cost of mitigation}$$

$$CBA = (\$375,000 - \$61,875) - \$92,400$$

$$CBA = \$220,725 \ (USD)$$

With the positive variance of $220,725, there is a good chance the Contoso Stock Photos board of directors will vote to approve the purchase of Azure Security Center and Azure Backup as a ransomware security mitigation control for the Azure VMs that are revenue generating.

■ **Note** The budget increase by $90,000 is used in the calculation for the CBA and not the entire IT budget for all eight servers. Only the additional four servers are considered because they are included as part of the security mitigation. The cost to include Security Center on each VM and to include Azure Backup on each VM covers all eight Azure VMs. This CBA is used to justify the purchase of cybersecurity software to mitigate the risk of ransomware for the entire business.

There are additional timelines that are needed by companies when considering a backup strategy.

- Recovery time objective (RTO)
- Recovery point objective (RPO)
- Maximum tolerable downtime (MTD)

The critical point is for a company to "tier" data based on the importance to the organization and the frequency of use. With the more time-sensitive data being replicated off-site, many customers are choosing the Azure cloud backup as part of their disaster recovery plan. The RPO is the objective of the business to bring system back online, and the RTO is the actual amount of time required for systems to be recovered. The most important backup time consideration is how long a business can be down before it impacts the business permanently, which is the MTD.

Other Considerations (Security Sensitive)

Additional considerations that are often overlooked and underestimated include hard dollar product licensing and soft dollar training or security knowledge in the cloud. These features are often part of the overall Azure infrastructure. However, they are highlighted here because of the layered security support that is needed. The additional costs described in this section are not necessarily the cost of licenses but the cost of architecting and operational costs of security control placement and auditing. You should consider the security features needed to create a virtual protection ring around the corporate data security in a hybrid network that spans from on-premises to the Azure cloud.

Azure Active Directory

Azure Active Directory (AAD) provides directory authentication to grant access to core Azure services that enable the configuration of governance controls and application access. The basic (free) tier provides the ability to manage groups and users and supports synchronizing with Microsoft Active Directory Domain Services (AD DS). Microsoft AD 2016 supports needed security features such as the following:

- Bastion Active Directory forest provisioned with Microsoft Identity Manager

- Shadow security principals to access resources without changing control lists

- Kerberos ticketing changes to "time-enabled" access

These are just a few of the many supported delegations of rights focused on security, and the point of highlighting these features is twofold. First, all the features, not just the few mentioned here, are available and included during a role installation with Microsoft Active Directory Domain Services. Second, all the features in the latest version of AD DS are not currently available in Azure Active Directory, so there is a gap in security features that can be synchronized between the two authentication services. This is important when considering synchronization between on-premises AD DS and Azure cloud AAD using Azure Active Directory Connect.

■ **Note**   Read more about the features provided by different Azure AD editions at `https://docs.microsoft.com/en-us/azure/active-directory/active-directory-editions`.

AD Connect supports the synchronization of groups, users, and other AD objects between the cloud and the local datacenter. You should not expect to replicate all on-premises attributes into the Azure cloud because of the gap in functionality.

■ **Security Tip**   You can download Microsoft Azure Active Directory Connect from `https://www.microsoft.com/en-us/download/details.aspx?id=47594`.

Azure Active Directory Basic should not be the only consideration when evaluating additional features that are supported by AAD Premium P1 and AAD Premium P2. These are both license cost considerations, so it's easy to get the price for them. However, most companies upgrade to higher tier levels once they review the flexibility of services offered.

Multifactor authentication (MFA) is a critical security feature included for all users and service accounts in the premium versions of AAD. MFA identifies impossible travel to a typical location. The Security Center algorithm uses machine learning, and a baseline is needed to weed out false positives. "Impossible Travel" from familiar devices may give a false positive if you have sign-ins from VPNs that are used by other users from a (Microsoft) directory. The pricing is intentionally not listed because the price you pay depends on the way Azure can be purchased. Your company may purchase using a pay-as-you-go Microsoft enterprise agreement, the Open Volume License Program, or the Cloud Solution Providers program. Pricing is less expensive when purchased through an EA agreement, so the point of this information is to identify Azure AD) premium as another cost consideration of Azure, not necessarily Azure Security Center.

Azure Support Plans

Azure support options are another overlooked consideration, but they add tremendous value to your internal team. The support plan has many options to consider such as it is a tangible cost to the IT budget, yet this is an incredible value that very experienced Azure support engineers provide. Basic support is included with Azure for support online, self-help, and billing questions using e-mail. The support is available in most Azure regions during business hours, from 9 a.m. to 5 p.m. There are some minor exceptions to this rule and requirements for languages, so evaluating the support options is important.

Support options at a higher level like Professional Direct or Premier may be a more valuable option for customers who are new to the Azure security infrastructure and require a faster support option. The two options mentioned have greater costs but provide faster initial response times. The Professional Direct initial response time is less than an hour, and the Premier initial response time is less than 15 minutes. There are other support plans to review and consider if budget is your only concern; they are the Developer and Standard plans.

Enterprise and global companies often choose the Premier support plan because of the response time and the assignment of a Microsoft technical account manager (TAM). The account service management features include monthly reviews, planning times, and operational guidance and onboarding. Additional services can be proactive such as "risk assessments" and product support workshops.

■ **Note**   You can review the current options for Azure support plans at `https://azure.microsoft.com/en-us/support/plans/`.

Application Gateway

Azure Application Gateway (AG) operates at Layer 7 of the Open Systems Interconnection (OSI) model, which is an abstraction layer that specifies the share protocols and interfaces used by host-to-host communication over the network. In an Azure infrastructure, Azure Application Gateway provides Hypertext Transfer Protocol (HTTP) load balancing, cookie-based affinity, and Secure Sockets Layer (SSL) offloading and provides health monitoring using Azure health probes.

The Azure AG pricing is another cost to consider; Table 2-3 provides the details. Another security service to consider is the Azure Application Gateway Web Application Firewall (WAF), which protects the applications similarly to AG. The WAF protects applications against many, but not all, of the Open Web Application Security Project (OWASP) top ten web vulnerabilities.

Table 2-3. *Azure Application Gateway Charges per Month*

Size of Application Gateway	Basic Gateway in Hours	WAF Application Gateway
Small	$0.025 per gateway (~$19/month)	TBD
Medium	$0.07 per gateway (~$52/month)	TBD
Large	$0.32 per gateway (~$238/month)	TBD

The Web Application Gateway and the Web Application Firewall costs are small with a single implementation; however, some of the new features include protection from SQL injection, cross-site scripting, and session hijacks. Every size company leveraging the cloud needs redundancy for their web app gateways with active-passive or active-active configuration. Web application protection using a medium gateway easily doubles the monthly cost for redundant security needs. The cost is small for the overall consideration; however, it is another component when considering costs.

■ **Security Tip** OWASP is a not-for-profit program you and your developers can join to learn more about the security of software. Learn more at the community portal at `https://www.owasp.org`.

Other considerations include the use of traditional firewalls and security information and event management (SIEM) integration. Some of these options are discussed in detail in Chapter 6, and companies evaluate the solutions because they can leverage current on-premises knowledge for these devices. The learning curve is then the pivot point for training the current security team to learn the Azure infrastructure or investing in training the Azure cloud operation teams as virtual application security experts. Some of the third-party virtual applications that have another price point to consider include more than 70 applications from the many Microsoft Azure partners. Figure 2-6 shows a snapshot of the partner applications; however, the pricing for a partner solution is a separate bill from the partner and not included in your Microsoft Azure monthly billing.

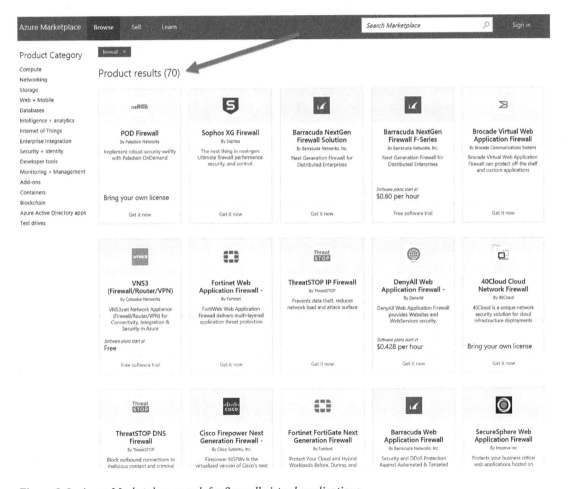

Figure 2-6. *Azure Marketplace search for firewall virtual applications*

Enterprise Security Architecture

The topic of enterprise security architecture can be extensive. Security architecture is a discipline that includes several design solutions to address system-level and network-level security across the infrastructure and applications. In the security industry, there exists a shortage of cybersecurity experts for all areas, but some of the more demanding positions include the following:

- Cloud security professional (CCSP)

- Certified expert penetration tester (CEPT)

- Certified security software lifecycle profession (CSSLP)

- Certified security analysis (CSA)

- Certified information systems security professional (CISSP)

There is a specific reason to remind managers of the need for a cloud security focus when migrating to the cloud, and it's that there is a shortage of security experts in supporting roles with expertise for nontraditional infrastructure, such as securing software-defined networks, cloud storage, network security groups, and Security Assertion Markup Language (SAML) for authentication. A need for new cloud designs is driving the necessity for cloud expertise. Companies require cloud security architects who design hybrid identity and access management solutions to authenticate valid users, grant authorization for cloud resources, and support a secure software development life cycle for applications.

A strategic security design focuses on the long-term strategy for business security services and is aligned directly with the business. Figure 2-7 shows a visual representation of all the business drivers in alignment with the support system of the business.

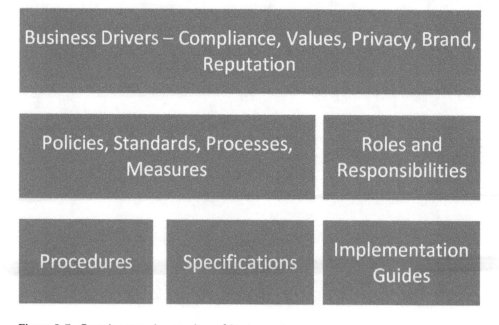

Figure 2-7. *Generic enterprise security architecture system*

There are cybersecurity frameworks available for companies looking for guidance for the enterprise. The National Institute of Standards and Technology (NIST) has an updated version of the Cybersecurity Framework. To support the framework that a company has in place, there are several enterprise security frameworks to consider, but you may want to focus on these two:

- Zachman framework

- Sherwood Applied Business Security Architecture (SABSA) framework

The enterprise architecture for the Zachman framework allows for the communication and collaboration for all areas of the infrastructure. Table 2-4 shows the Zachman framework from a high level.

Table 2-4. *Zachman Framework Example*

	What	How	Where	Who	When	Why
Scope	Importance to the business	Business processes	Business operations	Business organizations	Events or cycles	Business goals
Model	Semantic	Process model	Logic	Workflow	Schedule	Business plan
Designer	Data model	Application architecture	System architecture	Human interface	Process structure	Business rule model
Implementer	Physical data	System design	Technology architecture	Presentation architecture	Control structure	Rule design
Subcontractor	Data	Program	Network architecture	Security architecture	Timing Definition	Rule definition
Functioning System	Data	Function	Network	Organization	Schedule	Strategy

The framework focuses on the enterprise as a logical stricture but is not specific to a security architecture. The Sherwood Applied Business Security Architecture framework focuses on the security architecture with phases for strategy, concept, design, implementation, and metrics. Table 2-5 shows the SABA framework.

Table 2-5. Sherwood Applied Business Security Architecture Example

	What Assets	Why Motivation	How Process	Who Staff	Where Location	When Timing
Contextual	The business	Business risks	Business process	Business org relationship	Business geography	Dependencies
Conceptual	Attributes profile	Control objectives	Security strategies	Security Model Trust model	Security domain	Security lifetime
Logical	Information model	Security policies	Security services	Privilege Schema	Domain definitions	Security processes
Physical	Data model	Security procedures	Security mechanisms	Users, apps, interface	Network infrastructure	Control execution
Component	Detailed data structure	Security standards	Security products tools	ACL	Nodes, addresses, protocols	Security steps, timing
Operational	Assurance, continuity	Operational risk management	Security services management	Application, user support management	Security sites, networks, platforms	Security operations schedule

---

■ **Security Tip**   To learn more about the Sherwood Applied Business Security Architecture framework, refer to `www.sabsa.org/`.

Other frameworks include the Open Group Architecture Framework (TOAF) for organizations starting to design and build an enterprise. There are a lot of building blocks and components that can be used as reference models for companies that are looking for best practices and would like to use TOGAF.

Ransomware Lessons Learned

There are many different forms of malware that make security difficult to protect against and prevent, but if there were a single type to focus user training on, it would be ransomware. Ransomware prevents you from using your computer by holding your files "ransom" and preventing the recovery of the infection until you pay.

Many forms of ransomware have been recorded that have attacked indiscriminately by compromising large corporation workstations or single home computers. The attack "payload" uses encryption software deployed with malicious scripts via e-mail to quickly change the files on your systems so they cannot be accessed. If you're in a large enterprise and have network shared storage, the version of ransomware could encrypt those files even if your user account has the correct permissions. The bottom line is, no matter if you are at work or at home, files on the PC can't be accessed until the demand for money is paid.

The number of ransomware victims targeted has increased, as you read in Chapter 1, and the attackers specifically target their victims through e-mail phishing attempts. The phishing can be referred to as *whale phishing*, targeted to executives, or as *spear phishing*. An unexpecting e-mail recipient may click a malicious attachment that is cleverly disguised as an invoice from a company they know or have purchased from in the past.

You may think a phishing e-mail is easy to identify and that the typical weaponized payloads, like ransomware e-mail, are easy to identify, but they are not. If you look at the real-world example in Figure 2-8, this phishing e-mail made it through two different enterprise spam filters and a sophisticated endpoint protection and was not identified as a potential risk. The e-mail is slightly different, but it does not have any easily recognized signs from the usual suspects, like spelling errors, bad gramer, or a suspcious URL.

Figure 2-8. *Phishing email that looks very much like a real invoice*

This is a fake e-mail and not a real QuickBooks e-mail. However, if you don't normally pay business expenses, the e-mail looks legitimate for a business in specific areas of the world.

Figure 2-9 provides the Verizon DBIR report view of the top five malware varieties with ransomware in the second position. The business need for reviewing can be bolstered by a more technical review of the different families to identify "like" cyberattack methods.

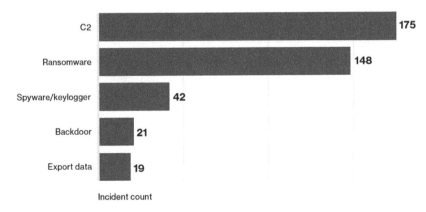

Figure 2-9. *Verizon DBIR top five malware varieties*

The technical-minded response for the validation of ransomware would include details about the most commonly encountered families worldwide. Using the current DBIR, SIR and other Cyber Security reports, help identify patterns, types, and similar industry attacks to "your" company.

■ **Security Tip**   Learn more about ransomware at the Internet Storm Center at `https://isc.sans.edu/`.

There is no substitute for end user awareness training in order for users to recognize suspicious e-mails and files that could harm their workstations. There is no single security program to stop the current variants of ransomware families, so having layers of security solutions starting at the network edge, next-generation firewalls, and intrusion detection and prevention systems for corporate enterprises are still a best practices. Many small and home businesses have budget-conscience solutions to help with the layering of network security.

Being prepared for ransomware requires two steps.

1. Back up your data and move the backup to an offline location. The fact that the backup from your system is saved to a location not connected by a network to your computer is key.

2. Create a second copy of your data and move it to a separate offline location.

If your computer and the backup location are not connected, it cannot be encrypted by ransomware.

■ **Security Tip**   Home users can get up-to-date advice from the University of California at `http://cnc.ucr.edu/security/userbp.html`.

Summary

In this chapter, you learned more about the cloud support models and what customers are responsible for when using IaaS, PaaS, and SaaS and what the cloud provider is responsible for maintaining. This groundwork was necessary to introduce you to a similar shared security model where you learned the shared matrix provided by the Azure cloud and what you are still responsible for supporting.

Next, you took a deep dive into not only the license costs of Azure Security Center per node but of the added Azure data changes for keeping security data in the cloud. To help justify the cost of purchasing the license for Security Center, I walked you through a quantitative risk assessment to justify the cost of security risk controls. Finally, you were guided through additional costs for Azure security components that are indirectly connected to Security Center such as Azure Active Directory, Microsoft Azure Premier plans, and Application Gateway. With a short introduction to enterprise security architecture, you were able to realize the cost of cybersecurity from more than a license perspective but as one that affects staff training and expertise.

In the next chapter, you will learn about creating an Azure subscription to deploy a typical virtual network infrastructure in detail.

Cloud Security Operations

Part II of this book provides you with a corporate deployment that can be used to configure Azure Security Center and enable a cloud security service foundation for your company's daily use of Security Center. This part also provides proactive recommendations that reduce real risk for your company and reduce exposure from cyber-threats.

Cybersecurity is not a difficult process. It is, however, a topic weighing on every company, and it is a problem that constantly shifts because the attackers are extremely agile, even using prebuilt frameworks. This part of the book covers the following topics that every security professional needs to know:

- How to assess the current security level (good/bad/really bad)

- How to improve compared to last year's metrics

- How to purchase effective security solutions wisely

- How to mitigate a new current risk or how to transfer it

CHAPTER 3

Getting Started with Azure Security Center

Prevent, Detect, Respond

In Chapter 2 you learned about the cost model beyond licenses and identified additional cost considerations required in an Azure cloud such as storage, static IP addressing, Domain Name System (DNS) servers, and other cloud infrastructure costs. Chapter 2 also covered the Azure infrastructure details required to evaluate the true financial impact of Azure Security Center on the business. You justified a budget increase through a real-world example using the financial impact of a ransomware attack in a quantitative risk assessment. You can use the same formula in your business analysis with the clear definitions of the model explained in Chapter 2. You then walked through some of the differences in standard business frameworks and how customization is needed to integrate cybersecurity as a service with existing IT business programs. Minor cybersecurity program changes may be necessary because of the diversity of different businesses.

In this chapter, you'll learn about some of the challenges of cloud security and get a high-level overview of exactly what Azure Security Center provides for intrusion detection and prevention. Additionally, you'll learn ways Azure Security Center can be positioned to support a cybersecurity framework for defense. You will learn best practices to support businesses using the IT life cycle and the layered security model.

Specifically, this chapter provides guidance to leverage Azure Security Center in the following areas:

- Prevention (overall compliance and applied best practices)

- Detection (Security Operations Center 24/7)

- Response (incident response process notification and event handling)

This chapter introduces a typical Azure cloud deployment example. This Contoso.com example is used in all the exercises in the remaining chapters. The cloud deployment infrastructure example includes virtual networks (vnets), virtual machines (VMs), and SQL Server instances. These cloud assets are designed to highlight the features of Azure Security Center based on real-world customer deployments, including mistakes.

Note This deployment example is also designed to follow standard cloud deployments that are often completed in Azure infrastructure deployments by new-to-the-cloud IT teams. The Contoso.com example provides security improvements that can and should apply to real-world deployments to strengthen a business's cybersecurity posture in the cloud.

© Marshall Copeland 2017
M. Copeland, *Cyber Security on Azure*, DOI 10.1007/978-1-4842-2740-4_3

Finally, this chapter discusses Azure subscription types that can be used for educational purposes before going into production. You'll learn how to enable a 30-day free Azure trial specifically for testing Azure Security Center.

Cloud Security Challenges

Small, medium, and enterprise-scale companies as well as government agencies are moving to the public cloud to take advantage of the elasticity and commodity of scale from trusted providers. Companies need to enable the best cloud security methods to extend their on-premises security layering to protect customer data, systems, and assets in the cloud.

Cloud infrastructures, in most companies new to cloud management and cybersecurity, are greatly distributed, and management is sometimes difficult. Chief information officers (CIOs) and chief information security officers (CISOs) are still responsible for the security of these environments even though the cloud infrastructure is more dynamic. A CISO requires best practices for security from on-premises environment integrated into the cloud. Customers with larger teams and longevity have on average 30 different security or cybersecurity-related solutions. Many of these tools create alerts that require attention, and the expertise required for each security solution creates another challenge for experts to use each solution and gain value from the data.

Sunset applications are ones that may no longer have engineering support, and these older applications are greater targets for cyber-attacks. In fact, some of the older applications were created under nonagile methods and could take more time and resources to be reviewed by a current software assurance program.

Every size company using Security Center leverages continuous security data analyses from Azure-deployed virtual machines, virtual networks, platform as a service (PaaS) services (think Azure SQL database), and partner solutions such as Barracuda, Fortinet, or Check Point. Companies gain visibility into the current security state, which extends across all subscriptions, so for customers that leverage parent-child Azure subscriptions, like a sandbox, those subscriptions may be used by system admins to improve their cloud knowledge.

Senior executives must rethink their approach to cloud security beyond traditional on-premises security expertise. Enterprise organizations may have greater numbers of staff members labeled as experienced cloud security experts; however, investment in cloud expertise introduces new challenges. Moving data to Azure cloud resources challenges administrators in the management of access and auditing of cloud security for those assets. Small and medium-size companies have the same compliance requirements as larger organizations with the additional competitive struggle to attract and maintain crucial cloud security experts. In addition, the support for secure DevOps is challenging for companies that want application development to include cloud agility.

It is important to understand the attack targets that bad actors are attempting to compromise inside an organization. The same type of attack surfaces can be seen in the Azure cloud, as shown here:

- Impersonation of a user (social media)

- Credential theft and elevation of privileges (admin or developer)

- Installing code to enable backdoors

- Gaining access to data and data resources (cloud resources)

- Azure subscription owners (top-level administration)

- Pivot attacks from on-premises to the public cloud

- Cloud resource compromises by hijacking or other exploitation

- Privilege elevation to move between subscriptions

- Public storage secret credential keys (GitHub)

- Misconfiguration of credential keys

- Imperva "man-in-the-cloud" token synchronized

- Side-channel code enablement

- Ransomware on cloud resources

The added training requirements that are needed to ramp up for cloud administrators and the additional need to improve knowledge to extend cybersecurity expertise to the cloud can be overwhelming. Every organization that chooses Microsoft Azure as part of their hybrid infrastructure can leverage Azure Security Center.

Security Center Overview

As you know, Microsoft Azure Security Center is a cloud-based service providing intrusion detection and intrusion prevention for a customer's Azure virtual infrastructure. It increases visibility by providing security control recommendations during automated configuration scanning and protects against cyber-threats attempting to compromise assets in Azure. Security Center provides integration using next-generation monitoring and policy management for the detection of threats that could go unnoticed. The collection of data from systems such as virtual machines, networks, or SQL Server instances is used to assess the current state of security. If evidence of a compromise is identified, security administrators are alerted to potential threats. In addition, Security Center uses the security state of systems and networks to provide best practice security recommendations to improve security readiness and reduce cyber-risks.

From a functional perspective, Azure installs a lightweight agent on the Windows or Linux VM, and the agent is enabled to automatically collect health monitoring, security configuration, and event data for all virtual machines in the subscription. The agent enables extensions to collect the data with minimum impact on the server performance. The security policy is set at the subscription level, and the data collections flow up from the group level. The events are collected and automatically prioritized based on the billions of security attributes and millions of Windows systems events accumulated across Microsoft's data intelligence.

Azure Security Center accumulates events and other data in your Azure subscription by monitoring the network and identifying suspicious machines communicating to command and control sites.

■ **Note**   Command and control servers may be directly controlled by the malware operators or themselves run on hardware compromised by malware. If you'd like to know more about command and control, review the Wikipedia page at `https://en.wikipedia.org/wiki/Command_and_control_%28malware%29`.

Many Internet addresses are identified as known sites for cyber-terrorists and are challenging for network providers to remove from the Internet. The information used in Security Center is collected from Microsoft's Digital Crimes Unit, Microsoft's Security Response Center, and leading security providers that have partnered with Microsoft specifically for security analytics.

The following are the advanced detection capabilities enabled out of the box:

- Anomaly detection for statistical profiling used for baselines

- Behavior analytics and known malicious behaviors and patterns

- Threat intelligence to identify known malicious attacks

- Synthesis, which is a mixture of events and alerts mapping of the kill chain timeline

- Secure Shell (SSH) or Remote Data Protocol (RDP) brute-force attacks and failed exploitation attempts

- Web application exploitations

Companies can leverage the current investment from on-premises security information and event management (SEIM) systems by importing the data into Azure Security Center or exporting it out of Azure for on-premises analysis or archiving. The preconfigured collections are set to 30 days for a baseline to understand the changes and to leverage machine learning in a supervisory manor with the data that is collected. Security center is detecting the threats and tagging them as true positive events and reducing false positives so customers can focus on the real threats.

This provides your cloud security team with clearly identified security alerts. These alerts are automatically analyzed from log data about the network, firewall configuration, and partner solutions like anti-malware. Threats are detected, and the corresponding alert is sent as a notification. Additional information from the correlated data provided by Security Center, with analysis and best practice recommendations, is also part of the overall solution.

If you are part of or have a traditional Security Operations Center (SOC), the goal is to retrieve the individual system event information and pool it for SIEM data use and then analyze it for known and unknown patterns. The event data reviewed is based on the SOC generation capabilities for log analysis. The systems have moved far beyond manually analyzing huge amounts of information to using an automated process. Vulnerability management takes place as described in NIST Special Publication 800-40 Revision 3, "Guide to Enterprise Patch Management Technologies." From a pure cybersecurity risk analyst perspective, a vulnerability is discovered and confirmed, and corrective measures (i.e., best practices) are identified.

Traditional log analysis collects large amounts of data (big data) from host systems, networks, and endpoints (nodes), so when an attack starts, much of the data is not visible in this limited view. In other words, this limited information from the host or network does not provide a complete and clear view of the attack attributes.

■ **Note**   The feature called Event Tracing for Windows (ETW) provides a mechanism to trace and log events that are raised by user-mode applications and kernel-mode drivers. ETW is implemented in the Windows operating system and provides developers with a fast, reliable, and versatile set of event tracing features.

Security Center Placement

As you learned in earlier chapters, a cybersecurity defense framework provides measured controls and security protection for external and internal security threats. As you start to leverage additional security solutions, such as Azure Security Center, a seasoned CISO or CIO must expect the worst outcome and plan accordingly. To be more specific, the resources from a determined nation make greater threats available that can defeat most if not all of the security layers put in place. Clearly, no amount of financial resources or even company-supported, well-trained security resources can sustain continued attacks from a cyber-army because of their unlimited resources to overpower.

The placement of Azure Security Center may very well depend on the results from testing completed in your environment. Security Center is viewed by many security teams as an intrusion identification service with the added features of recommending changes to improve security. Defensive design allows Azure Security Center to detect attacks and potentially breached networks and systems. Organizations can leverage the strength of Security Center discussed earlier as part of the layered cybersecurity defense framework and strategy. It uses next-generation solutions to actively identify attackers at the beginning of the attack before they can be successful.

Another key feature to help identify how to best use Azure Security Center is that the solution allows you to leverage the strengths of Microsoft's global cybersecurity knowledge and its global partners that previously required multiple products and highly skilled cybersecurity team members. After evaluating the solution, you may find it provides the necessary coverage in the cloud so additional licenses for on-premises solutions that overlap features of Security Center are not required. Additional insight is provided by standards from the Open Web Application Security Project (OWASP), which focuses on the improvement of software security. Read more at https://www.owasp.org.

■ **Note** "The national and economic security of the United States depends on the reliable functioning of critical infrastructure. To strengthen the resilience of this infrastructure, President Obama issued Executive Order 13636 (EO), 'Improving Critical Infrastructure Cybersecurity,' on February 12, 2013." To learn more about this quote from the NIST Cybersecurity Framework or more about the framework, visit https://www.nist.gov/cyberframework.

In Chapter 2 you were introduced to some best practices; for example, the Information Technology Infrastructure Library (ITIL) is IT guidance and not a security framework. You also discovered that governance is a key focus for cloud deployments specifically around security requirements such as lease privileged. Many professionals point out that the NIST Cybersecurity Framework does not fully address all cybersecurity areas; some security control areas are missing. For our discussion, we'll use the NIST Cybersecurity Framework so you have a single framework for referencing the NIST "Framework for Improving Critical Infrastructure Cybersecurity" document so that you can clearly place the components of Azure Security Center in support of this framework. If your business has a custom cybersecurity framework, the placement should be transparent also. Refer to Table 3-1 as you identify the placement of features for the exercises in the following chapters.

Table 3-1. *Cybersecurity Framework Function and Identifier Categories*

Function Unique Identifier	Function	Category Unique Identifier	Category
ID	Identify	ID.AM	Asset Management
		ID.BE	Business Environment
		ID.GV	Governance
		ID.RM	Risk Assessment
		ID.RM	Risk Management Strategy
PR	Protect	PR.AC	Access Control
		PR.AT	Awareness and Training
		PR.DS	Data Security
		PR.IP	Information Protection Processes & Procedures
		PR.MA	Maintenance
		PR.PT	Protective Technology
DE	Detect	DE.AE	Anomalies and Events
		DE.CM	Security Continuous Monitoring
		DE.DP	Detection Processes

(continued)

Table 3-1. (*continued*)

Function Unique Identifier	Function	Category Unique Identifier	Category
RS	Respond	RS.RP	Response Planning
		RS.CO	Communications
		RS.AN	Analysis
		RS.MI	Mitigation
		RS.IM	Improvements
RC	Recovery	RC.RP	Recovery Planning
		RC.IM	Improvements
		RC.CO	Communications

Azure Security Center provides support for areas in the framework to do the following:

- Protect (AC, AT, DS, IP, PT)

- Detect (AE, CM, DP)

- Respond (CO, an, MI, IM)

As you complete the exercises in later chapters, I will identify the specific connection to the cybersecurity support feature. In addition, I will explain the share support model between the cloud provider and customer as the customer expands their hybrid cloud model, as shown in Table 3-2. You will be provided specific guidance when using Security Center features to enable a gap feature.

Table 3-2. *Share Security Support Table to Identify Areas for Customers to Reference*

PaaS	IaaS
OS updates = Azure automated	OS updates = Customer manual
Logging = Azure automated	Logging = Customer manual
ACSs = Azure automated	ACLs= Customer manual
OS configuration = Hybrid	OS configuration = Customer manual
RDP = On demand	RDP/SSH = Customer manual

Preventing an Azure Infrastructure Breach

Security controls are in place to reduce the risk of an Azure subscription security breach. Some of the infrastructure safeguards include just-in-time administration (JIT) and role-based access control (RBAC). Security in the cloud is similar to on-premises after going through a security life cycle.

An organization can use their current security framework (or NIST Cybersecurity Framework) as a key part of its systematic process for identifying, assessing, and managing cybersecurity risk. The framework is not designed to replace existing processes; an organization can use its current process and overlay it onto the framework to determine gaps in its current cybersecurity risk approach and develop a road map to improvement. Utilizing the framework as a cybersecurity risk management tool, an organization can determine activities that are most important to critical service delivery and prioritize expenditures to maximize the impact of the investment. The framework is designed to complement existing business and cybersecurity operations. It can serve as the foundation for a new cybersecurity program or a mechanism for improving an existing program. The cybersecurity framework provides a means of expressing cybersecurity requirements to business partners and customers and can help identify gaps in an organization's cybersecurity practices. It also provides a general set of considerations and processes for privacy and civil liberties implications in the context of a cybersecurity program. The following sections present different ways in which organizations can use the framework.

Basic Review of Cybersecurity Practices

The Cybersecurity Framework can be used to compare an organization's current cybersecurity activities with those outlined in the framework's core. Through the creation of a current profile, organizations can examine the extent to which they are achieving the outcomes described in the core categories and subcategories, aligned with the five high-level functions: identify, protect, detect, respond, and recover. An organization may find that it is already achieving the desired outcomes, thus managing cybersecurity commensurate with the known risk. Conversely, an organization may determine that it has opportunities to (or needs to) improve. The organization can use that information to develop an action plan to strengthen existing cybersecurity practices and reduce cybersecurity risk. An organization may also find that it is overinvesting to achieve certain outcomes. The organization can use this information to reprioritize resources to strengthen other cybersecurity practices.

While they do not replace a risk management process, these five high-level functions will provide a concise way for senior executives and others to refine fundamental concepts of cybersecurity risk so they can assess identified risks, how each could be managed, and how their organization stacks up at a high level against existing cybersecurity standards, guidelines, and practices. The framework can also help an organization answer fundamental questions, including "How are we doing?" Then the organization can move in a more informed way to strengthen its cybersecurity practices where and when deemed necessary.

Establishing or Improving a Cybersecurity Program

The following steps illustrate how an organization could use the Cybersecurity Framework to create a new cybersecurity program or improve one that is currently in place. These steps should be repeated as necessary for a continuously improved cybersecurity life cycle. The high-level steps include the following:

1. *Prioritization*: The business identifies mission objectives and reconfigures the priorities based on the goal. Using this new prioritization, the business makes strategic resolutions for cybersecurity implementations. The Cybersecurity Framework can easily be customized for larger enterprise businesses or for unique business lines. Many customers have different business needs and associated risk tolerance.

2. *Rationalize*: The next step for the cybersecurity team is to identify related systems and assets. Accommodate the requirements and overall risk guidance based on the direction. The cybersecurity team can then identify specific types of threats with more focused vulnerabilities based on those systems, data, and other assets.

3. *Delineation*: The cybersecurity team provides analysis of specific business lines based on category and subcategory. Both of these parent-child businesses are products of the rationalization achieved.

4. *Assessment*: The risk assessment is the guide for the business to address the overall risk management process. The cybersecurity team and the business together analyze the operational environment to ascertain any security event and provide US Dollar value to the business of the event impact. Companies should continue security analyses for evaluating emerging risks and threat. Proactive vulnerability data, used by the business units to mitigate issues, is like using a "wide net" for information, business cost, business needs, by understanding potential impact of cybersecurity events.

5. *Targeted*: The cybersecurity team creates a persona that focuses on the assessments of the business and business lines. The characteristics describing the organization's desired cybersecurity expectations are used to develop additional subcategories to address unique organizational risks.

6. *Gap analysis*: To truly provide mitigation on all exposed business assets, the cybersecurity team must allow identified gaps to be addressed. It is the gap analysis that is used to recommend changes to address specific gaps. The business can then better determine the necessary steps to remediate and address any budgetary concerns.

7. *Implement*: What are the exact actions to carry out based on the gap analysis? Continuous improvement is leveraged with reevaluation following the cybersecurity best practices you just enabled. You can gain additional guidance using the Cybersecurity Framework references.

Azure Virtual Networking Example

The fundamentals of networking are not exactly the same as on-premises because Azure is a hosted multitenant model. If you are new to Azure, then creating Azure virtual networks is often first done from the portal, and security features used on-premises are not configured for the vnet. There are two main reasons for this, listed here:

*   You are new to Azure and are just learning the functionality.

*   System administrators are not network security experts.

As cloud administrators work through the portal wizard to create subnets, Azure windows prompt you with guidance and try to be helpful when building networks. Each Azure vnet subnet permits network traffic from one vnet to other Azure vnets by default unless you specifically prevent the TCP/IP communication. Perimeter networks of on-premises IP subnets are isolated by firewalls to prevent Internet attacks that try to gain access to other network subnets on-premises.

How do you secure specific subnets from the Internet and really design the Azure virtual network to resemble your on-premises network? If you have the skill set for IP subnets and networks, then you could architect the entire infrastructure. In addition to knowing TCP/IP subnetting, you also need to know details about subnetting and security in Azure. Another point to consider is whether you are working in a small IT shop and you wear many "hats" and don't have time to invest in Ethernet networking classes and additional classes for Azure. Azure Security Center scans and discovers the current Azure infrastructure with best practices to implement based on your deployment.

A security architecture needs to consider the network aspects of Azure as an extension of its on-premises network design. The values used for TCP/IP subnets cannot be duplicated in Azure. In other words, the IP subnets are managed and maintained by the same IT business team. Extending your company's network into Azure is important, and you must get it right. To show how Azure Security Center provides best practices and guidance for Azure vnets, I have created a simple design for discussion purposes only.

The virtual network shown in Figure 3-1 is how most Azure administrators start creating virtual networks before they start to place VMs into the individual networks. This example shows how Azure Security Center reviews the network configuration and suggests security measures to help improve your security posture. Other exercises in the other book "*Microsoft Azure: Planning, Deploying, and Managing Your Data Center in the Cloud, Apress Publishing ISBN-10: 1484210441*" will build VMs like in this foundation network example for the single purpose of identifying additional security-enabled features recommended by Azure Security Center so you can increase security protection in your Azure subscription.

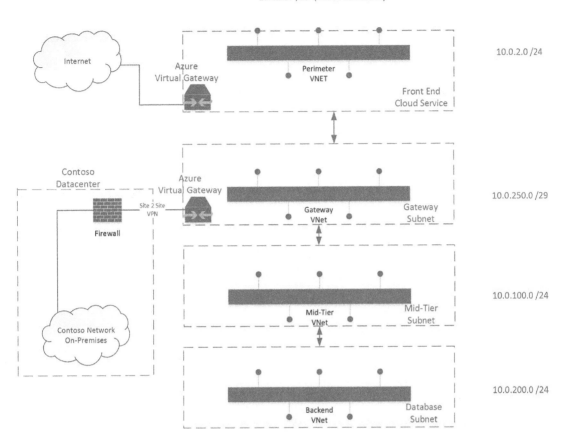

Figure 3-1. Azure vnet example of Contoso used in chapter exercises

---

■ **Tip** If you need detailed guidance on Microsoft Azure services, you can read my book *Microsoft Azure: Planning, Deploying, and Managing Your Data Center in the Cloud* (http://tinyurl.com/h5vktdg).

ON-PREMISES TO AZURE VPN CONNECTION

You will now gain a brief overview of your options for moving a hybrid environment from your on-premises network into Azure. Most customers extend Azure on-premises into Azure using one of the three options, listed here:

- Point-to-site (P2S)
- Site-to-site (S2S) VPN
- ExpressRoute

A P2S connection is used for remote branch sites or to connect a developer's laptop to Azure. Small and medium-sized companies often use telecom services to enable access from IT datacenters or IT data closest to the Internet. Companies have hardware devices that support a static public IP address, and they can be used to create a VPN connection into Azure. A P2S configuration supports a secure connection from an individual client computer, like a laptop, to an Azure virtual network. A P2S connection is useful when you want to connect to your vnet from a small office or from a mobile user's location such as a home office or a conference or when only a few clients need to connect to an Azure virtual network.

The connection most medium and large customers start with is an S2S VP connection. This type of connection enables companies to use a routed connection between separate offices or with other organizations into Azure. One point to make is the S2S connection is completed over a public network (i.e., Internet) connection. A routed VPN connection across the Internet connects your company's on-premises network over the Internet to a router in Azure. A site-to-site VPN connects a private network using mutual authentication. Then, using this site-to-site VPN connection, the packets are sent from either router across the VPN connection to pass TCP/IP packets to and from your hybrid network on-premises to your Azure subscription.

Azure ExpressRoute requires a network service provider (NSP) to create private connections between Azure and on-premises infrastructure to enable the network to connect into your Azure subscription. ExpressRoute connections do not allow TCP/IP traffic to traverse the public Internet. ExpressRoute requires the configuration of hardware by the network service provider to enable faster speeds, lower latencies, and higher security than typical Internet connections. Depending on the amount of traffic in and out of Azure, ExpressRoute's unlimited SKU allows the transfer of data between on-premises systems, and Azure can enable significant cost savings over an S2S VPN connection. ExpressRoute directly connects to Azure from your existing WAN network provided by a network service provider.

Select an Azure Subscription

If you are new to Microsoft Azure, then a free trial subscription might be the best first option to start becoming familiar with the portal interface to create services in the cloud. Before walking through that option, though, you should understand there are four options to purchase a Microsoft Azure subscription, with other options possible in the future.

The options are as follows:

- *Pay-as-you-go*: This plan is the most flexible for customers that want to utilize a competitive pricing option without a long-term commitment. Since it requires only a valid business or personal credit card, this option allows cancellation at any time.

- *Microsoft reseller*: The program includes many software resellers that may offer Microsoft Azure through the Open Volume License Program. Once the contract is purchased, you can activate a new subscription or add credits to maintain your Azure infrastructure.

- *Prepaid subscription*: Purchase Microsoft Azure services at a discount by prepaying for 12 months. You can add additional prepayments to continue the discount for services or pay as you go by using a business invoice or credit card.

- *Enterprise agreement*: Large corporations often sign a Microsoft enterprise agreement (EA) to make up-front monetary commitments with annual payments. One of the benefits of adding Azure to an EA is the ability to "true up" at the end of the year if additional services are needed for other business areas to leverage Azure. You don't have to ask the board of directors for an increase in budget in the middle of the year with other subscription options. You have an option to purchase an Azure subscription as shown in Figure 3-2.

■ **Note**   Customers that have opted for the pay-as-you-go option have seen a delay in increasing some of the core services once they are ready to radically ramp up more virtual machines or utilize more core services. The delay comes when the request is made to increase core services by several hundred and a credit report is exercised by Microsoft Azure to help substantiate payment. The report may take a day or longer to validate the financial change request and could possibly impact your production build-out timelines.

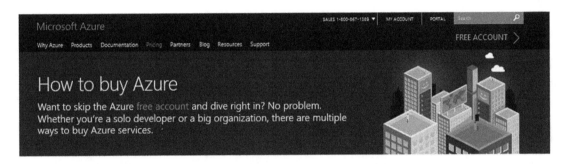

Pay-as-you-go

Competitive pricing. No minimums or commitments.

Cancel anytime. Our most popular and flexible payment plan.

Buy now >

Learn more

Prepaid subscriptions

Our 12-month prepaid subscription for Azure services lets you earn discounts on the amount you prepay. If your service consumption exceeds the prepaid amount, you can make an additional prepayment to continue getting the discount, or simply pay as you go for future usage. You can pay by credit card as well as by invoice.

Learn more

Buy from a Microsoft Reseller

Work with the same resellers that you may purchase Microsoft software from currently under the Open Volume License Program. Already have an Azure in Open license key? Activate a new subscription or add more credits here.

Figure 3-2. *Options to purchase as shown in Figure 3-2 an Azure subscription*

■ **Note** To learn more about these payment options, follow the guidance at `https://azure.microsoft.com/en-us/pricing/purchase-options/`.

Before you choose the best option to support your business, you should enable a free Azure subscription to ramp up your knowledge on utilizing Azure. It is recommended that you have a test/dev Azure environment to create a more specific rollout plan with customized documentation. If you have a current Azure subscription, you can create a new subscription that consumes services from the same parent subscription. The new environment would be separate from the current production environment. The free subscription can be created by anyone with an Internet connection and currently does not require a credit card to start. Azure services provide a $200 credit to try any combination of Azure resources.

The free trial is limited to 30 days, and it's available to all countries and areas where Azure is commercially available. Remember that you need to prepare to have all your services decommissioned at the end of that 30 days. However, you do have the option to convert the trial subscription to a pay-as-you-go subscription.

■ **Note** To choose the free one-month trial, follow the instructions at `https://azure.microsoft.com/en-us/pricing/free-trial/`.

CREATING A FREE MICROSOFT AZURE ACCOUNT

This example walks you through the process of creating a 30-day trial of Azure with the option to convert the account to a pay-as-you-go account later. You'll then use the same Azure subscription to build the necessary cloud infrastructure to host the Contoso.com example site to test Azure Security Center.

1. Open a browser with in-private windows and follow the options to create a free Azure trial at `https://azure.microsoft.com/en-us/pricing/free-trial/`.

   A free Hotmail account is used in this example; you can do the same to prevent configuration issues if your current e-mail is already associated with an e-mail account. After visiting the previously mentioned URL, choose the option to create a free e-mail account. In this example, the account used is `contosomgr@hotmail.com`.

2. After the e-mail account is created, complete the necessary information on the sign-up page (Figure 3-3). Click Next.

   Enter the information and note there are two mandatory verification processes: by phone and by credit card.

Create account

Microsoft account opens a world of benefits.

contosomgr   @hotmail.com

••••••••••••••••••

☐ Send me promotional emails from Microsoft

Use a phone number instead

Use your email instead

Choosing **Next** means that you agree to the Microsoft Services
Agreement **and** privacy and cookies statement.

Next

Microsoft

Figure 3-3. *The Hotmail account creation for a Contoso manager*

■ **Note** Your credit card is not charged; it is for verification processes only to validate the identity of the free Azure account.

3. If you click the link in the top left to learn more, as shown in Figure 3-4, the information provides the credit limits of the free account. Click Next.

Figure 3-4. *The form to fill out contact information for a free Azure subscription*

■ **Note** The text "$200 Windows Azure Credit" refers to the legacy name before the product was rebranded on the Microsoft cloud service to Microsoft Azure.

4. Once both the phone and credit card validation processes are complete, take the time to read through the subscription agreement, as shown in Figure 3-5, and click the sign-up button.

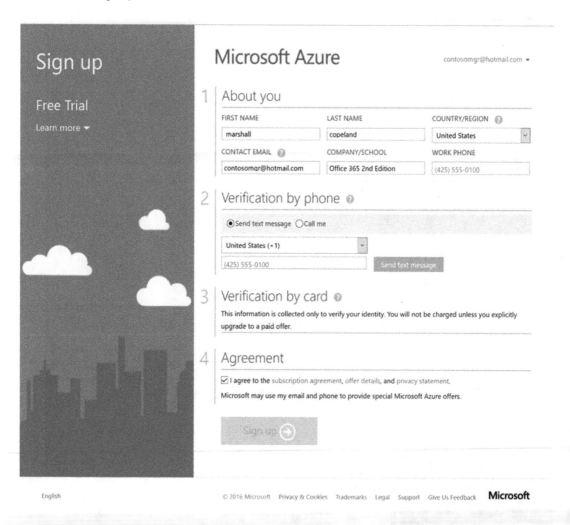

Figure 3-5. Credit card verification for account creation

This free account grants access to all Azure services. Operating system licenses are included in the VMs you are going to build to enable the infrastructure. The next few screens display that your new Azure subscription is being created and may take up to four minutes.

Your Azure subscription is ready, as shown in Figure 3-6, when the screen changes; click the green button to start managing your service.

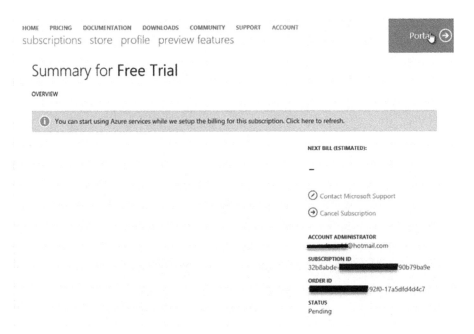

Figure 3-6. Final page of the free Azure subscription wizard

5. The next screen, shown in Figure 3-7, provides the last step and is an easy option to convert your free subscription to a paid subscription using the credit card entered in step 4. You always have the option to convert to a pay-as-you-go account, so for now click the top-right button to gain access to the Azure portal.

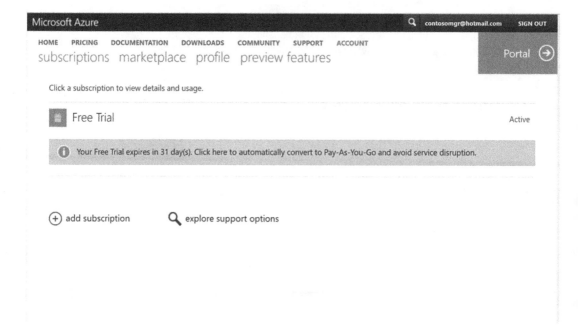

Figure 3-7. *Confirmation page and guidance to log on to the Azure portal*

6. The Azure portal is now created. This is where you build the infrastructure to maintain the Contoso.com and AD Connect servers. You can start building the networking and VM infrastructure from the Microsoft Azure portal, as shown in Figure 3-8.

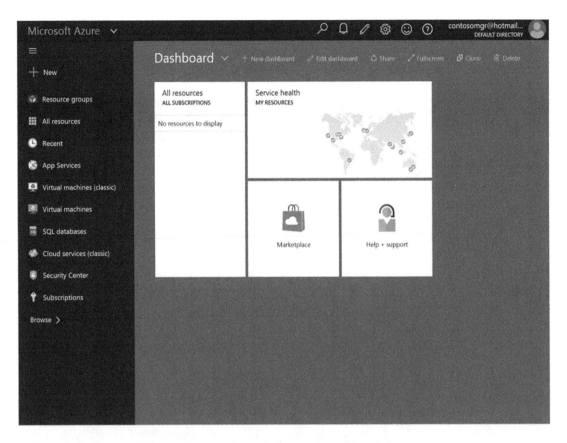

Figure 3-8. Azure portal after you log on to learn the limits of your subscription

This process has just enabled access to one of the world's largest, cost-efficient, and most secured datacenters. This newly created Microsoft Azure subscription provides any company with the ability to start creating IT services without having to wait multiple years to construct an on-premises datacenter, order server hardware, and hire IT staff to manage the datacenter.

Navigating Microsoft Azure

Cloud computing is easy to use and navigate once you have an understanding of what IT services are available and how to use the interface to activate the infrastructure to support your business. You need to have a clear understanding of the type of services to enable in your new Azure subscription, including the following:

- Understanding IaaS in Azure

- Understanding PaaS in Azure

Once your subscription is completed, you can access it by logging into the Azure web portal and becoming familiar with this new IT infrastructure. The portal provides access to all the Azure cloud services and entire IT infrastructure with the click of a mouse. The current portal provides the ability to create new resources such as virtual networks and virtual machines, create control access, manage and monitor resources, and review billing information.

The Microsoft Azure portal shown in Figure 3-9 gives you the ability to create any services, including the ones needed for this chapter, to enable federation in Azure: cloud services, virtual machines, and virtual networks. This chapter provides the steps for the necessary configuration; however, there are many additional Azure features that could be used to support your business that are not discussed in this chapter.

Figure 3-9. *Azure portal to start building Contoso.com test infrastructure*

> ■ **Tip** If you need detailed guidance on Microsoft Azure services, you can refer to my book *Microsoft Azure: Planning, Deploying, and Managing Your Data Center in the Cloud* (http://tinyurl.com/h5vktdg).

Once you have created the Azure subscription, you can click any of the properties to gain access to individual IT components. Understanding the individual components needed for the IT infrastructure is the next process.

Summary

In this chapter, you learned about some of the challenges of cloud security and got a high-level overview of just what Azure Security Center is and the ways Azure Security Center can be positioned to support a cybersecurity framework for defense. You were introduced to some of the issues an Azure consultant may encounter via a typical Azure cloud deployment example for Contoso.com.

The Contoso.com example is used in all the exercises in the remaining chapters. The cloud deployment infrastructure example includes vnets, VMs, and SQL Server instances. These cloud assets are designed to highlight the features of Azure Security Center based on real-world customer deployments, including mistakes.

Finally, in this chapter, you created an Azure subscription for testing but also learned about the types of Azure subscriptions that customers can use.

In the next chapter, you will learn how to leverage Azure Security Center with step-by-step exercises.

CHAPTER 4

■ ■ ■

Azure Security Center Configuration

Security as a Service

In Chapter 3 you learned about a few of the challenges that all cloud security professionals are confronted with. The previous chapter was intentionally written at a high level to not overwhelm cloud administrators with details of cybersecurity examples. It also touched on the recurring theme of prevention, detection, and response.

This chapter leverages the 30-day free Azure trial specifically for testing Azure Security Center using Contoso.com as a typical Azure cloud deployment example. If you skipped Chapter 3, go back and read it now before continuing. The Contoso.com network example has typical servers deployed into TCP/IP Subnet and is used in all the exercises in this chapter and remaining chapters. A typical infrastructure deployment includes virtual machines (VMs) in the perimeter IP subnet and infrastructure IP subnet and SQL Servers in the database IP subnet.

The next few exercises in this chapter will walk you through Azure Security Center and focus on the main configuration topics. You'll look the Contoso.com example in greater detail with screenshots, and then you'll go through some configuration exercises to see how to leverage the security as a service (SaaS) feature in Azure Security Center. Specifically, you'll learn how to do the following:

- Enable data collection

- See security policy details

- E-mail security alerts

- Review console recommendations

This chapter deepens your knowledge no matter what role you may have in your company. For example, if you are an Azure cloud administrator, you will gain insight into the world of cybersecurity and how to lower risks. If you're a security architect, this chapter provides insight into Azure configurations for your infrastructure.

■ **Note**   The example network was introduced in Chapter 3, so to gain background information about the network infrastructure, you should make sure to read that chapter before proceeding with these exercises.

By the end of this chapter, you will better understand that the Azure operations team roles and security architect roles are destined to merge. Security is necessary in every Azure cloud deployment, which is why security is built into the Azure fabric and other Azure services and needs to be enabled. Infrastructure design best practices have a long history in on-premises design, so adapting to a cloud deployment introduces new security challenges. The processes and stages are different in Azure cloud security deployment, but the end results are focused on the same goal: a secure deployment that mitigates security risks.

© Marshall Copeland 2017
M. Copeland, *Cyber Security on Azure*, DOI 10.1007/978-1-4842-2740-4_4

Azure Infrastructure Design

Typical network designs in customer deployments on-premises leverage routers, switches, and access control lists (ACLs) to secure communication between IP subnets and servers. Similar network security processes are used in Azure to leverage the software-defined network (SDN) without physical routers or switches. Networks in Azure leverage control by using a different and flexible network security group (NSG) configuration on the vnets configured in your subscription.

The Contoso.com design was intentionally enabled using the Azure portal to quickly create a standard infrastructure to support virtual machine deployment. This type of design by cloud administrators often skips the security design phase for a proof of concept (POC) because the initial IP subnet configuration is not scheduled to become a production deployment. The challenge is that all too often what begins as a learning experience quickly enables other technology team members to test SQL Server or web apps, and the verbal agreement for a testing-only use is soon forgotten. In addition, the networks, VMs, and systems created are excellent targets for cybersecurity hackers to compromise a system and penetrate the network.

Figure 4-1 provides the same example design as shown in Chapter 3 using a different view from the Azure portal.

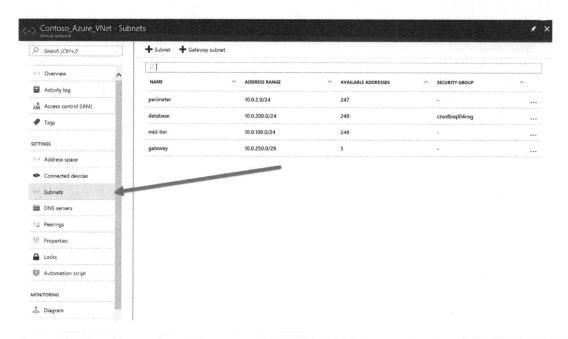

Figure 4-1. *View of Azure subnet deployment typically used in POC designs*

The individual IP subnet titles and classless inter-domain routing (CIDR) selected are often used in production cloud deployments. To the Azure administrator, this view does not provide the VMs deployed or the security that should be enabled to reduce Internet security risk from bad actors. Figure 4-2 shows the virtual machines that were deployed into the individual subnets.

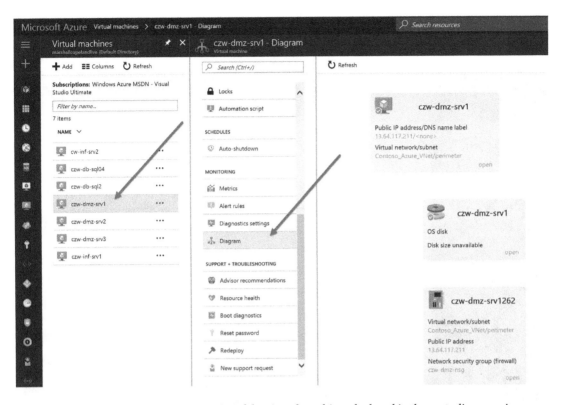

Figure 4-2. *Azure administrator perspective of the virtual machines deployed in the vnets diagram view*

Figure 4-1 and Figure 4-2 orient you to the deployment used in the Contoso.com example used throughout the exercises. You can get to these views in the Azure portal by selecting the Contoso_Azure_VNet view and then selecting either the Subnets or Diagram view. The exercises in this chapter and the remainder chapters use the Contoso.com details discussed in Chapter 3.

■ **Caution**   As mentioned in Chapter 2, there is a small agent installed on each VM. The agent is necessary for Azure Security Center to collect data and provide a history for the systems. For more details on the agent installation, refer to Appendix A.

ENABLE DATA COLLECTION IN AZURE SECURITY CENTER

This exercise walks you through the process of reviewing the initial screen of Azure Security Center and is used to orient you to the information provided. The additional steps enable data collection based on the default standard tier cost.

1. Open a supported browser of your choice to connect to the Azure portal (https://portal.azure.com) and log on with your Azure account and password to gain access to your subscription.

2. From the main portal dashboard, select the Security Center option, as shown in Figure 4-3.

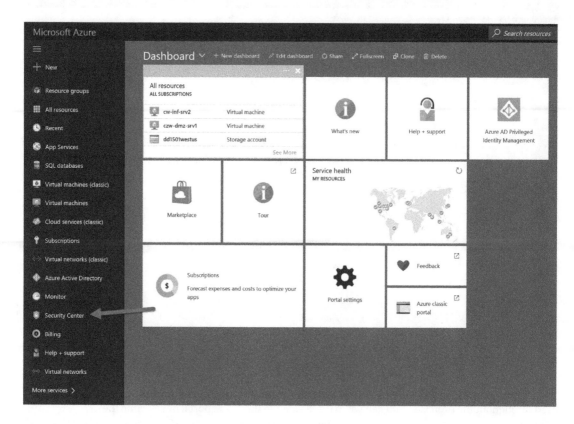

Figure 4-3. *View of the Azure portal to select Security Center for first use*

3.   The next screen you see should be similar to Figure 4-4 for the first usage. Click "Yes! I want to Launch Azure Security Center."

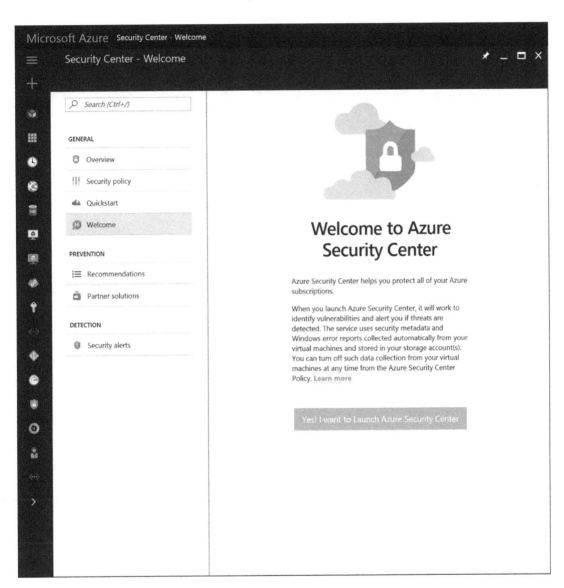

Figure 4-4.   *View of the first use with a welcome message*

4. The first view of Azure Security Center from your subscription will look slightly different from the Contoso.com example created for these exercises. You need to enable data collection. From your Security Center view, shown in Figure 4-5, click Policy to expand the portal blade to show the subscription name. Click the subscription name, as shown in Figure 4-5.

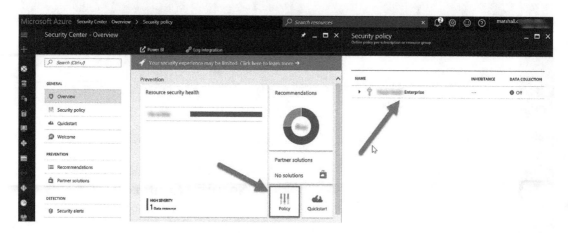

Figure 4-5. *Portal view of Policy blade and Security policy blade journey*

5. The first time you view the data collection for virtual machines, the configuration is set to Off, as shown in Figure 4-6. You can click the option to choose the storage account, but there is nothing to select. The storage account is necessary to collect data from the same geographic areas as your virtual machines.

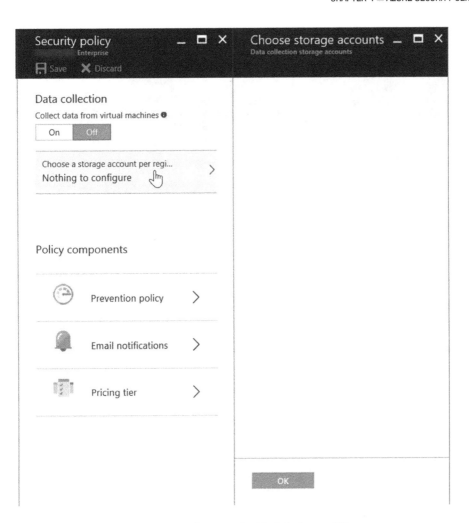

Figure 4-6. *Default "Security policy" view in the blade before enabling a storage account*

■ **Tip** Policies for Azure Security Center are set at the subscription level and the resource group level. However, selecting a storage account to keep data in the same geographic areas for privacy and data sovereignty is done at the subscription level only.

6. Change the "Data collection" option to On, as shown in Figure 4-7, and click the Save button.

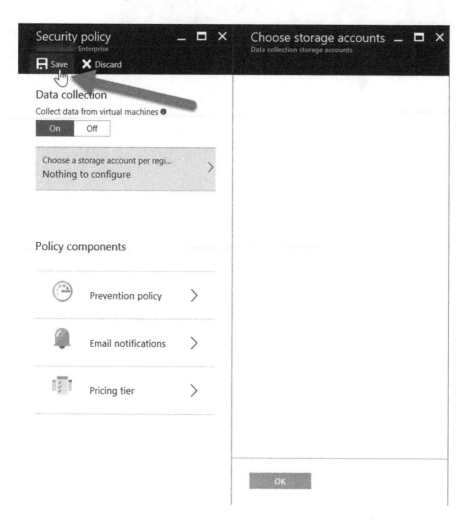

Figure 4-7. *View of the data collection options to enable and save the options from the Azure blade*

7. Once you click Save, an important pop-up message appears that may disappear too quickly to read. Simply click the Azure alert icon (a bell), as shown in Figure 4-8, to read the message. The message should inform you that the data collection agent installation process has started and may take several minutes. The amount of time taken to install the agents is directly related to the number of VMs running in the Azure subscription.

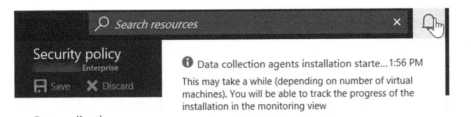

Figure 4-8. *Azure alert icon view to show the details of the last few portal configuration changes*

8. The final step is to go back to the main Azure Security Center screen to wait for the agents to be installed. You can click the browser option to refresh the view. In the Contoso.com example, the wait time was approximately 20 minutes for seven virtual machines.

Azure Security Center Pricing Tier

In Chapter 2, there was a great deal of discussion about the overall cost of Azure Security Center from a business perspective. That chapter focused on more than just the pricing tier model and allowed chief information officers (CIOs) and chief information security officers (CISO) to gain insight into the total cost of support for Security Center as part of the security layering defense strategy. Before moving onto further configuration, you need to consider the difference between the two tiers.

- Basic (free)

- Standard (not free)

The next set of exercises show how to configure the data collection storage account and enable the basic tier to start using the security service. The standard price is intentionally identified as not free for some specific reasons. First, the way your company purchased the Azure subscription may affect the price, and you may use many Azure services at a discount if you have an enterprise agreement (EA) with Microsoft. Second, the prices change often as major cloud providers change prices for their cloud features to remain competitive. Third, you may see the retail price and after a quick calculation decide the overall cost is too great without understanding the full breadth of features provided by Azure Security Center. Undercutting the value of any security product without comprehending the fullness of features does a disservice to your company and how security features benefit the overall security posture. If you are a cloud administrator, you should include the security architect in the decision-making process. Azure Security Center is not a solution that is used to simply check the box for security; it provides a breadth of value that should be evaluated based on merit.

Figure 4-9 provides a view of the two pricing costs at this time; as stated, the pricing could change in the future as competition between cloud security products continues.

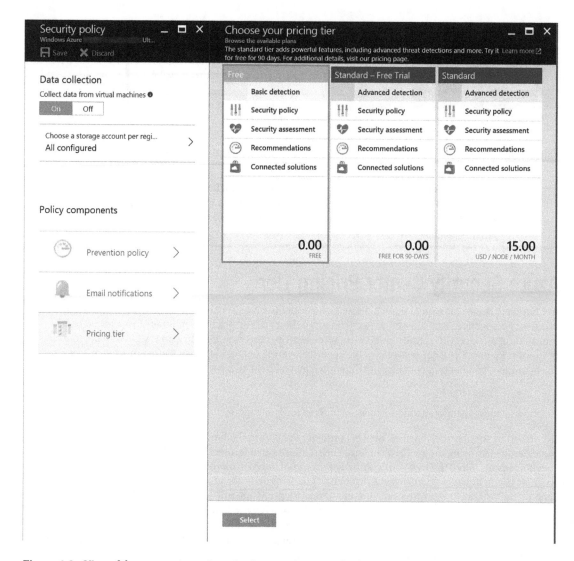

Figure 4-9. *View of the current Azure Security Center pricing tier for free and standard options per node*

Let's review the features between the two tiers before continuing with the exercises and other configurations. The free option does provide a great deal of insights; however, you get more functionalities with the standard tier pricing model. Notice the standard model, as of this writing, provides a 90-day trial period. If you are a novice to Azure Security Center but not to Azure, this may be a good choice to formally review the features before the cost per VM per month is charged at the end of the 90 days.

Table 4-1 provides an overview of some of the feature differences between the free and standard tiers.

Table 4-1. *Feature Comparison, Standard Tier vs. Free Tier*

Feature	Standard	Free
Security policy with assessments and recommendations	✓	✓
Third-party partner integration (additional cost)	✓	✓
Security alerting	✓	✓
Advanced threat detection	✓	
Anomaly detection	✓	
Crash analysis	✓	
Threat intelligence	✓	
Behavioral analysis	✓	

■ **Caution**   Moving from the free tier to the standard tier enables an automatic cap of 500MB of data per VM per day that was not applicable with the free tier.

The services supported by Azure Security Center are constantly changing at the pace of cloud innovation, so even though you are reviewing reviewing virtual machines in the exercises, additional preview features on the road map include Azure cloud services and SQL Server databases.

Standard Tier Advantages

As an Azure architect, you are undoubtingly evaluating the security features found in the standard pricing tier but may not have the background to understand the depth of the individual features and how Azure Security Center leverages the breadth of global information to protect server assets.

You should carefully consider the additional features beyond the free tier. Make sure to look at the standard tier features when evaluating other security products, which may not have the advantage of integrating with a cloud solution that is global in deployment and leverages millions of data sensor points.

Advanced Threat Detection

This feature is extremely informative to security teams because it provides details about sophisticated attack detection using the Microsoft cloud-based security analytics. The threat protection provided may be a tipping point for security professionals in favor of Azure Security Center because timely intelligent security data is a cornerstone that enables a successful solution. As an individual, you can become good at identifying intelligence from log files, accounts, and other security data. If you work in a team, the individuals combine the data points to make the discovery and decisions faster and more accurate. If you don't have a team of security specialists or the budget to hire them, then advanced threat detection provides insight that doesn't require the CISO or CIO to ask the board of directors for more money.

The advanced threat detection technologies and methodologies detect threats using machine learning analysis on big data. The security graph of data analytics aggregates what you as an individual may interpret as an anomaly, namely, recognized behaviors by the millions of data points of anonymized information.

The daily collection from Windows Defender and behavioral sensors (individual contact points) alone is astonishing. With integration with Windows Defender, the daily data includes the following:

- Millions of Microsoft Windows devices

- Indexed web URLs

- Online reputation lookups

- Millions of suspicious files

Other methods of detection are included as individual components to support the overall detection effectiveness of Azure Security Center. For instance, atomic detection leverages current information on the history of malicious patterns to provide known indicators of compromise (IoC). Atomic detection uses log entry data for software malware that, in the past historical data analysis, does not mutate. Atomic detection using log file attributes can most closely be correlated to active network packet analysis in an IDS. Because the patterns are known attributes, there is a very low level of false positive rates, and common malware can be found with this type of detection.

Anomaly Detection

The security graph of data analytics aggregates information in order to recognize certain behavior and detect threats. Building a system baseline is necessary to alert on deviations from the standard. It is possible that no alert is sent because the deviation did not have supporting evidence and no other attributes were detected to cause the alert threshold to be crossed.

Anomaly-based algorithms, such as repeated failed logon attempts based on statistically significant levels of failures, are identified. The type of information that can trigger an alert would include if the failed logon attempt was attempted with existing or nonexistent users.

Crash Analysis

Security Center analyzes data looking for future malware that is being designed and tested to compromise systems, including in results from system crash dumps. This analysis can find evidence of failed exploitation attempts and immature malware code.

Microsoft has integrated the crash dump data into Azure Security Center to detect indicators of failed attempts, and this crash data is surfaced to algorithms to identify potential failed attempts of threats on your systems.

Threat Intelligence

Microsoft has many global cloud services that provide threat intelligence telemetry such as Office 365, Microsoft CRM online, MSN.com, Azure, the Microsoft Digital Crimes Unit (DCU), and the Microsoft Security Response Center (MSRC).

Other partners have contracts with Microsoft to provide researchers with threat intelligence information including other cloud providers and third-party solutions. One of the many intelligence data points includes the communication from a compromised system to a known IP address of a malicious actor. Threat attributes include emerging threats or existing ones with specific indicators, implications, and other mechanisms. After the raw data is collected, it is augmented by a global team of threat protection "hunters" to analyze the data effectively and integrate it into Azure Security Center. The security team hunters run algorithms against customer data sets to validate results and reduce false positive alerting.

Behavioral Analysis

This form of analysis for threat detection is different than simply matching signatures and patterns; it focuses on "actions" taken by suspicious programmatic behavior. The collection of data changes compared to patterns that are known and are not just signatures. Malware can quickly generate many variants, which means the hash tables change just as quickly. As bits and bytes change on the malware, a new signature is required to identify the same malware based on the current attributes. This is a major reason behavioral analysis is a strength of Azure Security Center.

With Security Center, the technology can correctly articulate the behavior actions of a variant of malware, which provides necessary identification without pattern matching. With future malware movements and unidentified behavior correlated, false positives can be detected because of the initial suspicious properties.

ENABLE SECURITY CENTER STANDARD TIER

You get the benefit of additional security features when upgrading from the free tier to the standard tier. This provides the best opportunity to evaluate the Security Center functionality for your subscription.

1. Open your web browser to https://portal.azure.com, log in, and open the Security Center view, as shown in Figure 4-10.

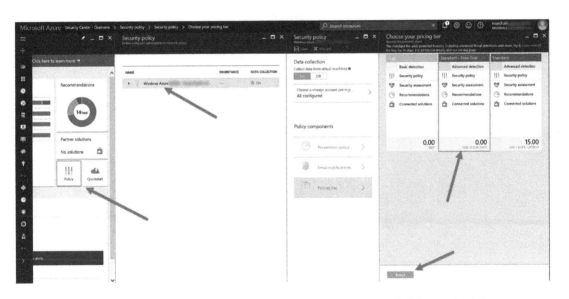

Figure 4-10. View of the selections when moving to the 90-day free trial period of the standard tier

2. Select Policy, then Subscription, and then Pricing Tier. Then select the Standard - Free Trial option. Click the Select button at the bottom of the tier blade.

3. The "Choose your pricing tier" view will close, and you must click the Save button from the "Security policy" blade, as shown in Figure 4-11.

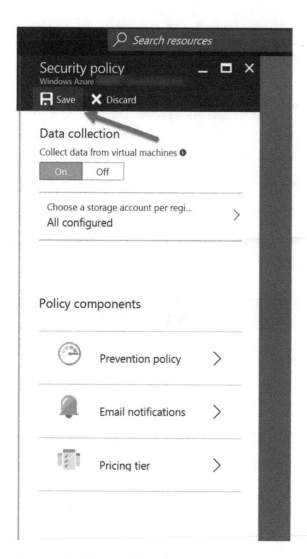

Figure 4-11. *View to click the Save button to commit to the standard tier change policy*

4. You can validate the change is being committed and the changes are in the process of updating on the Azure subscription by clicking the notifications bell at the top right of the portal view, as shown in Figure 4-12.

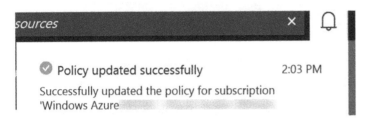

Figure 4-12. Notification view of the policy change moving from free to standard tier

Now that you have made the policy change to migrate to the standard tier, there are additional configuration options that need to be set before you learn more about the alerts and recommendations.

ENABLE E-MAIL ALERTING IN SECURITY CENTER

There are notification options you can enable from the "Security policy" blade in the Security Center solution. Most companies have an e-mail distribution list (DL) that is used to send notifications to a single e-mail account.

1. Open your web browser to `https://portal.azure.com`, log in, and open the Security Center view, as shown in the Figure 4-13.

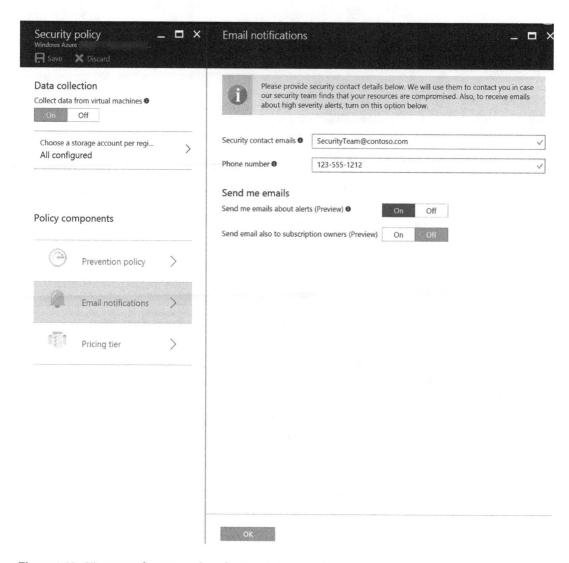

Figure 4-13. *View to configure e-mail notification for Security Center*

2. Enter the e-mail address of the DL that you'd like Security Center to send notification alerts to. Notice the option to also enter a phone number to receive notification. This phone number could be the 24/7 help desk and not necessarily an individual. Click the OK option at the bottom of the portal blade.

■ **Tip** Notice on the e-mail notification page there is an option to notify the subscription owner as a preview option. This is because the subscription owner may be a team or even a cloud service provider that may require an Azure Security Center notification.

3. Use your mouse to save the changes from the "Security policy" blade, as shown in Figure 4-14.

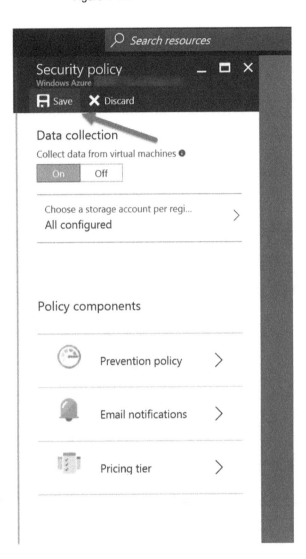

Figure 4-14. *View of the Azure portal to save changes to e-mail notification policy*

4. If you don't save the information changes, you will be prompted by the pop-up window shown in Figure 4-15.

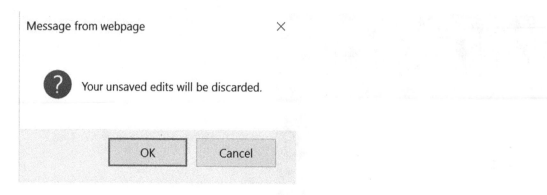

Figure 4-15. *Notification window message if policy changes are not committed*

The exercises have been designed so you gain the most benefit from the Azure Security Center functionality. You've made changes to enable e-mail notification and configure the standard tier; however, after moving to the standard tier, an additional policy change should be made before the initial configuration is completed.

ENABLE POLICY CHANGES

1. Open your web browser to https://portal.azure.com, log in, and open Security Center. Select the subscription blade and policy view, as shown in Figure 4-16.

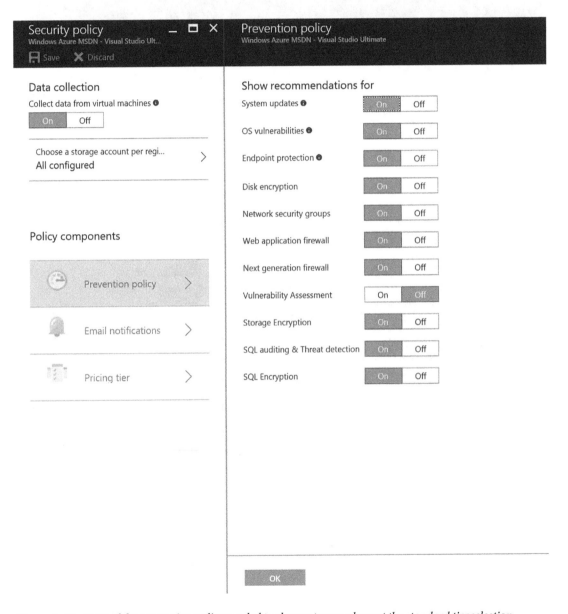

Figure 4-16. View of the prevention policy needed to change to complement the standard tier selection

2. Since making the change from free tier to standard, the policy change to enable "show all recommendations" may need to be configured. Validate that all recommendations are set to On, as shown in Figure 4-17, and click the OK button.

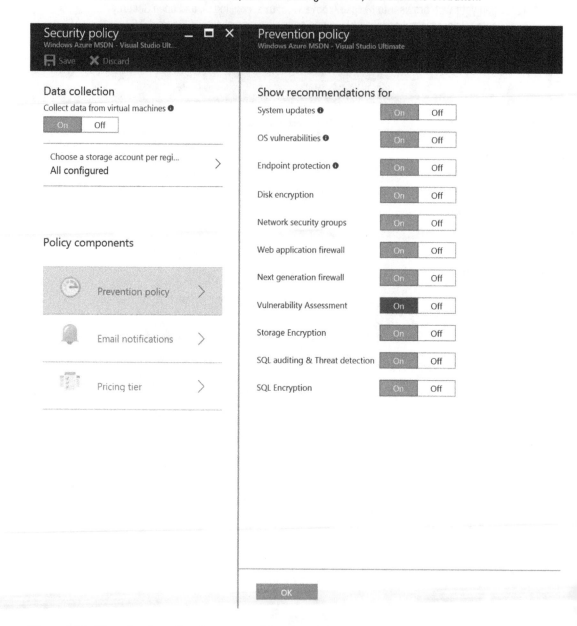

Figure 4-17. *View after the policy change to enable vulnerability assessment*

3.   Use your mouse to save the changes on the "Security policy" blade, as shown in Figure 4-18.

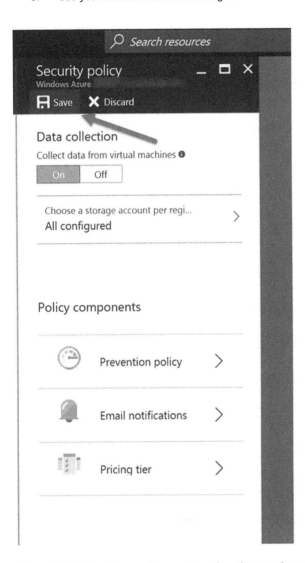

Figure 4-18. *View to save the security policy change after enabling*

Using Security Center

Now that majority policy changes are enabled for the initial Azure Security Center configuration, you should take the time to review the information that has been identified using this solution. The testing configuration discussed in Chapter 3 and re-introduced at the beginning of this chapter provides a different view than your Azure network infrastructure. In the Contoso.com infrastructure, the information provided is centered around eight virtual machines and three IP subnets; this represents a typical Azure first-use deployment. Security Center identifies all the missed configurations for each VM that has an agent installed and provides recommendations to protect the individual systems.

Review the information in Figure 4-19 as you learn more about the features of Security Center.

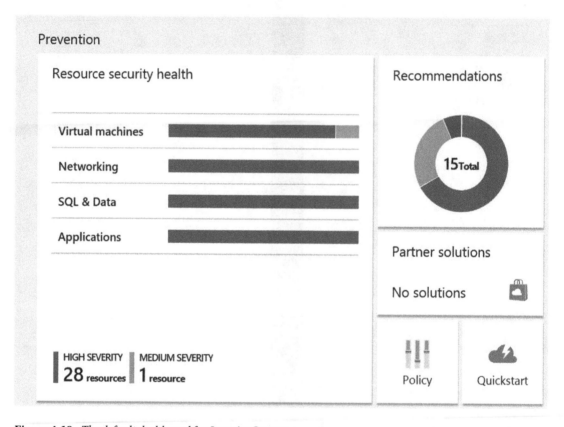

Figure 4-19. The default dashboard for Security Center

Your view should be similar to this information based on the size of your vnets and virtual machines. With the deployment of the Contoso.com Azure core infrastructure, Security Center identifies healthy components and unhealthy components using the virtual bar chart. The four main areas in the health view are as follows:

- Virtual machines
- Networking
- SQL & Data
- Applications

You can see in Figure 4-14, in the lower-left view, there are 28 high-severity and 1 medium-severity resources that need attention. Begin by hovering your mouse over any of the components to see the specific data for each of the four main health resources. In the Contoso.com Azure infrastructure, the virtual machines are selected first. You can see the number of high- and medium-severity changes, as shown in Figure 4-20.

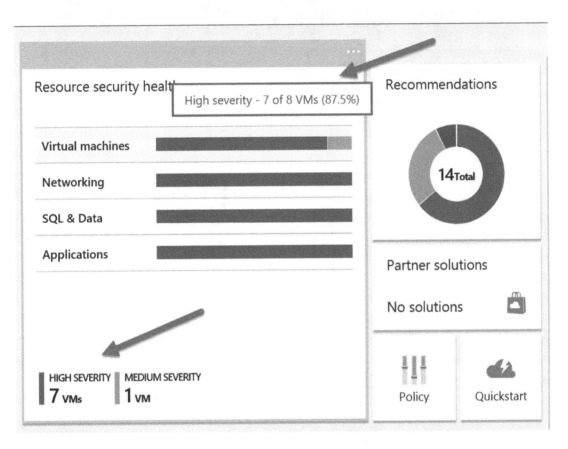

Figure 4-20. *View of the mouse hovering over the virtual machines' resource security health*

If you use the mouse to click the "Virtual machines" red bar, you will open a new dashboard blade that reports the security health of the virtual machines, as shown in Figure 4-21.

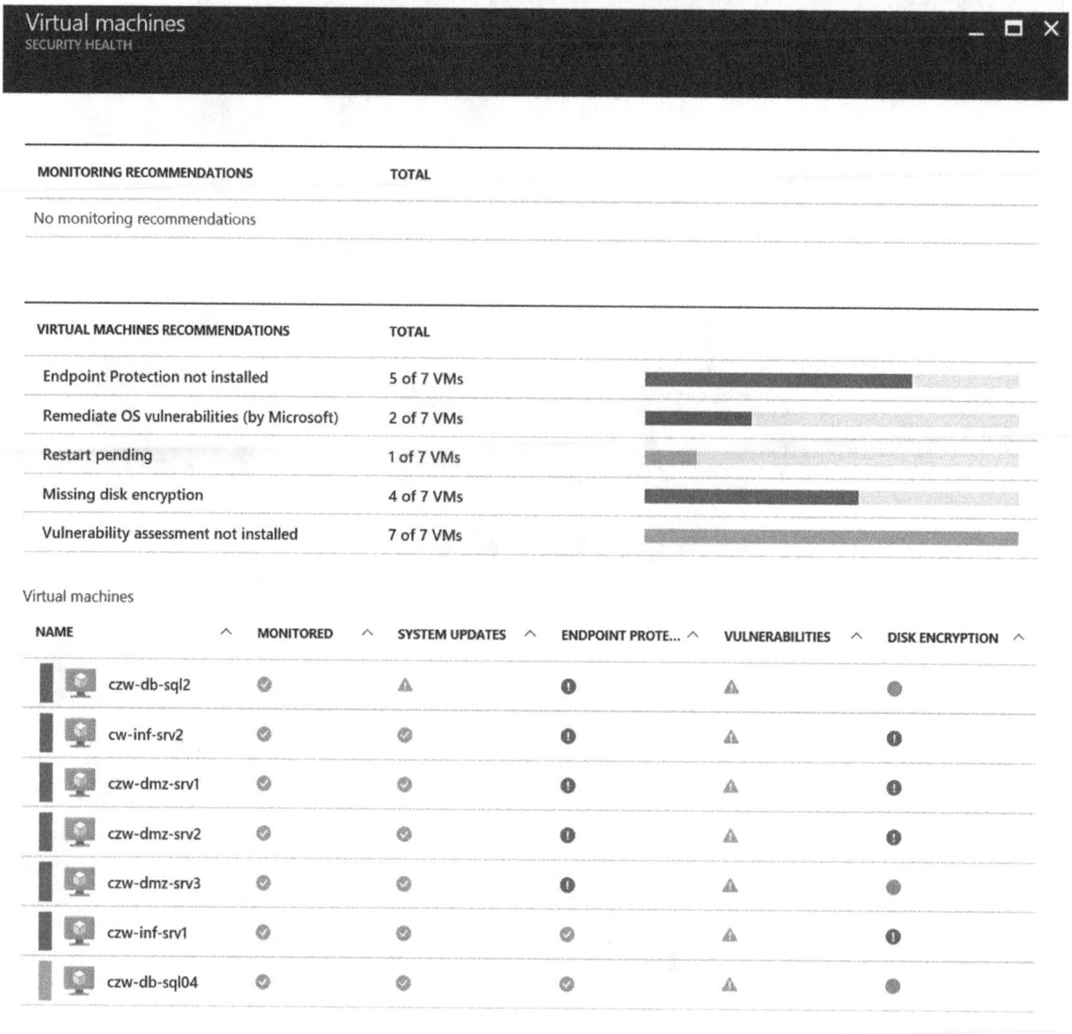

Virtual machines			— ▭ ✕
SECURITY HEALTH			

MONITORING RECOMMENDATIONS	TOTAL
No monitoring recommendations	

VIRTUAL MACHINES RECOMMENDATIONS	TOTAL	
Endpoint Protection not installed	5 of 7 VMs	
Remediate OS vulnerabilities (by Microsoft)	2 of 7 VMs	
Restart pending	1 of 7 VMs	
Missing disk encryption	4 of 7 VMs	
Vulnerability assessment not installed	7 of 7 VMs	

Virtual machines

NAME		MONITORED		SYSTEM UPDATES		ENDPOINT PROTE...	VULNERABILITIES		DISK ENCRYPTION	
🖥 czw-db-sql2		✅		⚠		❶	⚠		⬤	
🖥 cw-inf-srv2		✅		✅		❶	⚠		❶	
🖥 czw-dmz-srv1		✅		✅		❶	⚠		❶	
🖥 czw-dmz-srv2		✅		✅		❶	⚠		❶	
🖥 czw-dmz-srv3		✅		✅		❶	⚠		⬤	
🖥 czw-inf-srv1		✅		✅		✅	⚠		❶	
🖥 czw-db-sql04		✅		✅		✅	⚠		⬤	

Figure 4-21. Detailed view of the virtual machine security health

■ **Tip** This view is used to provide details of the virtual machines' security health based on the functionality of Azure Security Center. This is not the health of operating systems or applications, as you might see with Microsoft System Center Operations Manager or Azure Application Insight.

The information provided by this view is the type of data the security team needs to better remove security risks and maintain compliance standards. Also, this data is needed for Azure operations teams to support the business by improving the security posture for each VM deployed in the Azure subscription. This detailed view provides five specific areas to help focus security work, as listed here:

- Monitored

- System Updates

- Endpoint Protection

- Vulnerabilities

- Disk Encryption

Each of these five areas is identified with a security health rating of healthy, unhealthy, or NA because of the security data being analyzed. The color scheme is typical with alerting solutions in Azure.

- Red = high (critical)

- Yellow = medium (important)

- Green = none

These areas are color coded for security health, and a different scheme is used to show the priority of the component security recommendations. You will learn details about the recommendations in Chapter 5 when the details identifying the types of recommendations are presented and automatically remediated.

You should go back to the Security Center overview blade, as shown in Figure 4-19, and this time use your mouse to click the Networking resource security health bar. You should see a screen similar to Figure 4-22. The option to use a next-generation firewall (NGFW) is discussed in Chapter 6, where several OEM solutions are discussed in great detail as an advanced feature.

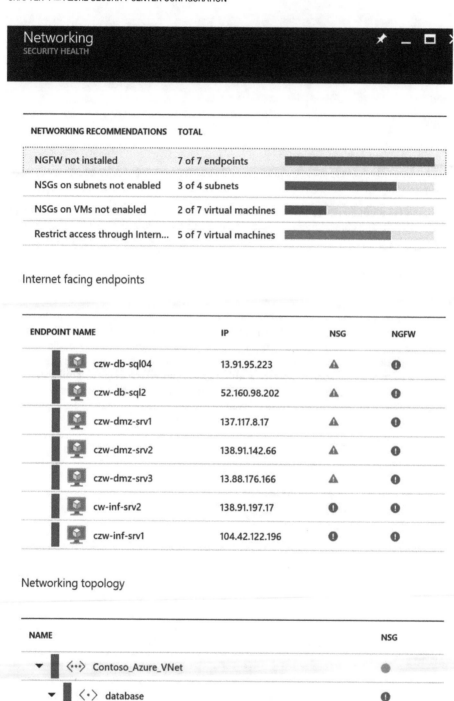

Figure 4-22. *A view of the networking security health including Internet-facing endpoints*

Security Tip   An NGFW detects and blocks sophisticated attacks by enforcing security policies at the application level, which supports information auditing.

In larger corporations, this type of visual data is normally viewed only by the subject-matter experts in the networking team and select systems administration teams. The security health of networks and computers exposed to the Internet is identified as critical and needs changes to reduce the risk of the current configuration. Chapter 5 discusses the recommendations and gives information about the security risk of the current security vulnerabilities identified by Security Center.

You should go back to the Security Center overview blade, as shown in Figure 4-19, and this time use your mouse to click the SQL & Data resource security health bar. You should see a screen similar to Figure 4-23.

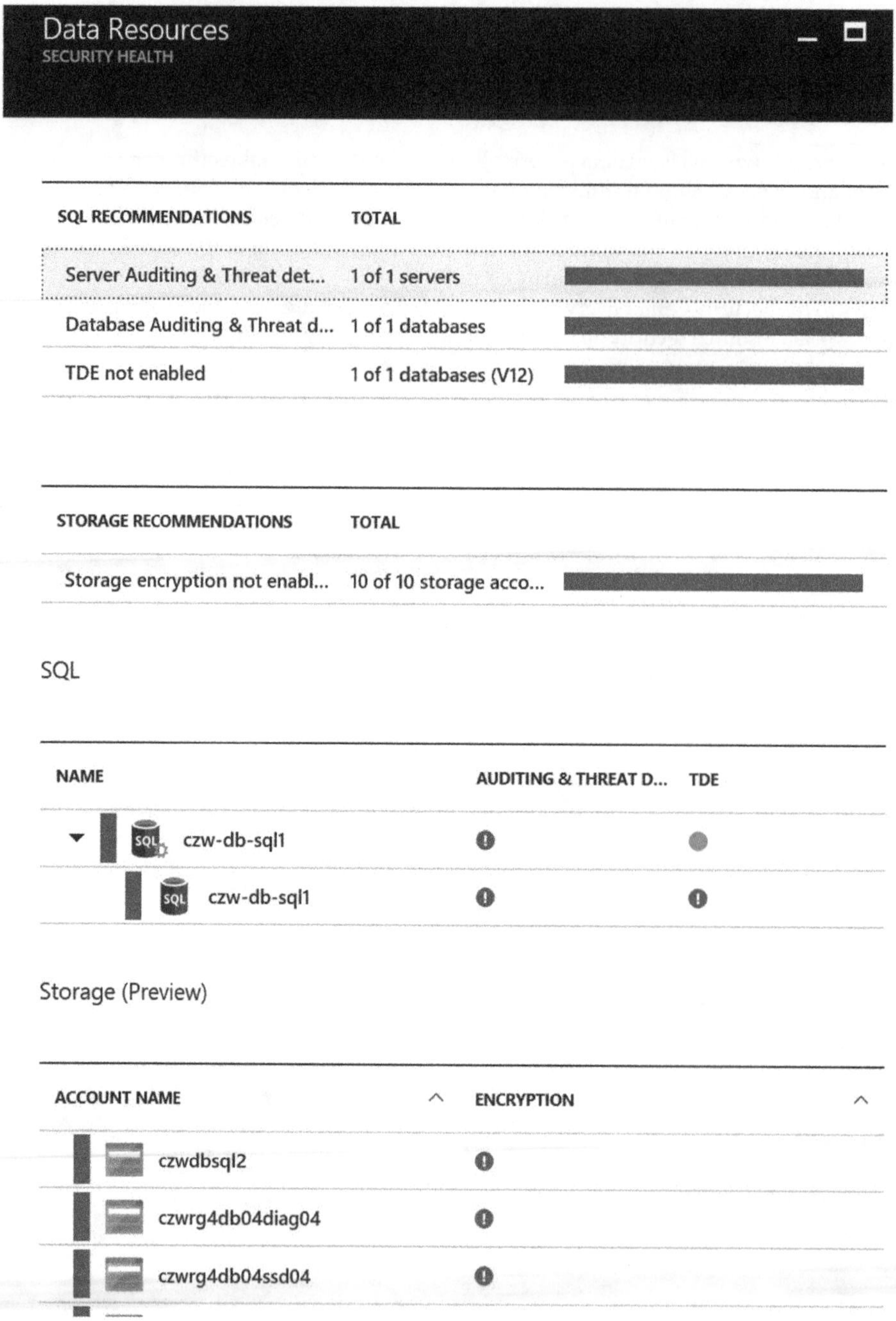

Data Resources
SECURITY HEALTH

SQL RECOMMENDATIONS	TOTAL	
Server Auditing & Threat det...	1 of 1 servers	
Database Auditing & Threat d...	1 of 1 databases	
TDE not enabled	1 of 1 databases (V12)	

STORAGE RECOMMENDATIONS	TOTAL	
Storage encryption not enabl...	10 of 10 storage acco...	

SQL

NAME	AUDITING & THREAT D...	TDE
▼ [SQL] czw-db-sql1	!	●
[SQL] czw-db-sql1	!	!

Storage (Preview)

ACCOUNT NAME ∧	ENCRYPTION ∧
czwdbsql2	!
czwrg4db04diag04	!
czwrg4db04ssd04	!

Figure 4-23. A view of the security health of Azure SQL servers and storage components

The Azure SQL & Data view provides guidance on security recommendations that improve the business security and exposure created by Azure SQL database default deployments.

Now go back to the Security Center overview blade, as shown in Figure 4-19, and this time use your mouse to click the Applications resource security health bar. You should see a screen similar to Figure 4-24.

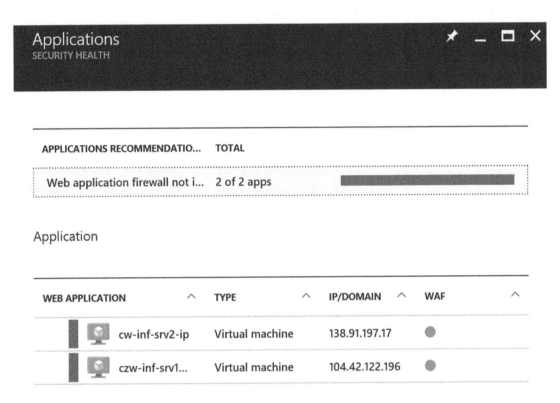

Figure 4-24. *A view of the security health of Azure web applications*

In the Contoso.com deployment, only two Azure web applications are identified, and Security Center has recommended security changes to reduce security risks.

■ **Tip**   Reducing security vulnerabilities and improving the infrastructure over all the security postures is a key delivery feature of Azure Security Center.

Summary

In this chapter, you configured Azure Security Center by enabling the clients to be installed on the existing VMs, and you migrated to the standard tier to obtain the most benefits using security as a service. You enabled e-mail notification and began receiving security health summaries.

You created the storage accounts needed to collect audit data and realized the value of the Security Center standard tier pricing option. You then learned how to configure e-mail alerts and started to leverage the best practices identified by Security Center. The additional policies provided details to enable a secure configuration for VMs, SQL servers, and network configuration.

Chapters 5 and 6 will guide you through the details of security alerts and how to implement the recommendations to improve the security of the business. Chapter 6 provides advanced configuration options that allow you to use many of the Microsoft Azure partners found in the Azure Marketplace.

CHAPTER 5

■ ■ ■

Azure Security Center Scenarios

Assume a Breach

This chapter gives you more details about the cybersecurity configuration recommendations from the example introduced in Chapter 3, the Contoso.com Azure deployment. The recommendations are based on the data provided from a Security Center evaluation of the infrastructure.

■ **Tip**   The guiding principle of Microsoft's security strategy is to "assume a breach." Microsoft's global incident response team works around the clock to mitigate the effects of any attack against the Microsoft business cloud. Learn more at https://www.microsoft.com/en-us/TrustCenter/Security/default.aspx.

The guidance that Azure Security Center provides is based on the specific identification of your Azure infrastructure over minutes, hours, and days. You should make and configure the security changes based on the recommendations, and after applying the changes, you should create a new baseline. Each Azure environment's discoveries are different. This is also an example of the power of security as a service (SaaS) because the configuration to identify security vulnerabilities requires a small client to be installed.

In this chapter's exercises, you will see specific recommendations about the following:

- Virtual machines

- Networking configuration

- SQL Server instances (including platform as a service [PaaS])

- Data

- Web apps

The exercises in this chapter will show you the steps necessary to enable the recommendations and will provide greater insight into each vulnerability. This allows you to use these Azure Security Center findings to strengthen your IT administration and extend Microsoft's cybersecurity expertise without investing in extensive cyber-classes.

To close out this chapter and further illustrate some of the features of automation and alerting, a specific controlled process was used to simulate security breaches and cyber-attacks. Please note that all legal and ethical guidelines were followed, and specific notification was completed to provide these events in the Contoso.com test scenario. Specifically, the Certified Ethical Hacker (CEH) code of ethics was used as guidance. You should not introduce foreign malware into your Azure subscription for the purpose of testing and evaluating Azure Security Center.

© Marshall Copeland 2017
M. Copeland, *Cyber Security on Azure*, DOI 10.1007/978-1-4842-2740-4_5

■ **Security Tip**   To read more about the CEH code of ethics, please read the 19 tenants of the code at the EC-Council site at `https://www.eccouncil.org/code-of-ethicks/`.

Also in this chapter you'll see several reference steps to enable endpoint protection and configure network security groups (NSGs). Then in Chapter 6 you will configure cryptography on Azure data and identify third-party extensions that provide security protection identified by Azure Security Center. These specific Microsoft Azure partner applications are configured in Chapter 6 to strengthen your Azure security posture and reduce security risk. These two chapters together provide steps that you need to complete in your Azure infrastructure.

Security Health Monitoring

The Contoso.com network design introduced in Chapter 3 has now been scanned by Azure Security Center. Security baselines were proactively created after a few minutes or a few hours depending on the type of virtual configuration. The timelines to identify security health are different for some VMs, blob data, and SQL components, and other health baselines are proactively created after a few hours. Once again, as a reminder, the Contoso.com deployment is a typical deployment used by many up-and-coming Azure cloud administrators. You should see similar recommendations after you enable Azure Security Center in your Azure subscription. In fact, in your Azure infrastructure, when the security vulnerability identified is the same, then you can reference these exercises to remediate the vulnerability following the exact same steps.

As a reminder, the configuration processes from the Contoso.com example, you should make sure to enable Azure Security Center using the standard pricing tier, as discussed in Chapter 4, and then begin scanning your Azure infrastructure. The Contoso.com example is provided as a common reference infrastructure and is very generic. The best way to implement the Azure Security Center remediation steps are to implement these exercises as processes for your Azure subscription. These processes are necessary steps to reduce the possible security vulnerability identified by Security Center based on your Azure virtual infrastructure configuration, whether it's an IaaS or PaaS. As different recommendations identified by Security Center based on the PaaS or SaaS property in your Azure infrastructure, these exercises provide the memory muscle to enable the necessary recommended security steps.

As a reminder, in Chapter 3 you were introduced to a standard Azure infrastructure deployment through a Visio network diagram. The Contoso.com example replicates the type of deployment often created from a cloud administrator who does not specifically have all the necessary Azure Cloud security best practices implemented. In Chapter 4, you learned how to configure the standard tier in order to take advantage of the enhanced automated security features based on your deployment. Now in this chapter, the exercises review the individual security recommendations, provide the steps necessary to reduce the security vulnerability, and provide guidance into the security risk.

Azure Security Center requires time to analyze your Azure VMs, vnets, web apps, and SQL-deployed applications. Baselines are created and used for recommendations to improve your security posture. First you will look at the results of implementing the standard tier, and then you can begin a methodical process to follow the recommended prioritization of the Security Center items.

Open the Security Center health blade overview, as shown in Figure 5-1, to review the current security status of your Azure infrastructure deployment.

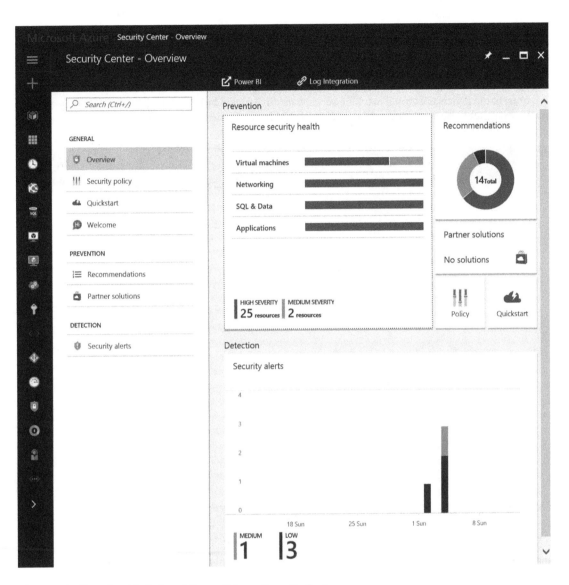

Figure 5-1. *Overview blade from Microsoft Azure Security Center*

The information in Figure 5-1 is based on the analysis of Contoso.com, so your overview will be provided in the same format, with results of the deployment analyzed by Security Center with tiles called Resource security health, Recommendations, and Security alerts. There should be minimal difference between the Contoso.com analysis overview in Figure 5-1 and your analysis overview relating to the level of resource security health. The number for the high, medium, low, and healthy severity levels will be different, and the number of recommendations will fluctuate because this is directly related to the security health identified by Security Center. As security is improved and the changes affect the baselines, the numbers change.

Azure Security Center monitors the security health proactively and identifies systems including VMs, web apps, SQL Server instances, vnets, and more. Enabling the standard tier provides proactive audits on your Azure resources to identify systems that fall short of security best practices and standard security configuration. The resources in your subscription are identified for potential security vulnerabilities, and a severity of high, medium, low, and healthy is provided based on the overall security state.

You should review the virtual machine security health in detail by hovering your mouse over the virtual machines health tile and clicking once to enable the VM health blade, as shown in Figure 5-2.

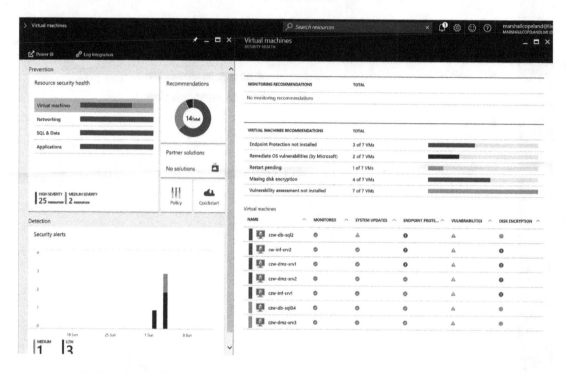

Figure 5-2. VM health identified by Azure Security Center on VM security health blade

■ **Tip** When everything is a priority, nothing is a priority. Security Center proactively identifies security health and prioritizes vulnerabilities so you can address them in a specific order.

As you review the VM health blade, notice that Security Center identifies vulnerabilities such as missing security updates, endpoint protection agent not installed, vulnerabilities, and disk encryption. In the next section you will walk through the initial installation steps from an Azure operations perspective and review Azure security background information to augment the cybersecurity insight from Security Center.

Security Recommendations Procedures

These are examples and not all the necessary procedures needed.

■ **Security Tip**   Azure Resource Manager (ARM) supports role-based administration access control (RBAC). RBAC is not available in the "classic" portal, so the ARM portal is recommended moving forward.
Many organizations do not have cloud security architect roles and responsibilities from a security perspective. These procedures were completed from an account authorization as Azure co-administrative, although least privileged access is a security best practice.

INSTALL ENDPOINT PROTECTION WITH AZURE SECURITY CENTER

This exercise walks you through the necessary steps to identify missing endpoint protection agents on VMs in your Azure subscription and then to install one or more agents into the VM operating system.

■ **Security Tip**   Not all endpoint protection supports the necessary extensions.

---

1. Open a supported browser of your choice, connect to the Azure portal at `https://portal.azure.com`, and log on with your Azure account and password. Open the Security Center blade, highlight the "Virtual machines" red bar, and click once with your mouse, as shown in Figure 5-3.

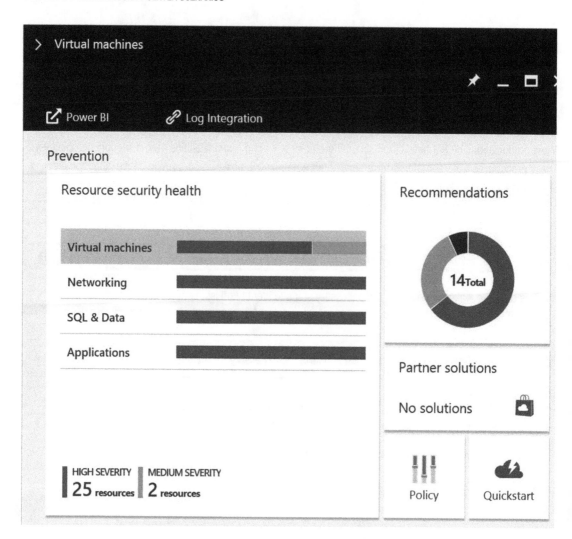

Figure 5-3. *Virtual machine view in Security Center, highlighted with a single mouse click*

2. The detailed "Virtual machines" pane opens and shows the overall security health of each VM in your subscription, as shown in Figure 5-4. Click the "Endpoint Protection not installed" recommendation.

Figure 5-4. *View of the VM security health*

■ **Security Tip** The "Virtual machines" pane provides many recommendations based on the security vulnerabilities category identified.

3. The Install Endpoint Protection blade opens, as shown in Figure 5-5. Select one or several VMs to install the agent on by clicking each check box and then click Install on VMs to continue.

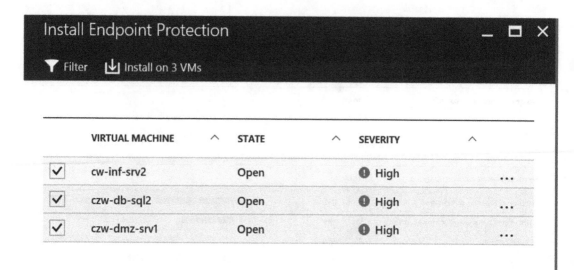

Figure 5-5. *View to install endpoint protection*

■ **Tip** Use the Filter option to select specific machines based on the service level agreement (SLA) you have in place with the business team for each VM. Degradation of the service or a VM reboot should be considered.

4. The Select Endpoint Protection blade opens. Notice the options in this example are TrendMicro and Microsoft, as shown in Figure 5-6. If you are not managing your enterprise with TrendMicro, then select Microsoft Antimalware.

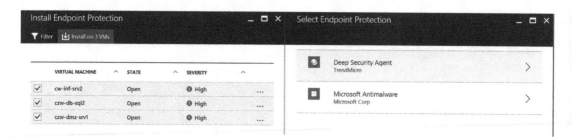

Figure 5-6. *View of the Select Endpoint Protection blade*

5. The next blade opens the legal terms and conditions of using Microsoft endpoint protection, as shown in Figure 5-7. Read through this information and click Create.

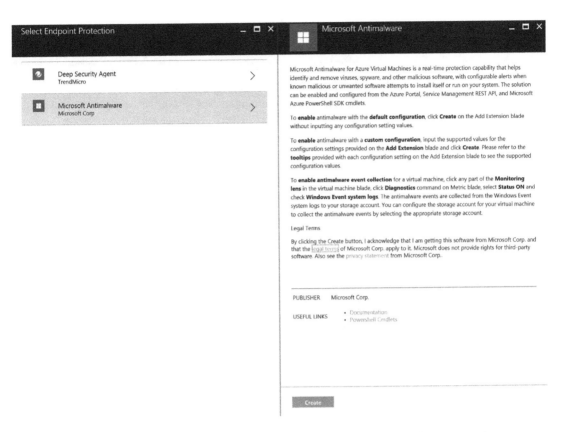

Figure 5-7. *View of the terms and conditions to use the Microsoft anti-malware endpoint protection extensions*

6. The pane to customize the installation opens, as shown in Figure 5-8, to allow for the following customization configuration settings for each of the VMs you selected endpoint protection to be installed on:

- Excluded Files and Locations

- Excluded Files and Extensions

- Excluded Processes

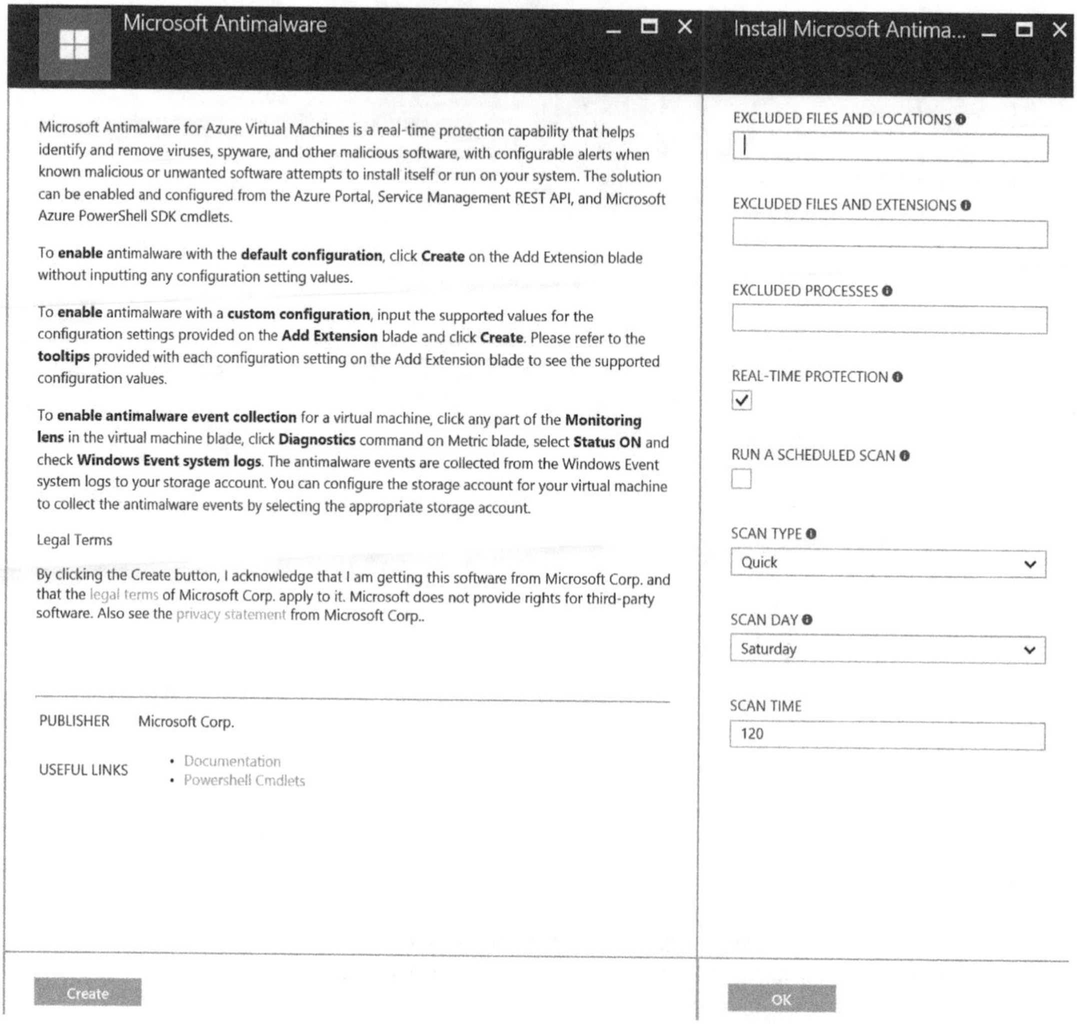

Microsoft Antimalware — ☐ ✕ | Install Microsoft Antima... — ☐ ✕

Microsoft Antimalware for Azure Virtual Machines is a real-time protection capability that helps identify and remove viruses, spyware, and other malicious software, with configurable alerts when known malicious or unwanted software attempts to install itself or run on your system. The solution can be enabled and configured from the Azure Portal, Service Management REST API, and Microsoft Azure PowerShell SDK cmdlets.

To **enable** antimalware with the **default configuration**, click **Create** on the Add Extension blade without inputting any configuration setting values.

To **enable** antimalware with a **custom configuration**, input the supported values for the configuration settings provided on the **Add Extension** blade and click **Create**. Please refer to the **tooltips** provided with each configuration setting on the Add Extension blade to see the supported configuration values.

To **enable antimalware event collection** for a virtual machine, click any part of the **Monitoring lens** in the virtual machine blade, click **Diagnostics** command on Metric blade, select **Status ON** and check **Windows Event system logs**. The antimalware events are collected from the Windows Event system logs to your storage account. You can configure the storage account for your virtual machine to collect the antimalware events by selecting the appropriate storage account.

Legal Terms

By clicking the Create button, I acknowledge that I am getting this software from Microsoft Corp. and that the legal terms of Microsoft Corp. apply to it. Microsoft does not provide rights for third-party software. Also see the privacy statement from Microsoft Corp..

PUBLISHER   Microsoft Corp.

USEFUL LINKS   • Documentation
                • Powershell Cmdlets

EXCLUDED FILES AND LOCATIONS ❶

EXCLUDED FILES AND EXTENSIONS ❶

EXCLUDED PROCESSES ❶

REAL-TIME PROTECTION ❶
☑

RUN A SCHEDULED SCAN ❶
☐

SCAN TYPE ❶
Quick ⌄

SCAN DAY ❶
Saturday ⌄

SCAN TIME
120

[Create]   [OK]

Figure 5-8. *View to customize the Microsoft anti-malware agent before installation*

The best practice is to exclude files and locations carefully. Exclusions set without forethought might lead to undetected malware. Excluding a folder could prevent a virus or worm from being detected.

7. Click the OK button, and the installation of endpoint protection begins. You'll see a notification displayed in a pop-up window, as shown in Figure 5-9.

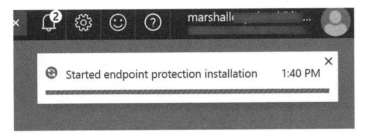

Figure 5-9. *Pop-up window notification of endpoint protection installation*

Identifying that endpoint protection is not installed or does not have the needed Azure extensions is important to protect the individual VM. It's also important so that Security Center provides alerts when corrective action is taken by the endpoint protection. The ability to have vulnerabilities identified is set by configuring the Security Center policy, discussed in Chapter 3. The next exercise walks you through the steps you need to implement to better understand what Security Center recommends and why.

REMEDIATE OS VULNERABILITIES WITH AZURE SECURITY CENTER

This VM example procedure is one example of a recommendation you may receive after Security Center scans your VMs. The configuration of your VM deployment may be greatly different than the Contoso.com example. If VMs are deployed from the Azure console, then few errors may be found. Use these steps for each OS vulnerability discovered. As you apply each recommendation, you will reduce your security risk. Stated another way, reducing the risk of vulnerabilities one at a time protects your business by securing the configuration identified by Security Center.

■ **Tip**   Some virtual machines and other PaaS offerings have specific security remediation recommendations identified by Security Center. Once enabled, they reduce risk.

---

1. Open a supported browser, connect to the Azure portal at `https://portal.azure.com`, and log on with your Azure account and password. Open the Security Center blade, and click "Remediate OS vulnerabilities by Microsoft," as shown in Figure 5-10.

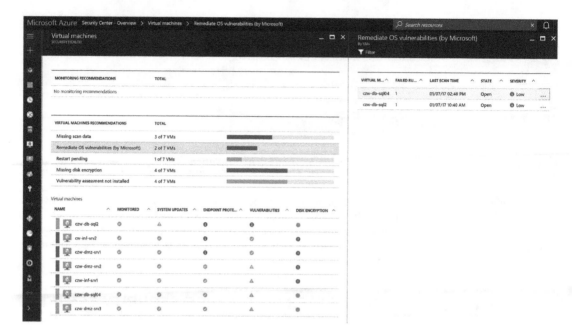

Figure 5-10. *View of VM security health with "Remediate OS vulnerabilities by Microsoft" enabled*

2. The "Remediate OS vulnerabilities" blade opens. Select the first item to gain greater insight into the security risk identified by Azure Security Center. In the Contoso. com infrastructure, the Azure administrator deployed SQL Server. You should see information like in Figure 5-11.

Figure 5-11. *Detailed view of automatic actions performed, memory quota adjustment*

3. Select the rule name to read more information about the specific change that was created. This specific change, shown in Figure 5-12, is to enable a group policy to remove or limit users in order to adjust the memory quota for a process. Notice the common configuration enumeration ID (CCEID) and the title "Adjust memory quotas for a process." Now that you have detailed information on what the automatic processes are, dismiss the notification to continue.

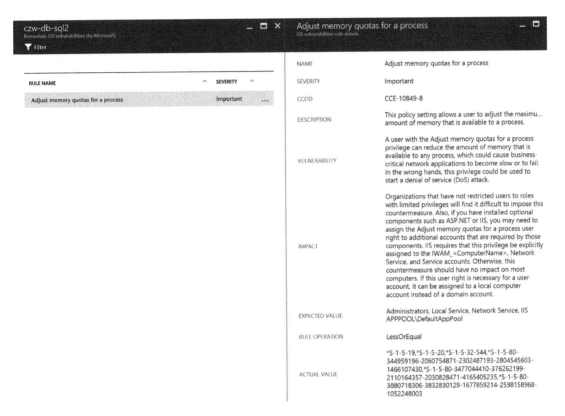

Figure 5-12. *Detailed view of the automatic adjustment of the memory quota for a process action*

▨ **Security Tip** User rights should be assigned to the appropriate accounts to remove the risk of a denial-of-service (DoS) attack. If this setting is not enabled, a compromised account, user, or service could increase the amount of memory available for the "compromised" process and reduce memory for the overall platform.

Prevention Blade

If you review the prevention blade and open the recommendation details from Security Center, it shows the individual Azure solution suggested after Security Center has analyzed your infrastructure. The recommendations are compared to security best practices after the agents complete their scanning of the Azure systems. You can see the security health of all properties of a resource at once by clicking the Recommendations tab, as shown in Figure 5-13.

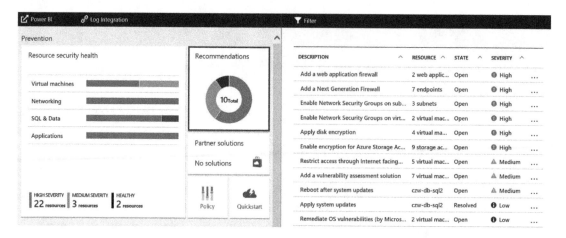

Figure 5-13. *View of security recommendations showing state and severity*

Security recommendations are displayed in a table format, to the right, and if a large number are displayed, you can filter them to focus on necessary tasks. The information provided in the columns includes the following:

- Description (topic of what needs to be completed)
- Resource (subnet, web app, VM, etc.)
- State (open, in progress, resolved)
- Severity (high, medium, low)

You can filter based on the type of recommendation you are reviewing. Azure Security Center prioritizes the severity for you and enables you to concentrate on critical systems first. The filtering can be enabled by clicking the Filter icon in the Recommendations blade, as shown in Figure 5-14.

Figure 5-14. *View of using the Filter option for recommendations*

The information provided helps Azure operations team members become more aware of the necessary security configuration and the security risk exposure. Some of the recommendations do not have an action that is performed from inside Azure Security Center, as shown in Figure 5-15.

Figure 5-15. *Detailed view of the VM recommendation blade to indicate a reboot is necessary to complete the security changes*

If you look in the top right above the Filter icon, you'll see the blade title is "A restart is pending to complete system updates." The systems listed here have been identified as having security updates installed; however, they will not take effect until the system is rebooted. You may think you can reboot the systems; however, many organizations have an SLA with the business that includes agreed-on times to perform maintenance on systems. Often with clusters of servers such as a SQL Server or SharePoint farm, individual nodes can be patched and rebooted one at a time to prevent an outage. Rebooting a server, or in this example a SQL Server instance, outside of the maintenance window would be considered an out-of-band operation. Use the Azure portal to restart the VM to complete the processes during the maintenance window or request a high-priority change request so all affected users of the system are properly notified.

Network Security Groups

Securing Azure virtual networks is an added security feature provided by the Azure portal's Azure Resource Manager deployment model. Before ARM, this security feature was implemented through PowerShell only. An NSG provides access control to Azure virtual machines and Azure vnets.

Implementing an NSG for a specific vnet provides agility for all the VMs in the subnet by controlling traffic for both inbound and outbound network traffic. Each NSG requires a name, and one or more rules are created that define the segmentation within a vnet. There are specific NSG rules that are required to be enabled for each NSG applied to a subnet. The NSG rules include the following:

- Rule name
- Inbound or outbound
- Priority integer
- Source IP address (from address)
- Destination IP address (to address)
- Protocol (TCP, UDP)
- Allow or deny access

Architecting and enabling zone security for the Azure network is an effective strategy for reducing security risks and the VMs inside the Azure vnets. The example provided for Contoso.com in Chapter 3 was used to deploy IP subnets to represent a real-world enterprise network infrastructure. The example included three networks and specific IP subnets, as shown in Figure 5-16.

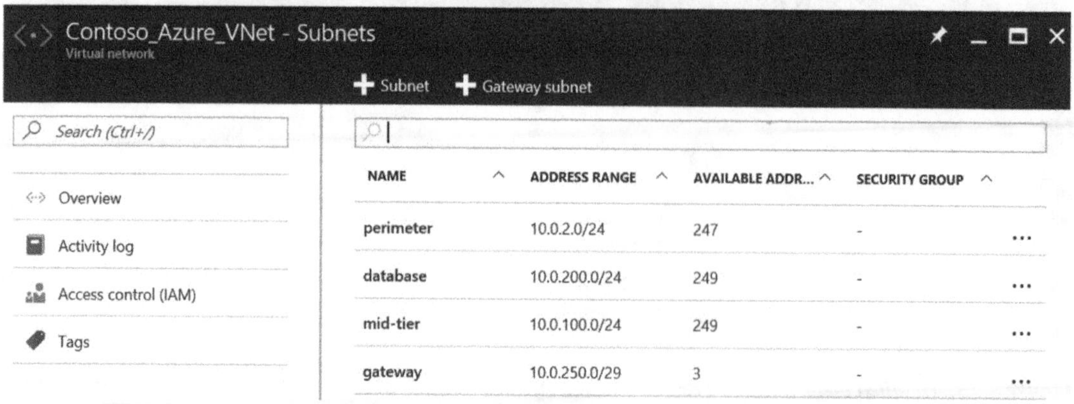

NAME	ADDRESS RANGE	AVAILABLE ADDR...	SECURITY GROUP	
perimeter	10.0.2.0/24	247	-	...
database	10.0.200.0/24	249	-	...
mid-tier	10.0.100.0/24	249	-	...
gateway	10.0.250.0/29	3	-	...

Figure 5-16. *View of the Contoso Azure vnet IP subnets*

The three networks for this discussion are the perimeter, database, and mid-tier; the gateway is not part of the discussion. If you start at the perimeter network, this IP subnet contains systems that are Internet-facing, but in this example you'd like to place them behind a firewall.

An Azure NSG should be configured to allow inbound Internet traffic to systems in the perimeter network and deny inbound Internet traffic to the mid-tier and database IP subnets. In addition, the database IP subnet would allow inbound traffic from the mid-tier IP subnet and deny inbound traffic from the perimeter IP subnet. The mid-tier IP subnet would allow perimeter IP subnet traffic and deny inbound Internet traffic. The way to configure Azure NSGs is to use a five-tuple (five-value) definition.

Source Network | Source Port | Destination Network | Destination Port | Protocol

If you have configured traditional firewalls on-premises, this is the same five-tuple rule, and the Azure NSG functions like a traditional firewall. The NSG allows or denies UDP or TCP protocols from the Internet or other Azure IP subnets. In this procedure, you will learn to create an NSG for each of the three subnets and then configure the IP subnet restrictions as follows:

- Perimeter | Allow internet inbound and outbound TCP port 443

- Mid-tier | Deny internet inbound and outbound TCP port any

  - Allow "database" inbound and outbound

- Database | Deny internet inbound and outbound TCP port any

  - Allow "mid-tier" inbound and outbound

There are other restrictions that may be set on inbound and outbound traffic; however, those details are enabled based on the applications being used and the ports those applications require. Once these changes are made, Azure Security Center will rescan the IP networks to validate that the NSG was created correctly. If additional security risks are identified, they are included in the updated security health and recommendation blade.

Every time an NSG is created, it includes default inbound and outbound rules that are predefined and cannot be edited or deleted. Table 5-1 shows the default NSG rules created with every network security group (note the astrik '*' is a wildcard, for all ports).

Table 5-1. Default Inbound Network Security Group Rules

Description	Priority	Source IP	Source Port	Destination IP	Destination Port	Protocol	Allow/Deny
Virtual network inbound	6500	Virtual_ Network	*	Virtual_ Network	*	*	Allow
Azure load balancer	65001	Azure_ Loadbalancer	*	*	*	*	Allow
Deny inbound all	65500	*	*	*	*	*	Deny

Table 5-2 shows the default outbound NSG rules that cannot be edited or deleted.

Table 5-2. Default Outbound Network Security Group Rules

Description	Priority	Source IP	Source Port	Destination IP	Destination Port	Protocol	Allow/Deny
Virtual network outbound	6500	Virtual_ Network	*	Virtual_ Network	*	*	Allow
Internet outbound	65001	*	*	Internet	*	*	Allow
Deny outbound all	65500	*	*	*	*	*	Deny

You can use the next exercise to enable inbound and outbound data traffic at each of the NSGs. Adjust the two options to allow or deny the NSG rules based on the applications in your network. The inbound rules are created and applied to the IP subnets, and separate outbound rules are created and applied to the same IP subnet.

The assumptions for this procedure are that you and Contoso.com would like to filter traffic to and from each VM identically inside the virtual network. One of the hard rules is that each network subnet can be associated to only one NSG, and the security rules are evaluated in the priority starting with the lowest number. The priorities can be set (low to high) from 100 to 4096. The NSG has separate inbound and outbound rules to allow or deny traffic.

ENABLE NETWORK SECURITY GROUPS WITH AZURE SECURITY CENTER

You have learned the basics of Azure NSGs and understand they provide similar security support as traditional firewalls. Azure Security Center provides recommendations about specifically how security should be enabled for the individual IP subnets. These procedures can be easily customized for your environment. There are some minor recommendations for naming and best practices that are introduced in the procedures. The best practices include the following:

- Start with a number or letter and end with a letter or number (case insensitive).

- Use 80 characters that are region unique (NSG name and NSG rule name).

- iba is an inbound rule to allow (traffic into the IP subnet).

- ibd is an inbound rule to deny (traffic into the IP subnet).

- oba is an outbound rule to allow (traffic out of the IP subnet).

- obd is an outbound rule to deny (traffic out of the IP subnet).

When creating the complete network security group configuration, you must have an NSG name and an NSG rule name, and you should use a standard naming convention that reveals details of the network security group and how it provides security for the IP subnet.

Here are the NSG name best practice naming standards, with an example:

Corp Region – VNet supported – Prod or Dev – Trusted or Not Trusted

Contoso West US – Perimeter - Production – Semi Trusted (long form)

cwus-perim-prod-semitrust (short form)

Here are the NSG rule name best practice naming standards, with an example:

Corp Region – VNet supported – inbound rule or outbound rule – port – protocol – priority

Contoso West US – Perimeter - inbound allow – 443 – TCP – 500 (long form)

cwus-per-iba-443-tcp-500 (short form)

Take into consideration the NSG name length and that this name can be used in a PowerShell script. A short name that follows a naming best practice is easier to type than a long name. Additionally, the NSG rule is a naming convention, while the rule properties also include the source and destination IP addresses. Both are required to be entered in the NSG rule properties but not in the NSG rule name.

The NSG plan for this procedure is to enable a network security group to create an NSG name for the database IP subnet and review the default NSG rules. Next you will create an NSG rule to allow inbound and outbound traffic for Remote Desktop Protocol (RDP) for the mid-tier IP subnet. You will then create NSG rules to allow database IP subnet inbound and outbound traffic to the mid-tier IP subnet. With these rules created from this one procedure, you can duplicate other inbound and outbound NSGs for any Azure IP subnet to remove security risks.

■ **Security Tip** Virtual machines require an RDP connection to connect to the system and manage the VM. If you connect to the system through the Internet, it is a best practice to create an NSG that allows an RDP connection from your workstation IP subnet and remove the RDP connection from all Internet IP ranges.

1. Open a supported browser, connect the Azure portal at https://portal.azure.com, and log on with your Azure account and password. Open the Security Center blade and highlight Networking, as shown in Figure 5-17.

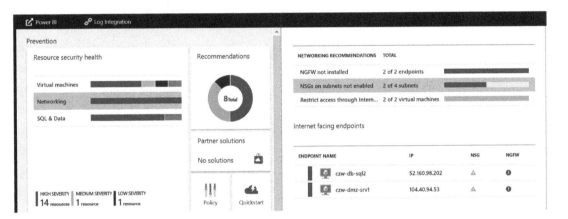

Figure 5-17. View of Security Center prevention blade with Networking recommendations selected

2. Click "NSGs on subnets not enabled" on the Networking security health blade, as shown in Figure 5-18.

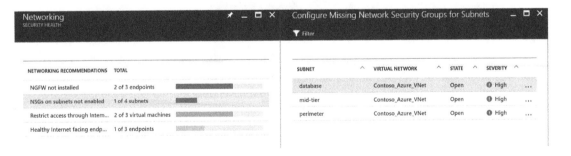

Figure 5-18. View of the NSG subnets that are not enabled

3. With the Configure Missing Network Security Groups for Subnets blade open, select the database vnet. This will open the option to choose a network security group or create a new one, as shown in Figure 5-19.

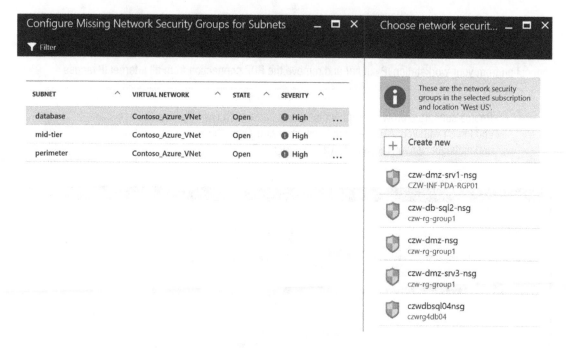

Figure 5-19. *Choosing the network security group view*

4. If you do not have an NSG to select, then click the "Create new" option and name the NSG following the guidelines provided at the beginning of this exercise. For the Contoso.com example, the NSG selected is czwdbsql04nsg. After selecting an NSG or creating a new NSG, wait for this step to complete. Wait approximately 30 seconds while the pop-up window displays, as shown in Figure 5-20.

Figure 5-20. *View of the pop-up window creating the NSG*

5. Return to the Security Center Network recommendation blade, as shown in Figure 5-21.

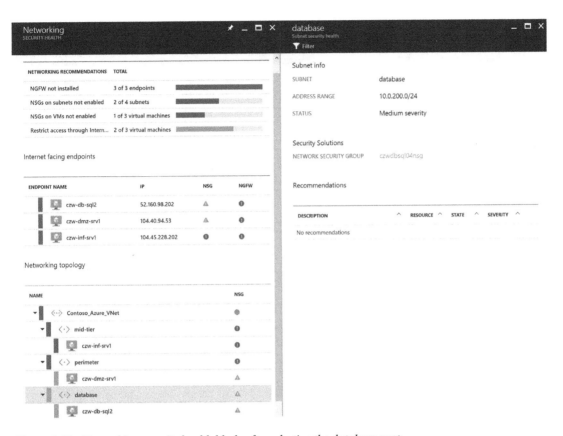

Figure 5-21. *Networking security health blade after selecting the database vnet*

6. Select the network security group, as shown in Figure 5-22. Notice there is one highlighted rule that was created automatically, called default-allow-rdp, from any IP source to any IP source.

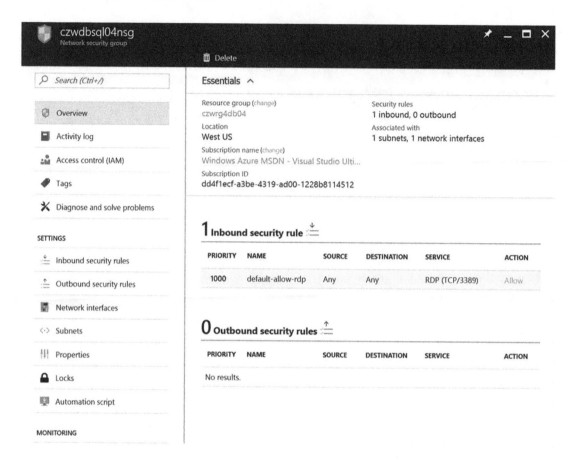

Figure 5-22. *Selected NSG name needed to configure the NSG rules to apply*

7. With the NSG blade open, from the Settings view, click the inbound security rules and then click "Default rules," as shown in Figure 5-23.

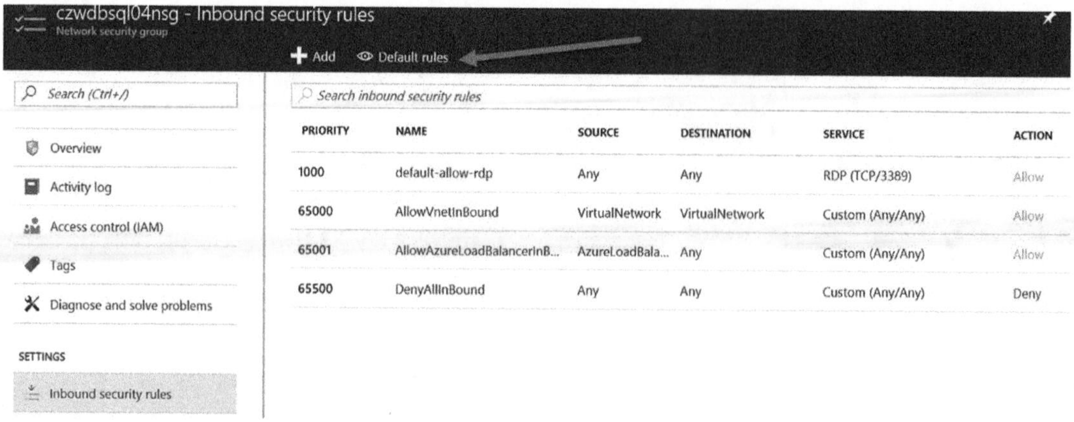

Figure 5-23. *Default rules of the database NSG with inbound security rules selected*

8. Select the Add rule option shown in Figure 5-24. Now you can enter the name of the rule, **AllowMidTierInbound**, and enter the mid-tier IP subnet using CIDR notation and the Microsoft SQL port 1433. Press Enter to create the rule and apply this rule to the network security group created in step 4.

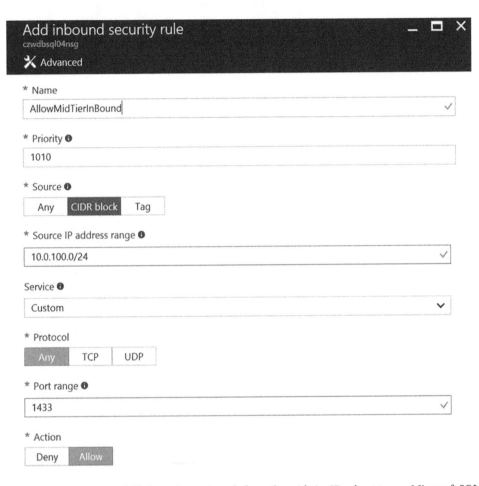

Figure 5-24. *View to add inbound security rule from the mid-tier IP subnet to any Microsoft SQL Server instance on port 1433*

9. To create an outbound NSG rule, return to the settings and select the outbound security rules. Select the default options to review the default outbound rules and click the Add option, as shown in Figure 5-25. Enter the name **AllowMidTierOutBound** and the IP subnet in CIDR notation and choose the custom option, as shown. (This optional port depends on the application ports required by the VM in the mid-tier IP subnet.) After you select the service and port, click Save to continue.

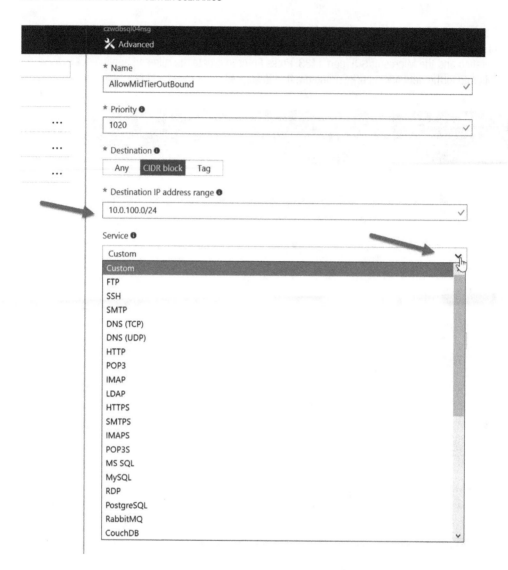

Figure 5-25. *Add outbound NSG rules view with custom settings options*

10. Finally, you can review the network security group (named czwdbsql04nsg), shown in Figure 5-26, and the default NSG rules for inbound IP traffic and ports and NSG rules for outbound IP traffic and ports.

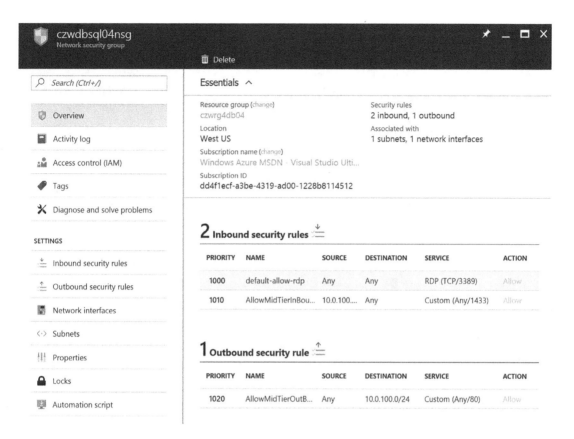

Figure 5-26. *Overview of the NSG named czwdbsql04nsg with NSG inbound and outbound security rules*

11. Continue to add inbound and outbound rules to this NSG if necessary. Return to the Azure Security Center networking recommendations and create NSG names for other IP subnets. Follow the same processes to block IP addresses (inbound) from the Internet and block IP addresses (outbound) to the Internet.

■ **Security Tip** The reason IP subnets are blocked from unknown Internet IP subnets is obviously for tighter security. One reason outbound Internet address are blocked from database and mid-tier IP subnets is to prevent communication of a compromised system back to a "command and control" server on the Internet.

You should use this procedure as a best practice to enable network security group naming and NSG rules that apply to the IP subnet. You should create an NSG name that will be applied to each VM inside the IP subnet. You can then create more NSG rules that allow or deny IP traffic from other Azure vnets or the Internet.

Summary

With the security work you completed in this chapter, you created procedures using the recommendations identified by Azure Security Center. These procedures included best practices to deploy the Azure-supported Microsoft endpoint protection. The other option (currently) is using Trend Micro endpoint protection. These two options are the only two supported agents that include the Azure extensions to report up to Azure Security Center.

Next you created security procedures to identify OS vulnerabilities and secure the operating system from a possible denial-of-service (DoS) vulnerability by reducing accounts that have privileges to increase memory for VM services. You learned more about Security Center prevention recommendations, and in the final exercise you were introduced to network security groups. There was detailed security information about the differences between the NSG name and the NSG rules. You can create a single NSG name applied to a single IP subnet. However, you can create multiple NSG rules that allow or deny IP traffic to or from that IP subnet.

In the next chapter, your security deployment continues with the implementation of Azure virtual applications installed from the Azure Marketplace. You will learn about some of the current gaps in security event data (but not gaps in security) to use as extensions of your on-premises security platforms. Many examples will be provided, and greater integration between applications and Azure governance is detailed.

CHAPTER 6

Azure Security Center Extensions

Operational Security Assurance

In Chapter 5, you learned how Azure Secure Center provides recommendations to help your layered security design after analyzing your Azure infrastructure. You gained hands-on knowledge in the exercises when you installed endpoint protection on an Azure VM and resolved OS vulnerabilities based on your current configurations. Recommendations to improve your security posture were based on the security health and included hardening the IP subnets with network security groups (NSGs), with different rules for trusted and untrusted networks.

In this chapter, you will begin following the guidance provided by Security Center after the discovery process publishes recommended changes about disk encryption, SQL injection, and more. The following are the main topics identified:

- Detection and security alerts

- Security recommendations

- Encryption needed

- Pending actions

Next you will learn to extend security through real-world recommendations based on the network infrastructure after Security Center has evaluated the security needs. The processes enhance security by integrating Security Center with original equipment manufacturer (OEM) virtual appliance through the Microsoft Azure Marketplace. The following are the virtual appliances you will learn to deploy in this chapter:

- Web application firewall (WAF)

- Next-generation firewall (NGF)

- Vulnerability assessment integration

In this last chapter, the common theme builds on the foundation of Azure infrastructure services to help create a security framework that improves your skills and knowledge to gain cloud compliance through operational security assurance (OSA).

Security Center Updates

Before you spend more time reviewing the recommendations of Security Center, you might need to be reminded that as an Azure cloud service, its changes and innovation are at "cloud speed." In this section, you'll review a single product from the Microsoft System Center solution suite, Microsoft System Center Operations Manager (SCOM). Table 6-1 gives a timeline of the feature release dates.

© Marshall Copeland 2017
M. Copeland, *Cyber Security on Azure*, DOI 10.1007/978-1-4842-2740-4_6

Table 6-1. *System Center Operations Manager 2012 R2 Feature Release Timeline*

SCOM 2012 R2 Update Rollup	Month and Year	Months to New Features
Update Rollup 1	January 2014	0 (start)
Update Rollup 2	April 2014	4
Update Rollup 3	July 2014	4
Update Rollup 4	October 2014	4
Update Rollup 5	February 2015	5
Update Rollup 6	April 2015	3
Update Rollup 7	August 2015	5
Update Rollup 8	October 2015	3
Update Rollup 9	January 2016	4
Update Rollup 10	N/A	N/A
Update Rollup 11	August 2016	8

As you can see, the number of months between release dates for update rollups varies from three to five. One point to consider is that an update rollup is not a service pack release, which would require re-certification in some deployments. Another service point, related to time, would be to consider the traditional change management processes to install the update rollup. The change management processes include creating a deployment plan, creating a back-out plan, defending the update to the change management team, and then doing an after-hours deployment.

■ **Tip**   You can view the Microsoft System Center 2012 R2 release timeline in detail at `https://support.microsoft.com/en-us/help/3193857/cumulative-update-releases-for-microsoft-system-center-2012-r2-operations-manager`.

By contrast, changes in the cloud happen weekly and monthly. Specifically, for our security topic, there are new features on the road map for Azure Security Center and also bug fixes on the cloud service side. Figure 6-1 highlights new features for Security Center.

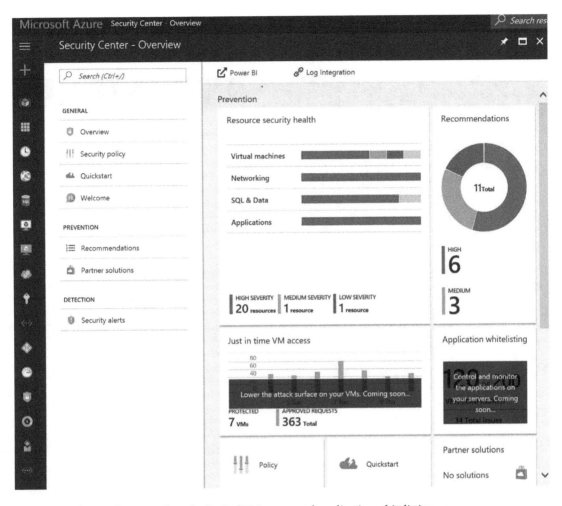

Figure 6-1. System Center updates for limited VM access and application whitelisting

The new features for Azure Security Center are highlighted in a gray window with details and the statement "Coming soon...." The change management processes may need to be evaluated by testing the new features in a controlled rollout with test and pilot systems.

■ **Tip** The Microsoft Azure team maintains a Cloud Platform News Byte Blog. You can read the updates and subscribe to notifications at `https://blogs.technet.microsoft.com/stbnewsbytes/`.

Detection and Security Alerts

You installed Microsoft endpoint protection on virtual machines in the Azure network infrastructure, and now you will start to see the integration between security endpoint actions and the Azure Security Center prevention. Return to the Azure Security Center blade and click the "Security alerts" detection.

The information provided by Security Center might be similar to the information shown in Figure 6-2, which detected activity on VMs deployed in the network. This information is related to bad actors that are attempting to gain access to your network.

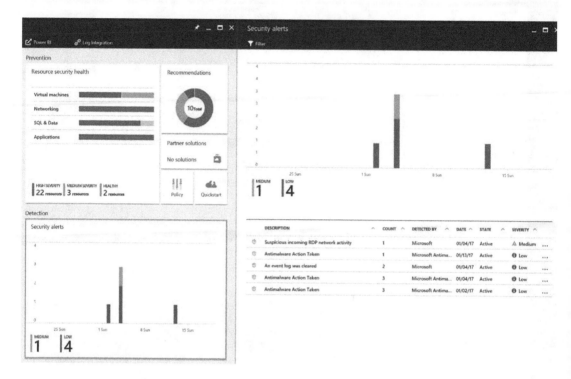

Figure 6-2. *Detection and security alerts identified on the VM infrastructure*

■ **Security Tip** The alerts displayed are real. The attacks were created quickly and easily with free hacking tools that can be found on the Internet. Azure security support requires notification before conducting any security test such as a vulnerability assessment.

Security Center also sends you a notification e-mail about this issue, which was set up when you configured the installation. Notification is necessary so you can gain insight into a potential attack; it is necessary to bring some attention to things beyond the normal activities on the cloud.

You can continue to learn from actions in previous exercises, such as when you deployed endpoint protection that integrated Security Center directly with an Azure VM. For the temporary 60-day trial period, the standard tier was selected as part of the Contoso proof of concept (POC). Now, you will gain specific guidance for security protection that is automatically enabled after the discovery of malware on servers. The malware discovered in Figure 6-3 is real and used as a powerful example of the layered security that is supported with Azure Security Center and endpoint protection.

Security Center prioritizes alerts based on these three levels:

- High
- Medium
- Low

If you review the details of some of the Contoso alerts in Figure 6-3, you'll notice the first priority description is "Suspicious incoming RDP network activity."

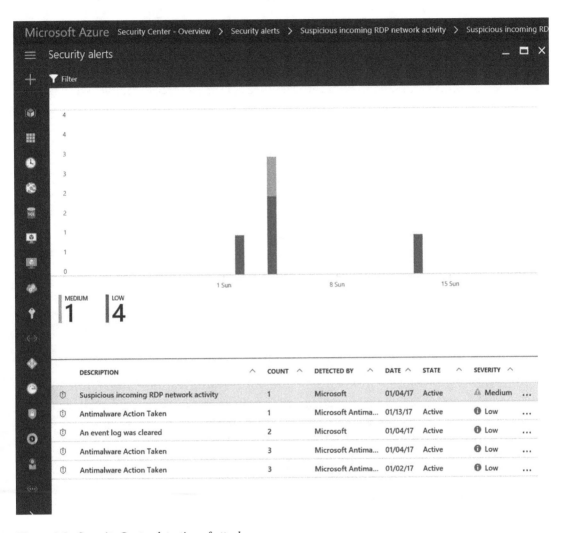

Figure 6-3. *Security Center detection of attacks*

The Remote Desktop Protocol (RDP) is used to connect to a Microsoft computer; RDP was developed by Microsoft specifically for connection over a network. In this example, the system integration has warned of incoming network activity that is suspicious. If you click the RDP alert, Security Center provides more details into why this alert was raised, as shown in Figure 6-4.

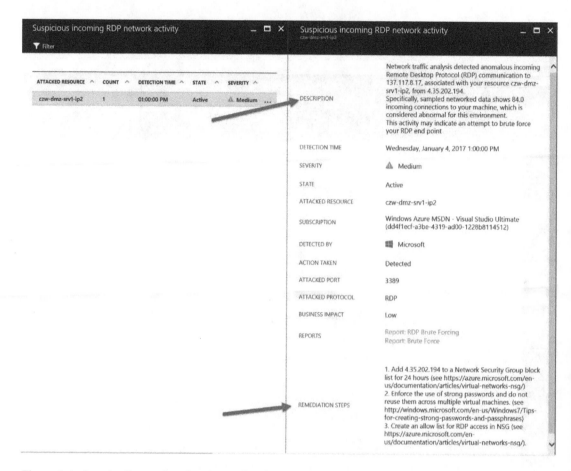

Figure 6-4. Security Center alert description details and remediation steps

Reviewing the description, you can see that the sampled network connections entry shows 84 attempts to connect to the VM from a specific IP address. In addition to the information, some remediation steps are suggested to block the specific IP address using an Azure network security group (NSG); the description also reminds you to enforce strong password usage. The use of very long passwords or passphrases makes brute-force attacks take years to be successful using off-the-self attacker utilities.

■ **Security Tip** A commodity-valued desktop workstation can easily support a Linux-based OS that accommodates multiple graphics processing unit (GPU) cards. This type of computer is a highly modified system configured to use several GPU cards, and individual computers can be assembled as a cluster. An attack, leveraging speed from this type of computer cluster, can cycle through more than 300 billion passwords (guesses) per second.

Without the automation found in Security Center and other solutions, an attack may go undiscovered by a busy cloud administrator. If you review this type of attack from the computer security event log, as shown in Figure 6-5, the remote connection is attempted using the account titled ADMINISTRATOR. If this server were on-premises, this account is the default account and could be vulnerable to a password dictionary attack. However, since this system was deployed directly in Azure, the administrator name is not a valid administration account name.

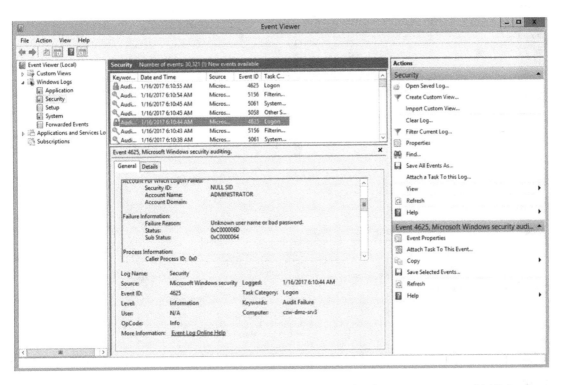

Figure 6-5. Security event log view from the Windows server view with administrator account highlighted

To review, Security Center provided notification of the anomaly, details of this specific attack, and recommendations to reduce the threat vulnerability. You may want Security Center to just take care of the attack problem for you automatically. The good news is that, in some attack profiles, the automation integration does automatically remediate the attack.

■ **Security Tip**   Strengthen your password policy. The RDP attack used to create the alerts is known as a *dictionary attack*. A password policy that requires eight characters with uppercase and lowercase letters, digits, and symbols can be cracked in about six hours.

If you review Figure 6-6, the next low-priority alert description is Antimalware Action Taken. There are several notifications, and the graph represents the totals by day of the week.

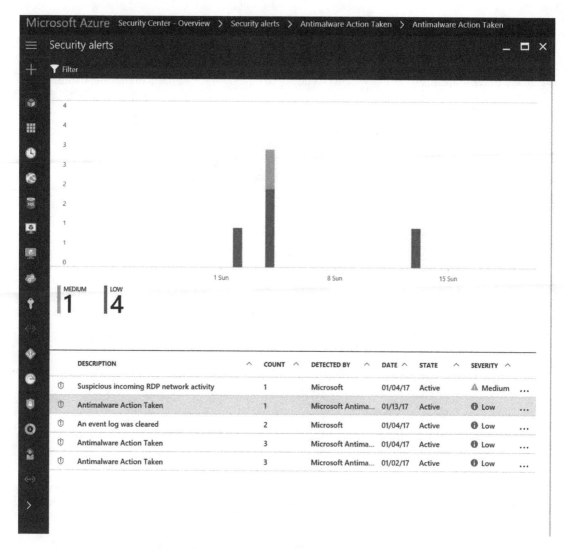

Figure 6-6. *View of anti-malware action taken by integration of endpoint protection and Security Center*

The action taken was completed by the Microsoft Endpoint Protection agent after System Center corroborated the identified anomaly. If you click this type of warning, you'll see details about it, as shown in Figure 6-7. The key areas to notice are the automatic action taken, listed as Block, and the remediation steps that say "No user action is necessary."

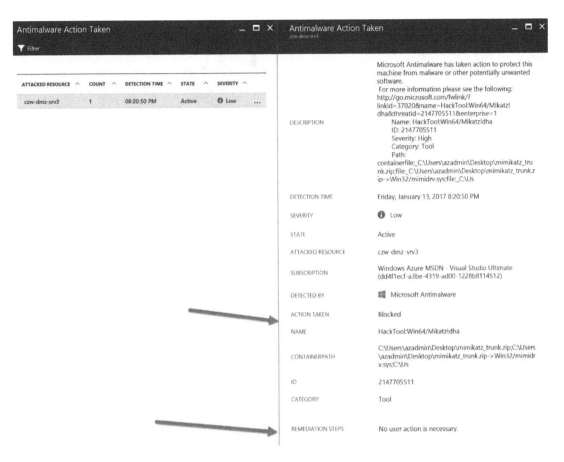

Figure 6-7. *Security Center view of automatic action taken and remediation steps*

The hacking tool identified in the description is a known tool called mimikatz and is used to gain credential data or to run remote code. This is a current attack tool that is kept up-to-date on GitHub, a code repository hosting service.

■ **Security Tip**   Many freely available hacking tools, like mimikatz, are considered useful for gathering Windows NT Lan Manager (NTLM) hash values of users who have logged onto a Windows OS computer. Hackers use the credentials to elevate privileges to an administrator level in an attack commonly called *pass-the-hash.*

The final recommendation in this series may be a simple notification and go unnoticed even if you have a full-time employee (FTE) reviewing the log files. In Figure 6-8, notice the highlighted activity of "An event log was cleared."

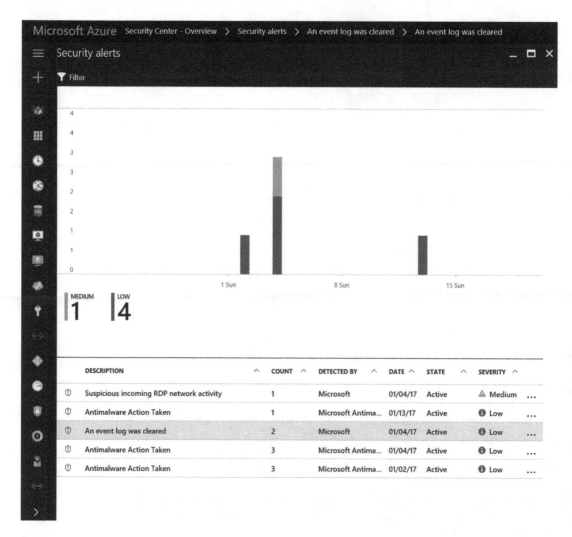

Figure 6-8. *Notification view from Security Center of an event log cleared action*

If you see this event in your deployment of Security Center, click the event to gain greater insight into the details. As you review the details provided in Figure 6-9, notice the description identified the Azure account used to clear the log files. Additionally, notice the remediation steps outlined for the security guidance.

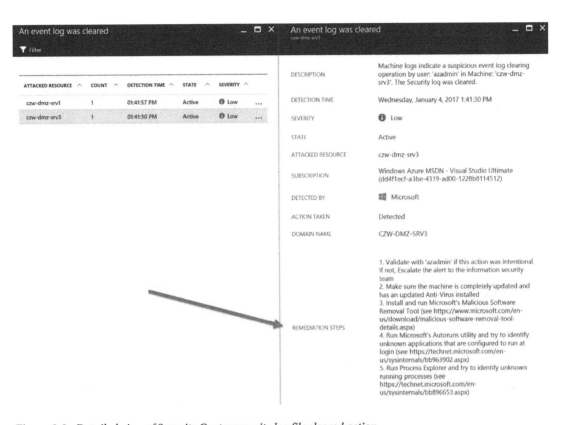

Figure 6-9. Detailed view of Security Center security log file cleared action

The automation behind Security Center provides intelligent recommendations after analysis of the events. These events could span the partner solutions as well as the virtual machines you build and place into different Azure IP subnets. A list of prioritized security alerts is presented in the console; an e-mail is also sent with severity recommendations needed to prevent an attack. You can see a few examples of additional security events in Table 6-2.

Table 6-2. Security Center Anomaly and Behavioral Attack Examples

Security Center Description	Security Consideration
Malicious SQL activity	SQL injection attempt
Failed RDP brute-force attack	RDP attack prevented by Security Center
Successful RDP brute-force attack	RDP attack that was not prevented (successfully); system is most likely compromised
Suspicious process executed	Unidentified execution of a processes; baseline anomaly
System binary discovered in dump file	Hacker code caused a crash dump; Security Center compared attributes through behavioral analytics

Responding to security alerts requires the security team to follow the "incident management procedures" to validate the alerts. All alerts are prioritized, and some actions are taken automatically to help you plan the most appropriate use of your time.

■ **Security Tip** Always verify a security alert of high priority. New systems, new applications, and new Azure administrators may cause a *false positive*, which is a System Center alert that may be false. Once you've validated that it's not a false positive, then take action. The best practice is always to "think before you act."

Recommendations

If you recall, the Contoso deployment of Security Center started in Chapter 4 and over time has been evaluating the infrastructure for several days or a week or more. Security Center requires many hours and sometimes days to identify and evaluate. The processes to review recommendations are highlighted in this chapter to provide greater understanding for interpreting the severity levels and insight provided by Azure Security Center.

If you go back to the main Security Cent blade and select the Recommendations blade from the left menu, you'll notice your installation may be similar to the discovered security risks in Contoso Azure deployment. Begin by reviewing the recommendations, as shown in Figure 6-10.

Recommendations					Enable storage encryption			
▼ Filter					▼ Filter			
DESCRIPTION	RESOURCE	STATE	SEVERITY		STORAGE ACCOUNT	STATE	SEVERITY	
Add a web application firewall	2 web applic...	Open	🔴 High	...	czwrg4db04diag04	Open	🔴 High	...
Add a Next Generation Firewall	5 endpoints	Open	🔴 High	...	czwrg4db04ssd04	Open	🔴 High	...
Enable Network Security Groups on sub...	2 subnets	Open	🔴 High	...	czwrgdb	Open	🔴 High	...
Enable Network Security Groups on virt...	2 virtual mac...	Open	🔴 High	...	czwrggroup1diagsrv1	Open	🔴 High	...
Apply disk encryption	4 virtual ma...	Open	🔴 High	...	czwrggroup1disks	Open	🔴 High	...
Enable encryption for Azure Storage Ac...	9 storage ac...	Open	🔴 High	...	czwsadmzsrv1	Open	🔴 High	...
Restrict access through Internet facing...	3 virtual mac...	Open	⚠ Medium	...	czwsadmzsrv2	Open	🔴 High	...
Add a vulnerability assessment solution	5 virtual mac...	Open	⚠ Medium	...	czwsadmzsrv3	Open	🔴 High	...
Reboot after system updates	czw-db-sql2	Open	⚠ Medium	...	dd1501westus	Open	🔴 High	...
Apply system updates	czw-db-sql2	Open	ℹ Low	...				
Remediate OS vulnerabilities (by Micros...	2 virtual mac...	Open	ℹ Low	...				

Figure 6-10. *Security Center recommendations based on the security vulnerabilities discovered*

In this example, the recommendation is to enable encryption for Azure storage accounts as a high priority. Protecting data at rest is a requirement for companies placing data in the cloud. If you review the details on this Contoso recommendation page, there are a total of nine storage accounts that need to have encryption enabled. It is an easy process, as shown in Figure 6-11, to simply highlight the database and wait for the Encryption blade to open.

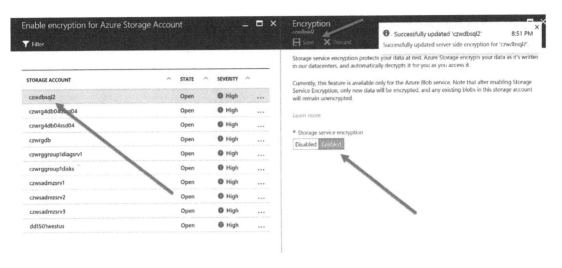

Figure 6-11. *Enabling encryption for Azure storage account*

The recommendation to encrypt the Azure storage account was identified after Azure Security Center evaluated the infrastructure. The process to encrypt the Azure storage account is easy; just select the option to enable it and then save the encryption change option before leaving the Encryption blade. You will see a small pop-up window on the right side of the console indicating the storage account has encryption enabled and was successfully updated.

■ **Security Tip**   A best practice is to enable Azure storage encryption before any data is copied to the blob storage. Notice the information that only new data written to the storage account is encrypted, so you should add the encryption step before storage is made available to applications and users.

Return the view to the Recommendations pane and notice that one of the systems, czw-db-sql2, requires a reboot before the updates to the system have been completed. By highlighting the system, as shown in Figure 6-12, you can see that the restart is necessary.

Recommendations

DESCRIPTION	RESOURCE	STATE	SEVERITY	
Add a web application firewall	2 web applic...	Open	⬤ High	...
Add a Next Generation Firewall	5 endpoints	Open	⬤ High	...
Enable Network Security Groups on sub...	2 subnets	Open	⬤ High	...
Enable Network Security Groups on virt...	2 virtual mac...	Open	⬤ High	...
Apply disk encryption	4 virtual ma...	Open	⬤ High	...
Enable encryption for Azure Storage Ac...	9 storage ac...	Open	⬤ High	...
Restrict access through Internet facing...	3 virtual mac...	Open	⚠ Medium	...
Add a vulnerability assessment solution	5 virtual mac...	Open	⚠ Medium	...
Reboot after system updates	czw-db-sql2	Open	⚠ Medium	...
Apply system updates	czw-db-sql2	Open	ⓘ Low	...
Remediate OS vulnerabilities (by Micros...	2 virtual mac...	Open	ⓘ Low	...

A restart is pending to complete system updates

RESOURCE	LAST SCAN TIME	STATE	SEVERITY	
czw-db-sql2	02/09/17 04:01 PM	Open	⚠ Medium	...

Figure 6-12. Recommendation that a system reboot is pending

This recommendation has identified a needed restart to complete the update because until the system is rebooted, the application or OS is still vulnerable to the risk. The remediation of some OS vulnerabilities through what is commonly called a *patching process* is completed by Security Center. The remediation of OS vulnerabilities is displayed on the Security Center blade, as shown in Figure 6-13. However, an automatic reboot may disrupt services to this application, so it is highlighted as a recommendation with a medium severity. This provides time for the Azure administrators to submit a change process and notify the business that a reboot is necessary.

Recommendations

DESCRIPTION	RESOURCE	STATE	SEVERITY	
Add a web application firewall	2 web applic...	Open	⬤ High	...
Add a Next Generation Firewall	5 endpoints	Open	⬤ High	...
Enable Network Security Groups on sub...	2 subnets	Open	⬤ High	...
Enable Network Security Groups on virt...	2 virtual mac...	Open	⬤ High	...
Apply disk encryption	4 virtual ma...	Open	⬤ High	...
Enable encryption for Azure Storage Ac...	9 storage ac...	Open	⬤ High	...
Restrict access through Internet facing...	3 virtual mac...	Open	⚠ Medium	...
Add a vulnerability assessment solution	5 virtual mac...	Open	⚠ Medium	...
Reboot after system updates	czw-db-sql2	Open	⚠ Medium	...
Apply system updates	czw-db-sql2	Open	ⓘ Low	...
Remediate OS vulnerabilities (by Micros...	2 virtual mac...	Open	ⓘ Low	...

Remediate OS vulnerabilities (by Microsoft)
By VMs

VIRTUAL M...	FAILED RU...	LAST SCAN TIME	STATE	SEVERITY	
czw-db-sql04	1	01/15/17 10:17 PM	Open	ⓘ Low	...
czw-db-sql2	1	02/09/17 04:00 PM	Open	ⓘ Low	...

Figure 6-13. OS vulnerabilities for SQL Server instances remediated by Microsoft

Return to the Security Center overview blade; then go to the "Partner solutions" blade and Recommendations pane, as shown in Figure 6-14. The recommendation has identified two web applications that are vulnerable to risks, and the severity is high.

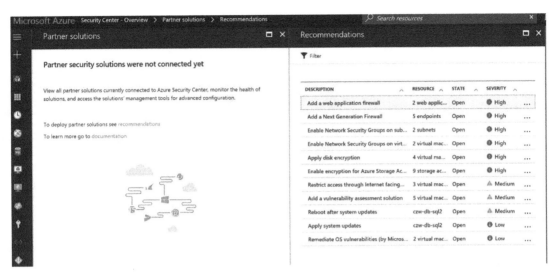

Figure 6-14. *Partner solution recommendation for a web application firewall*

A web application firewall (WAF) supports applications that communicate on the application layer of the Open Systems Interconnection (OSI) model. This layer is where web servers and web browsers communicate using the Hypertext Transfer Protocol (HTTP) and is the foundational method of data communication for the Internet. A WAF is used to prevent attacks with HTTP/HTTPS, such as cross-site scripting (XSS) and SQL injection. Both types of attacks are included on the 2013 OWASP Top Ten list (2017 Top Ten list updates have not been finalized) of most critical security risks facing organizations that develop web applications.

■ **Security Tip**   OWASP is a not-for-profit organization and community providing free security information and guidance focused on improving application security and trust. The organization is commercial free and provides unbiased, particle application security. To join the OWASP foundation and learn more, visit
`https://www.owasp.org/index.php/Main_Page`.

ADD A WEB APPLICATION FIREWALL

1. Select the first recommendation to add a web application firewall, as shown in Figure 6-15.

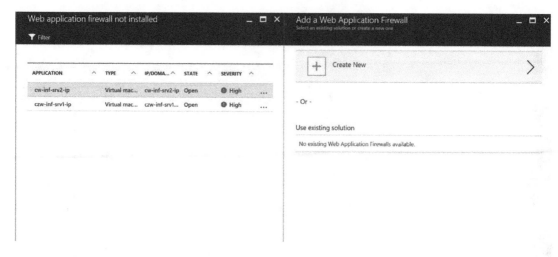

Figure 6-15. *Web application firewall recommended*

2. If this is the first time you have added a partner OEM web application firewall, there is no option to use an existing solution. Click the plus sign to create a new one.

3. The view shown in Figure 6-16 is only three of more than 100 web application firewall results when searched on the Azure Marketplace. Notice that Barracuda Networks has two packages available for the install. For this example, select the Barracuda Networks, Inc., firewall option.

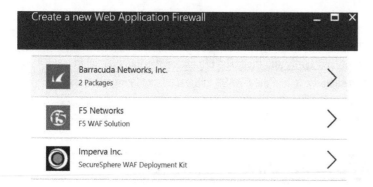

Figure 6-16. *Options recommended to create a new web application firewall*

4. Figure 6-17 displays the two different Barracuda web application firewalls.

Figure 6-17. *Automatically provisioned and semi-automatically provisioned*

5. Select the "Automatically provisioned" option (the top one) to read the details about the Barracuda network licenses, as shown in Figure 6-18.

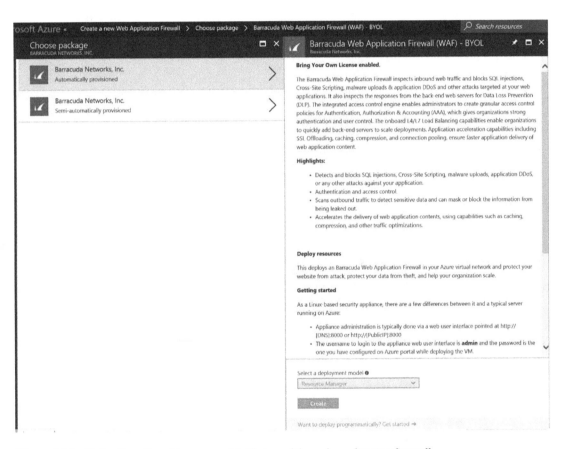

Figure 6-18. *"Bring Your Own Licenses enabled" view of the web application firewall*

6. Click the button at the bottom of the blade to create the WAF. This starts the wizard processes, as shown in Figure 6-19.

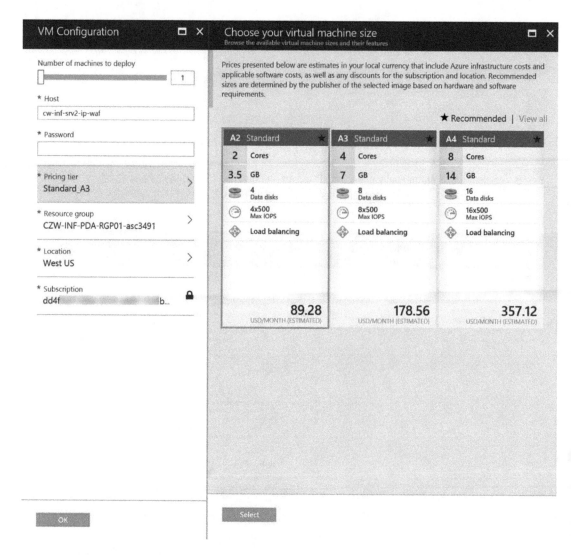

Figure 6-19. Choosing the VM size for the Barracuda web application firewall

7. The default setting is an A3 standard; however, for testing purposes, you could select the A2 standard before deploying in production. Enter a password for the Linux VM, validate the deployment is in the same region as your virtual machines, and click Select.

8. The next option is to request an evaluation license, as shown in Figure 6-20.

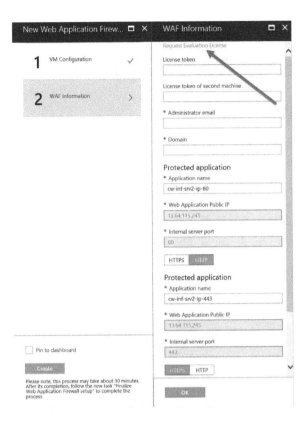

Figure 6-20. *Requesting a Barracuda evaluation license*

Click the Request Evaluation Licenses link to open your web browser to the Barracuda web site, as shown in Figure 6-21.

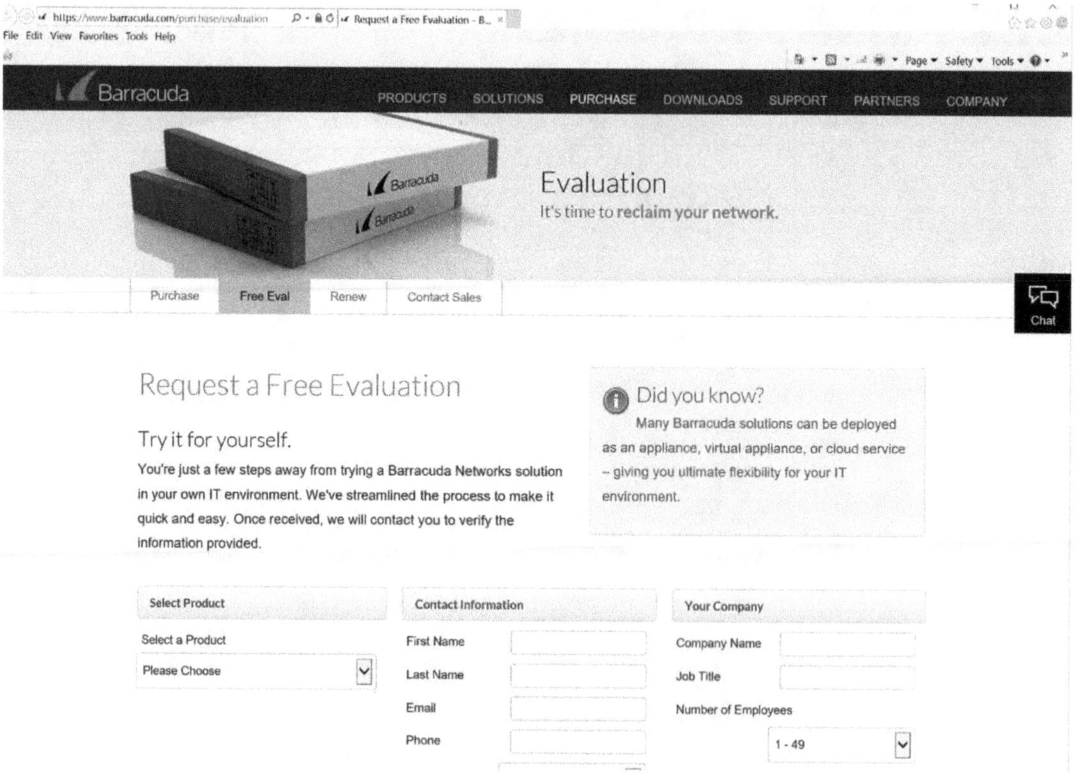

Figure 6-21. *Free evaluation licenses from Barracuda for a trial license*

9. Enter your information to complete the registration processes. To select the correct option, click the down arrow on the menu to select a product. Scroll down to the options, as shown in Figure 6-22.

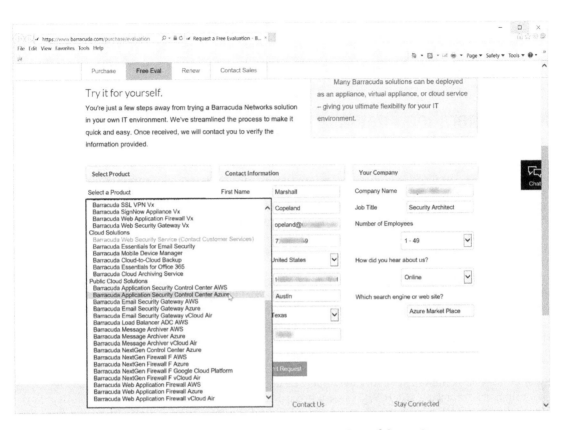

Figure 6-22. Selecting the product Barracuda Application Security Control Center Azure

10. You need to allow the automated Barracuda product trial license to e-mail you the trial code. Once you enter that code in step 8 (Figure 6-20), click OK to begin the trial of this web application firewall.

11. Notice after the WAF is in place, the "high" severity alert from Security Center is removed.

Security Tip If you want to see the features of the Barracuda WAF, you can try the demo simulator at the Barracuda web site at http://waf.barracuda.com/cgi-mod/index.cgi. The user name is *guest*, and the password is *admin*.

The web application firewall is a product that supports the OWASP Top Ten project. The overall goal of the Top Ten project is simply to raise awareness about application security by allowing developers to learn from the mistakes of other organizations. The long-term goal for business executives should be to create a web software application development life cycle or software development life cycle (SDLC). The Top Ten project is a representation banner that allows a common language for developers and security professionals to communicate, and it is just the tip of the iceberg. There are hundreds of security issues overall from a web application discussion topic. The 2013 OWASP Top Ten is based on eight databases from firms that specialize in application security and on the application vulnerabilities from hundreds of organizations totaling more than 500,000 vulnerabilities. (note, the Top Ten List is updated every 3 - 5 years, the 2017 Top Ten list is in "preview" and published after this books publication date.)

■ **Security Tip** The 2017 OWASP Top Ten update is underway. To learn more about the data collected in 2014 through 2016, visit `https://www.owasp.org/index.php/Category:OWASP_Top_Ten_Project`.

Next-Generation Firewalls

The early versions of firewall products were stateless types of firewalls that provided simple TCP/IP packet filtering. Firewalls can be compromised, so you can add a layer of defense by setting an access control list (ACL) with Azure. The packet filtering either accepts the network addresses and ports or denies the network address and port. The TCP/IP packet is competed to match the packet filter settings or what is called the *packet filter rules*. If the packet does not match, the packet information is dropped or rejected. If the packet information matches, it is allowed to pass. The packets are not maintained, so the traffic is considered to be "stateless," which means the firewall does not maintain any traffic streaming data. Each packet IP address, port number, and protocol (TCP or UDP) is handled separately. This type of firewall is supported on the TCP/IP Network layer of the OSI reference model.

Later came stateful packet inspection firewalls, which keep packet information to make a decision to allow or deny the packet, based on stateful rules about the overall state of the TCP/IP packets. The type of stateful data includes the identification of a packet as a new packet or part of an existing packet that should be allowed to continue to the destination IP address identified in the packet. From a security standpoint, this stateful packet inspection reviews whether the packet is not part of any connection and validates that it is not a denial-of-service (DoS) attack.

As attacks became stealthy, deeper packet inspection was required. With network attacks on the rise, the application layer firewall platform extends beyond the stateless and stateful firewall by evaluating applications and protocols. The TCP/IP packets use specific known ports for applications such as Hypertext Markup Language (HTTP), Doman Name System (DNS), and File Transfer Protocol (FTP), among others. Now the packets are inspected to make sure HTTP Internet traffic or DNS lookup traffic is not an attempt to be used as a hidden attack from a known protocol. The individual packets are inspected for inclusion as a valid stream of packets for conversations or compromised TCP/IP frames of data with an attack.

Next-generation firewalls (NGFs) leverage a combination of frame, packet, and application inspection but at a much deeper packet inspection level. Application layer firewalls must be combined with lower-level network security firewalls in order to implement a network firewall strategy that defends against low-level attacks as well as application-aware attacks. The complexity of the packet is inspected to identify viruses, spam, and intrusion criteria to validate the TCP/IP packet legitimacy. The NGF inspects by data mining, network management, and flow of packet data from the beginning to end of a packet flow.

A deeper packet inspection provides the ability to review packet data at Layer 2 through Layer 7 of the OSI model. The NGF can be said it is application aware to provide a greater level of granularity to ensure that the proper data is deeply inspected before allowed into the enterprise network.

Next-generation firewalls are data dependent, so the more up-to-date that the real-time signatures and anomaly data are kept, the more likely the NGF can provide the highest level of security. Next-generation firewalls have different details in their deep inspection processes to improve application awareness; these details may include a detailed application signature database from partners that profile known applications based on data attributes. NGFs can distinguish different applications running from the same web site or whether there is a change that may indicate a cross-site forgery or another web attack.

■ **Security Tip** Several NGF appliances support a trial period for as short as a few hours up to a few weeks. Review the many options from the Azure Marketplace and compare features to improve your security layering. Search for *NGF virtual appliances* at `https://azuremarketplace.microsoft.com/en-us/marketplace/`.

If you return to the Azure Security Center recommendations for the Contoso example, five endpoints are exposed to the Internet, and an NGF security device is recommended. A traditional firewall provides allow or deny access to or from endpoints. The NGF evolution is that of a stateful firewall that is application aware. The NGF is capable of recognizing and blocking applications according to specific patterns and fingerprints of the application. The overall security of a next-generation firewall is to prevent users from bypassing the layer of defense out of the network. Unlike a traditional firewall, which enforces the access control by an IP address, port address, and protocol, an NGF enforces the user based on the application.

■ **Note**   The NGF install procedure walks you through the deployment steps to make a purchase and not install a trial version as completed in the WAF procedure.

ADD A NEXT GENERATION FIREWALL

1. Open the Recommendations blade from the Security Center blade. Select the option to add a next-generation firewall, as shown in Figure 6-23.

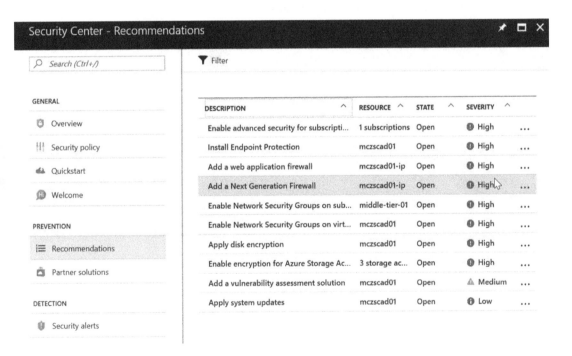

Figure 6-23. Recommendations blade to add a next-generation firewall

2. Select the Create New option to review the options presented in Figure 6-24.

Figure 6-24. Creating a new NGF

■ **Note** You should consider a bring your own licenses (BYOL) approach if the "buy" step does not support your testing plan.

---

3. Select the Fortinet single-VM next-generation firewall, as shown in Figure 6-25. Enter a unique name for the VM, administrator name, and password. Select the resource group or click "Create new" and then click OK.

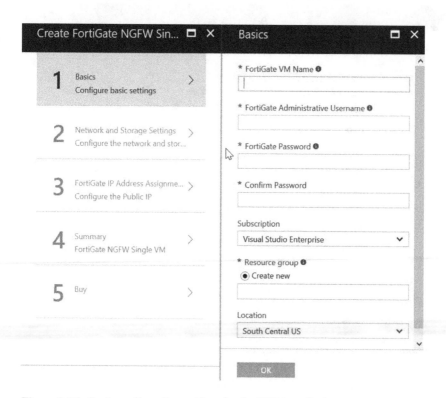

Figure 6-25. Basic configuration settings for the NGF installation

4. Add the virtual network to protect and select the subnets to support. You may keep the default standard D3 size VM and create a diagnostic storage account for all the event data, as shown in Figure 6-26, and click OK.

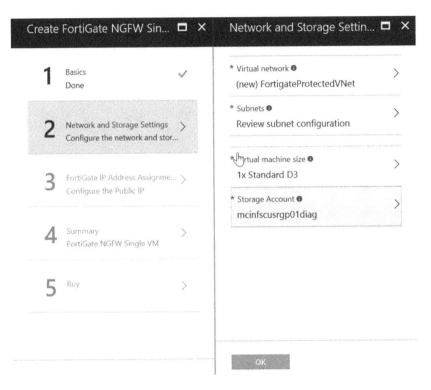

Figure 6-26. *Network configuration settings*

5. The public IP address name selection will be used for Internet access for the deep inspection provided by the next-generation firewall processes, shown in Figure 6-27. Enter the domain name label and click OK.

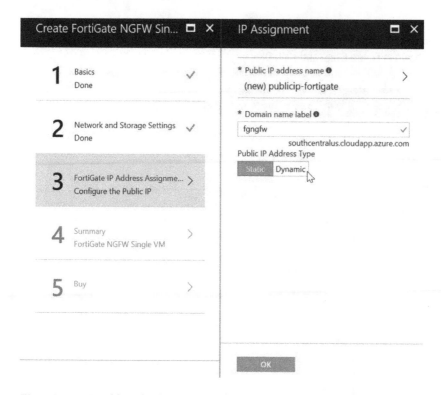

Figure 6-27. *IP address for the public-facing network connection*

6. Figure 6-28 shows the summary page, where you can review the selections. The last step is to click OK and in the next window click Buy to purchase the FortiGate NGF.

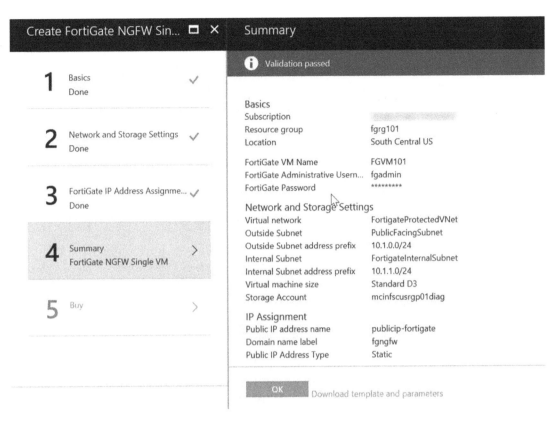

Figure 6-28. FortiGate NGF summary page

■ **Note**   If you select to purchase through the Microsoft Azure Marketplace, the cost for the Azure VM computing and storage appears on one bill. The second monthly invoice comes from Fortinet or the NGF you selected to purchase.

Vulnerability Assessment Integration

One of the strengths of Azure Security Center is the extension for partners to integrate a greater security management and monitoring service for your Azure infrastructure. The Qualys vulnerability solution is integrated into Azure Security Center's Azure Marketplace and offers a security risk assessment. Security Center provides the detection of the VMs without the solution and automates deployment of the Qualys agents. The agents gather vulnerability data and send it to the Qualys cloud platform, which, in turn, provides vulnerability and health monitoring data to your Azure Security Center, which can be used to strengthen your security posture.

ADD A VULNERABILITY ASSESSMENT

1. Open Security Center, highlight the Recommendations blade, highlight the Azure service, and choose the option to add a vulnerability assessment solution, as shown in Figure 6-29. Click the option to create a new solution.

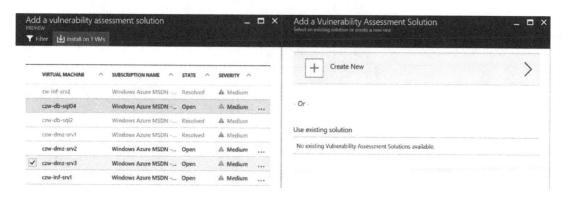

Figure 6-29. *Security Center view recommending to add a vulnerability assessment solution*

2. The solution has been added, so for the next Azure service that requires a vulnerability assessment, you could choose an existing solution. This option is in "preview," and there is currently one partner that offers an assessment, as shown in Figure 6-30.

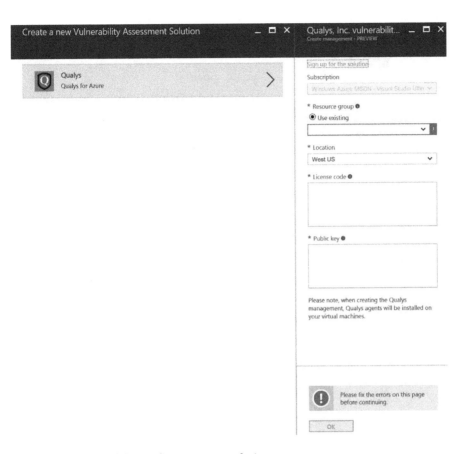

Figure 6-30. *View of the Qualys assessment solution*

3. Select the option at the top right to sign up for the solution trial, as shown in Figure 6-31. The license codes and public digital key are required to enable the trial for your Azure POC.

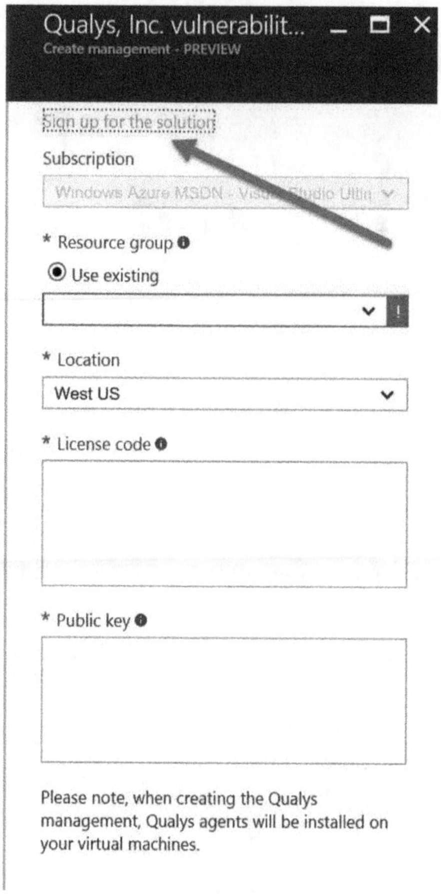

Figure 6-31. *Qualys option to sign up for a trial solution*

4. The web browser opens the Qualys web site, as displayed in Figure 6-32. Click the option to request a free trial.

Figure 6-32. Qualys solution to request a free trial

5. Once you click the Qualys free trial, a form is displayed with sizing options based on the proof of concept, as shown in Figure 6-33. Since this is a small POC, select Express Lite and click Create Account.

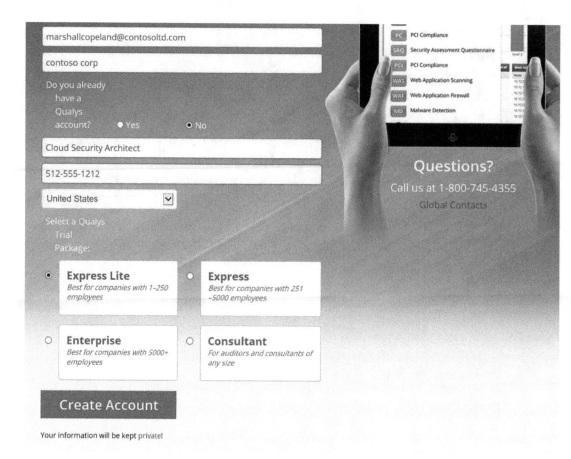

Figure 6-33. *Quays view to select a size for the POC and to enter your contact information*

6. Once the account has been created, the necessary licenses and public key are provided for the trial. As shown in Figure 6-34, enter the information and click OK.

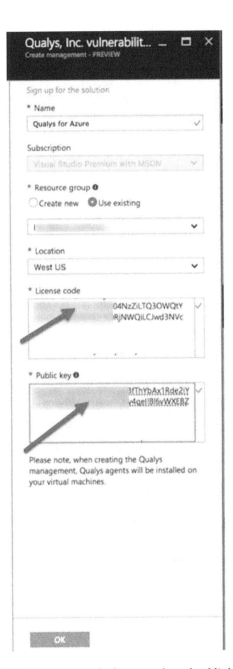

Figure 6-34. Qualys license code and public key

7. After the agents are deployed, the Qualys vulnerability assessment shows up for the virtual machines that Security Center recommended. Return to Azure Security Center and click the VMs under the Qualys partner solution you created to find the vulnerability assessment data.

Summary

This final chapter marks the beginning of your Azure Security Center configuration beyond a proof of concept and into the production deployment of your Azure infrastructure network. You've learned the necessity of a layered security approach that extends an on-premises security model into a hybrid deployment model for the Azure cloud for both IaaS and PaaS deployments.

In this chapter, you learned about Security Center recommendations, detections, and security alerts that provide guidance so you can remediate attacks. The security cloud service provided system attention on items like those that required encryption and specific pending actions, such as a reboot for a security patch to be effective.

You were introduced to real-world examples with recommendations based on the discovered Azure network infrastructure or asset. The security remediation steps enhance the overall security through Azure partner extensions. You now know the steps to deploy a web application firewall, next-generation firewall, and vulnerability assessment solution. Along the security journey, you gained insight into the value of Azure Security Center. As the Azure security architect, you gained security skills and knowledge to support operational security assurance, which in turn supports your business.

APPENDIX A

Troubleshooting and Cyber-Reference

Security Center Logs and Cybersecurity Vocabulary

Azure Security Center Diagnostics Troubleshooting

This appendix contains tips for troubleshooting Security Center that you may need during configuration and when trying to understand how data flows from the endpoint protection–extended client to Security Center. This appendix was written in response to technical questions that I have gotten in the course of my work; it helps security analysts understand how the communications and log data are handled in Security Center. Finally, cloud administrators in businesses large or small that are using Azure Security Center can gain insight into how to collect and share cybersecurity information.

You should begin by searching for data in the Azure Audit Logs view after logging into the Azure Resource Manager (ARM) portal. When you installed and configured Security Center, you configured the diagnostic log that collects information separately from the virtual machines (VMs) and other platform as a service (PaaS) services. The Azure portal provides a Monitor journey with information collected for more than Azure Security Center. Review the information in Figure A-1 to gain a better understanding of the Azure Monitoring view.

© Marshall Copeland 2017
M. Copeland, *Cyber Security on Azure*, DOI 10.1007/978-1-4842-2740-4

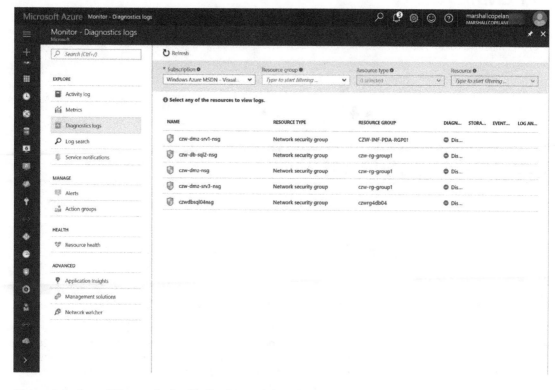

Figure A-1. *Azure "Diagnostics logs" collection portal service*

The log files for Windows Server contain records of information specifically used to write events on the services provided by the operating system (OS). The security log in Windows Server provides details for the Local Security Authority Subsystem Service (LSASS.exe), and this log is used to investigate any attempt to gain access by unauthorized intruders. If you are taking advantage of the Azure infrastructure as a service (IaaS), the specific logs for the Windows OS VM include the following:

- Windows Log

- Application

- Security

- Setup

- System

- ForwardedEvents

- Applications and Services

- Admin

- Operation

- Analytic

- Debug

Now that a VM is a supported OS type (in the Azure Marketplace) running in Azure, additional logs have been added to the OS. These logs can also be used in collecting and identifying health issues beyond the standard OS logs. Some of the Azure logs include Azure platform logs, which includes logs that might be related to Azure guest agents, the Azure extensions, and other Azure components.

▪ **Note**   You can find Azure log details at `https://azure.microsoft.com/en-us/blog/simplifying-virtual-machine-troubleshooting-using-azure-log-collector`, and you can find the Azure VM extension details at `https://docs.microsoft.com/en-us/azure/virtual-machines/windows/log-collector-extension`.

The Event-Logging service controls tracked events in the OS, and when the service starts, you can track activities such as user actions and system resource events. The generic data that is provided includes auditing data in categories by event audit, including the following:

- *Information*: Events that are informational, not a toggle between success and failure

- *Success Audit*: Events related to successful action

- *Failure Audit*: Failed execution of an action

- *Warning*: Details useful in future system actions

- *Error*: Failure for a specific action

When you look at log information, there is specific data that log files can provide including the following:

- *Source*: What application or service logged the action

- *Category*: Future description related to the action

- *Event*: Identifies the specific action

- *User*: User account that was logged during the event action

- *Computer*: Computer name during the event action

- *Description*: Details of the event action

- *Data*: Any data or error codes output by the event action

You now have a good understanding of the type of data provided in the Window OS event logs and the extended logs from the Microsoft Azure event logs. The logs and data can be searched for the action, who enabled it, when the action accrued, and other statuses or values of the event to help with troubleshooting.

In this book, you were introduced to three Azure Security Center agents that are installed on VMs, and these services all provide log file data. You should enable the monitoring of the agents' data collection when you configure the diagnostic service. The three services are as follows:

- `ASMAgentLauncher.exe`: Azure Monitoring Agent

- `ASMMonitoringAgent.exe`: Azure Security Monitoring extension

- `ASMSoftwareScanner.exe`: Azure Scan Manager

The extensions are needed to integrate the Azure-installed endpoint protection agent and to complete the automated removal of cybersecurity threats. If open a Task Manager or Sysinternals Process Explorer, you will see something similar to Figure A-2.

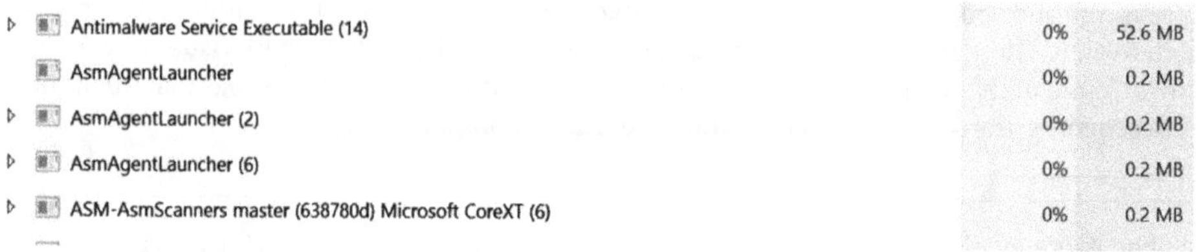

▷	Antimalware Service Executable (14)	0%	52.6 MB
	AsmAgentLauncher	0%	0.2 MB
▷	AsmAgentLauncher (2)	0%	0.2 MB
▷	AsmAgentLauncher (6)	0%	0.2 MB
▷	ASM-AsmScanners master (638780d) Microsoft CoreXT (6)	0%	0.2 MB

Figure A-2. ASM agents installed by Azure Security Center

SYSINTERNALS FROM A WEB BROWSER

Often IT professionals must configure tools to run on systems and provide details; for example, you might need a tool to review log files and run processes in memory and CPU utilization. However, installing the product is a post-configuration build step that is sometimes missed. Rather than install the Sysinternals tools on each server, with the proper firewall security in place, you can use the entire toolset available at https://live.sysinternals.com, as shown in Figure A-3. These Sysinternals tools, with proper administrative permissions, run on any server or workstation with a web browser.

live.sysinternals.com - /

```
       Friday, May 30, 2008   3:55 PM       668 About This Site.txt
   Friday, February 17, 2017   2:54 AM    777896 accesschk.exe
   Friday, February 17, 2017   2:54 AM    402608 accesschk64.exe
Wednesday, November 1, 2006   1:06 PM    174968 AccessEnum.exe
    Thursday, July 12, 2007   5:26 AM     50379 AdExplorer.chm
Wednesday, November 14, 2012  10:22 AM   479832 ADExplorer.exe
   Tuesday, October 27, 2015  12:13 AM   401616 ADInsight.chm
   Tuesday, October 27, 2015  12:13 AM  2425496 ADInsight.exe
Wednesday, November 1, 2006   1:05 PM    150328 adrestore.exe
   Saturday, August 27, 2016   3:15 AM   138920 Autologon.exe
   Friday, February 17, 2017   2:54 AM    50512 autoruns.chm
   Friday, February 17, 2017   2:54 AM   716456 autoruns.exe
   Friday, February 17, 2017   2:54 AM   844464 Autoruns64.exe
   Friday, February 17, 2017   2:54 AM   629928 autorunsc.exe
   Friday, February 17, 2017   2:54 AM   743088 autorunsc64.exe
   Tuesday, October 27, 2015  11:28 PM  2049168 Bginfo.exe
Wednesday, November 1, 2006   1:06 PM    154424 Cacheset.exe
   Wednesday, June 29, 2016    9:44 PM   139944 Clockres.exe
   Wednesday, June 29, 2016    9:44 PM   154792 Clockres64.exe
   Wednesday, June 29, 2016    9:44 PM   253600 Contig.exe
   Wednesday, June 29, 2016    9:44 PM   268960 Contig64.exe
    Monday, August 18, 2014    7:29 PM   892088 Coreinfo.exe
Wednesday, September 27, 2006  5:04 PM    10104 ctrl2cap.amd.sys
Wednesday, November 1, 2006   1:05 PM    150328 ctrl2cap.exe
   Sunday, November 21, 1999   5:20 PM     2864 ctrl2cap.nt4.sys
   Sunday, November 21, 1999   6:46 PM     2832 ctrl2cap.nt5.sys
Thursday, September 15, 2005   8:49 AM    68539 dbgview.chm
    Monday, December 3, 2012  10:10 AM   468056 Dbgview.exe
Wednesday, November 1, 2006   9:06 PM   158520 DEFRAG.EXE
Wednesday, October 17, 2012   5:28 PM   116824 Desktops.exe
   Tuesday, December 17, 2013 11:46 AM    40717 Disk2vhd.chm
    Monday, January 20, 2014   2:16 PM  7134400 disk2vhd.exe
   Wednesday, June 29, 2016    9:44 PM   143008 diskext.exe
   Wednesday, June 29, 2016    9:44 PM   158376 diskext64.exe
Wednesday, November 1, 2006   1:06 PM   224056 Diskmon.exe
    Monday, December 8, 2003   9:40 AM     9519 DISKMON.HLP
Wednesday, March 24, 2010    1:00 PM    580984 DiskView.exe
Thursday, October 14, 1999    1:45 PM     11728 DMON.SYS
   Wednesday, July 6, 2016     1:29 AM   169104 du.exe
   Wednesday, July 6, 2016     1:29 AM   191128 du64.exe
   Wednesday, May 20, 2015     2:24 AM   146232 efsdump.exe
       Friday, July 28, 2006   8:32 AM     7005 Eula.txt
   Wednesday, June 29, 2016    9:47 PM     <dir> Files
   Wednesday, June 29, 2016    9:44 PM   147112 FindLinks.exe
   Wednesday, June 29, 2016    9:44 PM   169136 FindLinks64.exe
    Saturday, July 2, 2016    12:08 PM   425624 handle.exe
    Saturday, July 2, 2016    12:08 PM   226464 handle64.exe
Tuesday, November 18, 2008    5:04 AM        16 healthmonitoring.html
   Wednesday, June 29, 2016    9:44 PM   150176 hex2dec.exe
   Wednesday, June 29, 2016    9:44 PM   164520 hex2dec64.exe
```

Figure A-3. View through a browser of https://live.sysinternals.com

If you scroll down to the Process Explorer and click the text to start the executable, you may see a browser pop-up window to allow the processes, as shown in Figure A-4.

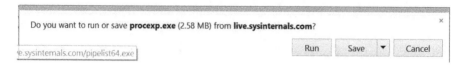

Figure A-4. *IE browser pop-up to run or save the Sysinternals procexp.exe program*

Click Run; the installation starts and requires permission to continue, as shown in Figure A-5.

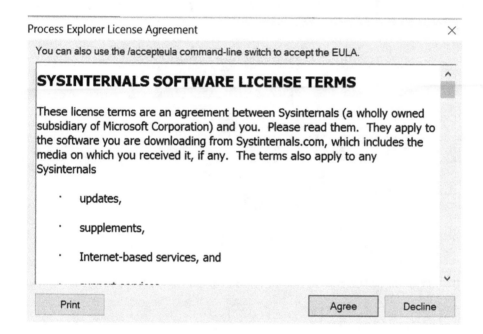

Figure A-5. *Sysinternals license terms*

Click Agree, and the Process Explorer program starts to run. Process Explorer is a feature-rich view, more than the built-in Windows Task Manager, as shown in Figure A-6.

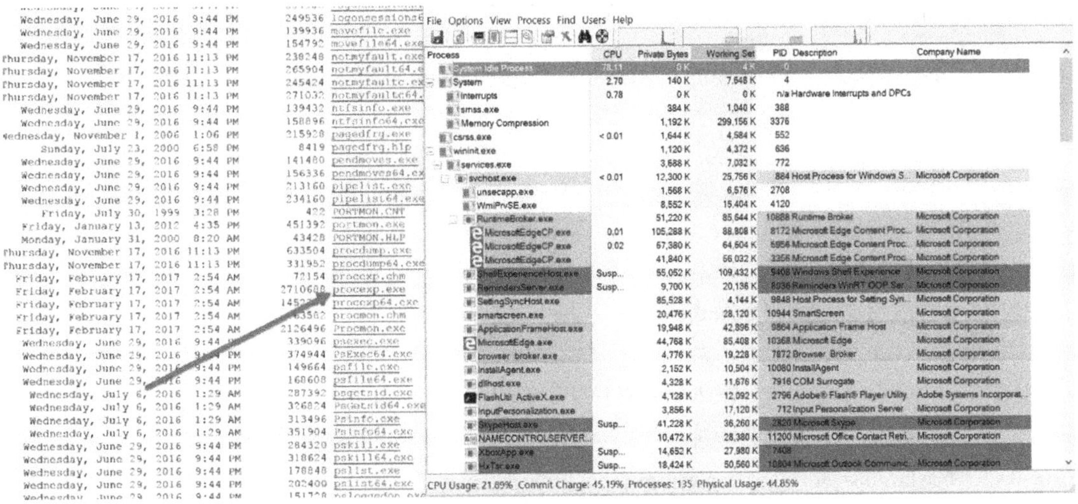

Figure A-6. *Process Explorer running after selecting the procexp.exe from the web browser*

The Azure Security Monitoring extension does the scan for event information, and each agent has a different responsibility, such as patch scanning. You can look at the log file information on the Azure VM in the installation directory's agent log folder.

- %systemdrive%\windowsazure\logs (i.e., C:\WindowsAzure\Logs).

One of the "unwritten" rules of cybersecurity analysis is to understand, based on log file data, the amount of data and correlation of events to classify work as "normal." If log file information is not updating as expected or is not what you would normally expect to see from the agent log files, you need to restart the VM because there is currently no PowerShell command to stop or restart the agent.

After the system reboots, you can remove the agent and then reinstall it to validate that any issues were resolved. Typically, on large installations, identifying a single Security Center agent installation that is incomplete is common. To uninstall the agent and then automatically reinstall it, follow these steps:

1. From the Azure portal, click the virtual machine.

2. Right-click Microsoft Azure Security Monitoring and click Uninstall.

The Security Monitoring extension will automatically reinstall (it takes about ten minutes).

The Security Center agent installation in Linux requires a different but similar log file location. The following are the log file locations:

- /var/log/mdsd.err

- /var/log/azure/

On a Linux system, the extension is downloaded to the following location: /var/lib/waagent/. Then you need to run the command cat /var/log/waagent.log.

Linux systems have daemons (similar to Windows OS services) and require listening via connections for specific ports based on the TCP or UDP requirements. The Linux agent communicates on port 29130 using TCP. From a command prompt, run the following:

```
netstat -plantu | grep 29130
```

General networking troubleshooting processes may include the endpoint protection of the anti-malware extension on the Azure agent.

■ **Security Tip** This tip is important to repeat. The System Center Configuration Manager agent installation is not compatible with Azure Security Center because it does not, currently, have the needed extensions. Even if you plan to support all Azure VMs through the Configuration Manager console, the integration with Azure Security Center must be installed from the Azure System Center portal.

The following are additional key points for troubleshooting:

- Remove and reinstall the agent: uploaded, custom image, and new installs.

- The Linux agent is different from the Windows agent.

- New agents update automatically. Older versions do not update correctly; you must reinstall them.

- Validate that the agent is running (Figure A-2); some software may disable the agent.

- A change request process may help identify when incorrect settings for an Azure network security group (NSG) were changed. Block network traffic to and from the guest agent.

There are other Azure-specific sites that you can review, including the Windows Azure – Troubleshooting & Debugging site. (The current site refers to Windows Azure still.) You can find it at https://blogs.msdn.microsoft.com/kwill/, as shown in Figure A-7.

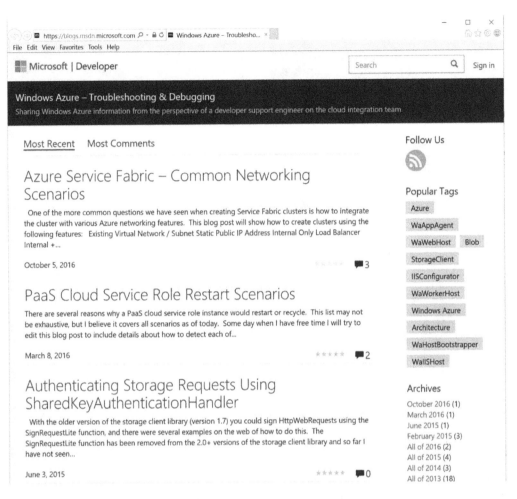

Figure A-7. *Azure troubleshooting blog*

Another location for helpful information on all Azure cloud subjects is the Microsoft Azure forum at `https://social.msdn.microsoft.com/forums/en-US/home?category=windowsazureplatform`, `azuremarketplace,windowsazureplatformctp`, as shown in Figure A-8. The top-right search option allows you to search for Security Center topics.

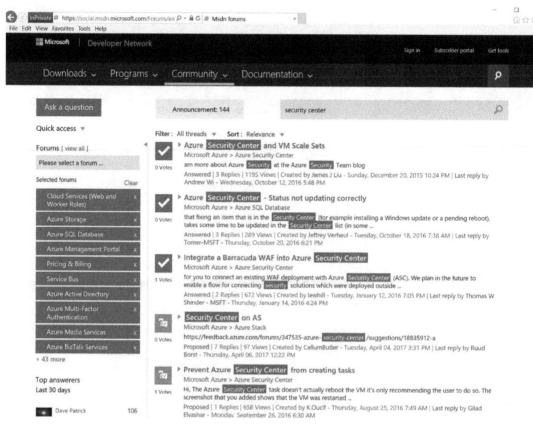

Figure A-8. *Azure MSDN forum for all Azure topics*

However, if you need further troubleshooting, you can open a new support request using the Azure portal. This is a cloud service, and sometimes after all the time spent to troubleshoot a specific issue, reaching out to product support is the fastest way to getting a resolution.

Cyber-Reference

Cloud network architecture is a software-defined network. Traditional brick-and-mortar businesses use local area networks (LANs) to support and restrict geographic locations such as office buildings and departments within larger enterprises and the home office. Arranging LANs along department divisions like Accounting or Sales and Marketing helps to separate LANS into workgroups.

Systems are often separated by the host type such as workstation (clients are laptops and mobile devices) or server (physical or virtual). Often these terms are used to describe "nodes" on the network, which includes any node that uses Transmission Control Protocol/Internet Protocol (TCP/IP). The need to understand both the OSI layer model and the Internet model is a requirement so you know what can and cannot be used in a hybrid network that connects traditional on-premises networks to Microsoft Azure virtual networks.

What's in a Name

You need to know the definition of some critical terms in order to understand the language of security so you can communicate with other security team members. The references in this section are not as in-depth as others that you may want to bookmark for review.

First, a great resource is the official web site of Homeland Security. Specifically, its NICCS cybersecurity lexicon at https://niccs.us-cert.gov/glossary serves cybersecurity communities in both the public and private sectors.

Second, the up-to-date glossary at https://www.sans.org/security-resources/glossary-of-terms/ is maintained by the Sans organization.

If you need a PDF copy to download for quick review, one option is from NIST and available at http://nvlpubs.nist.gov/nistpubs/ir/2013/NIST.IR.7298r2.pdf. Another option is available from the Information Systems Audit and Control Association (ISACA) web site at http://www.isaca.org/Knowledge-Center/Documents/Glossary/Cybersecurity_Fundamentals_glossary.pdf.

Glossary

Here is my own list of definitions.

Definitions

Advanced persistent threat (APT): This is a hacker who possesses sophisticated levels of expertise, software, or overpowering resources that create attacks using multiple attack vectors such as cyber-attacks, physical attacks, and deception.

Black hat: This is a person or group of people who are computer security experts and hack into a computer network with malicious or criminal intent.

Bitcoin: This is a digital currency or cryptocurrency (one of many types of payment with a cryptocurrency wallet) used as an electronic payment process developed by an unidentified group of programmers who go by the name Satoshi Nakamoto. Bitcoins are used by hackers and can be exchanged for other monies or currencies, products, or services.

BOT or botnet: This is short for "robot" and is a sophisticated type of software used in computer crime on the Internet. Bots are like worms and Trojans but provide a variety of automated tasks on behalf of the master server (cybercriminal or attacker or hacker) using command and control from a safe location across the Internet.

Breach: This is a security break from a hacker who exploits a vulnerability that leads to the damage of a system or unauthorized access to the system and loss of private data, personally identifiable information (PII), or confidential information.

Command and control (C&C): This describes the type of infrastructure that supports a number of servers used to control malware such as bots. Many bots linked by a single group of C&C systems become a bot army.

Exploit: This is a technique to breach the security of a network or information system in violation of a security policy.

Gray hat: This is a person or group of people who hack or a computer security expert who may sometimes violate laws or typical ethical standards but does not have the malicious intent typical of a black hat.

Hacker: This is someone or some group that uses computers to gain unauthorized access to data directly or creates a computer program, called a *bot*, that leverages the vulnerability (flaw) in the application, OS, or network.

Malware: There are types of computer software "infections" written with different features that classify them as viruses, worm, Trojans, or bots but that can be classified as malware. Malware is short for "malicious software." Malware is any software specifically designed to damage, disrupt, steal, or inflict some other evil action on corporate data, hosts, or networks.

Ransomware: This is malware that installs covertly on a victim's computer and enables an extortion attack using cryptography techniques called *cryptovirology* to encrypt computer data. The data is held hostage by the attacker until a ransom is paid using bitcoin.

Red hat: This is a computer company that supports a Linux OS distribution (aka distro open source OS) software.

Threat: This is a circumstance that has the potential to exploit vulnerabilities and adversely impact business operations and impact assets, individuals, or customers.

Vulnerability: This is a weakness or flaw that exposes your business to exploitation by a threat.

Weakness: This is an imperfection in software code, design, architecture, or deployment that becomes a vulnerability or contributes to a vulnerability. The weakness can be a physical or digital (code) flaw in the application, operating system, or hardware.

What hat: This is a person or group of people who are computer security experts and hack into a computer network to test or evaluate its security systems.

Zero-day: This is a vulnerability that is previously unknown or unpublicized that was released to the public. In some circumstances, the zero-day exploit may have a patch released the same day as the public information is released or no patch is available.

Security, Identity, and Cryptography

Algorithms: These include Data Encryption Standard (DES), Triple DES (3DES), Advanced Encryption Standard (AES), Rivest-Shamir-Adleman (RSA), and Elliptical Cure Cryptography (ECC). Algorithms (symmetric and asymmetric) can be used together. Some encryption techniques are slower than others but are more secure and often create a more secure (complete) method. As an example, key management (encryption and decryption) could be ECC or RSA. The strength of the protection for a public key in binary bits ranges from 512 for ECC up to 15360 for RSA to support the same security level.

Asymmetric cryptography: This is a division of cryptography using an algorithm that uses two different keys for communication. Often the two keys are referred to as the *private key* and *public key*. The public digital key is widely used in the communication between two or more parties. The private digital key is known only to the person who encrypts the message. The person sending the message uses their private key to encrypt, and the person reading the message uses the sender's public key to decrypt. This type of cryptography supports the CIA triad and resolves the issue of key exchange.

Availability: The data is available to be read or consumed without disruption (a denial-of-service attack has been mitigated and does not affect availability).

CIA: This refers to the confidentiality, integrity, availability triad.

Confidential: This refers to data that should not be read or altered.

Cryptography: This is a method or mathematical practice to secure communication. Often cryptography and encryption are used interchangeably. However, encryption is the actual mathematical methods used to secure the message.

Digital certificate: A digital certificate is an electronic "validation" that establishes source credentials when doing business or other transactions on the Internet. It is issued by a certification authority (CA). The certificate contains the company name, a serial number, expiration dates, a copy of the certificate holder's public key (used for encrypting messages and digital signatures), and the digital signature of the certificate-issuing authority. The CA establishes credibility so that a recipient (receiver) can verify that the certificate is authentic.

Digital security or security strength: This supports confidentiality, integrity, availability, and nonrepudiation through encryption.

Digital Signature Algorithm (DSA): This is an asymmetric cryptographic algorithm (public key and private key) that produces a digital signature. From a high level, the DSA is mathematically created using a pair of large numbers. The signature is computed using rules and parameters such as the identity of the sender to "sign" the communication, and the integrity of the signed data can be verified.

Encryption: This is a process, method, or technique for transforming plain-text data into cryptographic data. The process of encryption dates to Julius Caesar (the Caesar cipher) and is used to protect data and communication of information between computer systems. Often the encryption processes or techniques are referred to as encryption of plain text into cipher text to conceal the data's original meaning and prevent data from being usable. The encrypted data cannot be read or used without unencrypting the data.

Encryption techniques: These techniques include symmetric cryptography and asymmetric cryptography.

Hashing algorithm or hash function: This is a one-way mathematical process to create an arbitrary hash value based on the data's fixed size. If the data changes or is altered by a single bit or a single character, the hash value changes. The output of the hash function is called the *message digest*, and the one-way function means the input cannot be determined from the output.

Integrity: The data is authenticated from the sender or by the provider.

Mathematical algorithms (used for encryption): These can be identified as weak or strong. The security of data or communications requires using the strongest algorithm without creating an unnecessary cost of resources to encrypt and decrypt.

Nonrepudiation: This is needed to provide proof of origin and proof of receipt. It is used to identify the source of the secure message (proof of origin) and is used to validate that the intended recipient did receive the secure message (proof of receipt).

Strength: This is in the digital key length (binary mathematical size) and the algorithm (type of encryption) that uses the key size. Key length is in bits (low to high) such as 64, 112, 128, 168, 192, 156, 1024, 2048, 4096, and different mathematical methods (algorithms) are used to encrypt the data.

Symmetric cryptography: This is a division of cryptography involving algorithms that uses the same key for two different steps of the algorithm (such as encryption and decryption or signature creation and signature verification). Symmetric cryptography is sometimes called *secret-key cryptography* (versus public-key cryptography) because the entities share the key. The key is a word or number used to secure the communication via the encryption technique. The symmetric cryptography method supports the CIA triad; however, the challenge is the "key" exchange. Everyone who communicates using the same method requires the same key.

Attack Method

Now that the basics of security events and vulnerabilities were defined and you have a brief understanding of data security methods, this section provides a few definitions for types of attacks and attack methods.

Denial of service (DoS): This attack is designed to deny services, in this instance computing services. However, it could be a banking service, mail server, e-commerce web site, phone service, or any service (server) providing clients with access. A DoS attack is an attack on the "availability" in the CIA triad. Ay device that has an IP address or DNS address can be targeted by a single source DoS attack. When the attack is enabled from multiple sources, even hundreds or thousands of sources, this is a distributed denial-of-service (DDoS) attack. A common use of DDoS is to saturate the victim's system (services) with overwhelming requests.

▪ **Security Tip** When the term *application layer attack* is used, it is referring to the OSI model at Layer 7, the presentation layer. A Layer 7 attack can be a DDoS threat to overload a server by sending many requests requiring server-intensive handling by CPU processing.

The following are all types of DoS attacks:

Botnet DDoS attacks: These are created by a "zombie army" of compromised systems (baby cameras, home routers, or other hacked web-connected devices) to control the DDoS attack from a remote location. The zombie army of botnets sends connection requests to an innocent computer called a *reflector*.

Botnet arms: These are for hire from web services often being auctioned and traded among attackers on the Dark Web. Online marketplaces have sprung up with commercial entities trading in huge numbers of malware-infected PCs. A hacker or hacker wanna-be can rent a DDoS or other attack for a length of time as a service.

DNS amplification: This is when an attacker exploits vulnerabilities in DNS servers by manipulating public DNS services and flooding the target with large quantities of UDP packets.

Hacking as a service (HaaS) or DDoS as a service: This is making it easier for DDoS attacks to be carried out by hackers, competition, or disgruntled employees. You don't need to code or create malware with these services for rent.

HaaS platforms: These hide behind the ambiguous service definition of *stressers* or *booters* (stress testing services) that sell DDoS as a service. You pay with bitcoins and receive access to a richly featured toolkit, as well as a distribution network, to execute attacks on demand.

High Orbit Ion Cannon (HOIC): This is a free, open source network stress application developed by a hacktivist and used to create denial-of-service and distributed denial-of-service attacks by flooding target systems with improperly formed HTTP GET and POST requests.

HTTP flood: This is a DDoS attack that exploits legitimate Hypertext Transfer Protocol (HTTP) GET or POST requests to attack a web server. A GET command retrieves content such as images, while POST requests are used to access dynamically generated resources; this attack is effective when the victim's server or web application is forced to allocate maximum resources in response to the requests.

Low Orbit Ion Cannon (LOIC): This is a widely available open source application used as a network stress testing service or what hackers call a DoS and DDoS attack platform.

NTP amplification: The Network Time Protocol (NTP) is used by Internet-connected machines to synchronize their clocking devices on computers, and the NTP protocol queries a given NTP server for a traffic count. The attacker repeatedly sends a request to an NTP server and can cause the computer to be unavailable or even crash.

Ping flood: This targets a network computer or system using an ICMP packet that is sent rapidly with the ping command; the attacker does not follow the proper protocol by *not* waiting for replies.

Ping of death: This is another denial of service by an attacker who tries to crash, or freeze, the targeted router, server, or computer by sending malformed or oversized TCP/IP packets using a simple ping command.

Smurf attack: This is a DDoS attack that attacks at the network layer (of the OSI model) and is named after the DDoS.Smurf malware that permits the attack. A smurf attack is similar to a ping flood attack by using an unusual number of ICMP echo request packets. A smurf is an amplification attack that boosts its damage potential by exploiting unprotected networks that allow the broadcast of network traffic on the IP subnets.

SYN flood: An SYN flood is at the TCP/IP level and sends a victim's system (router, switch, network card) more TCP SYN packets (synchronize packets for opening a connection) than the software and hardware can process.

UDP flood: This takes place at the TCP/IP level; the attacker overwhelms random "ports" on the targeted victim's system with IP packets containing UDP datagrams.

Know Your Enemy

Vulnerabilities and Remediation

Many IT professionals ask after they start configuring Azure Security Center about the types of cybersecurity attacks they can expect. Attending professional cybersecurity training helps you prepare to understand the methods used, the speed and automation of cyber-attacks, and how to defend against these attacks.

There are many credible methods to receive professional cybersecurity training and certification for the purpose of learning what your enemy, the cyber-hacker, knows. The information available is needed as IT professionals and cloud administrators increase their security skills. You should consider learning more about cybersecurity to be a multiyear process. There are boot camps, multiday training, and online classes; basically, there are not enough hours in the day to learn everything you need. You may have heard the phrase "security is a journey" because of the multiple layers of security that exist. Cybersecurity for the cloud is a multiyear journey and could possibly result in a rewarding career change.

You need to know the skills required for a Microsoft Azure cybersecurity professional. Start by reviewing the following list of requirements from a recent online job posting (abbreviated for our purposes):

- Knowledge of system security vulnerabilities and remediation techniques
- Demonstrated expertise in a broad array of systems and network security technical controls and processes
    - Identity and access management, system hardening, network segmentation, data loss prevention, federated identity management, incident response, intrusion prevention, DDOS mitigation, threat intelligence
- Knowledge of cloud security design and architecture, cloud security–related certifications
- Knowledge of how public key cryptography includes Public Key Infrastructure (PKI) and how it differs from Secure Sockets Layer (SSL) as security over HTTP
- Responsible for developing cloud security strategies
    - Monitoring and integration into security operations
- Strong scripting skills Ruby, Python, or other scripting language
- Strong understanding of the security risk landscape and OSI model Layers 2–7
- Responsible for establishing security engineering
    - Operations frameworks for various cloud security technologies

© Marshall Copeland 2017
M. Copeland, *Cyber Security on Azure*, DOI 10.1007/978-1-4842-2740-4

- Knowledge of network and web-related protocols

    - TCP/IP, UDP, IPSEC, HTTP, HTTPS, routing protocols

- Experience with and responsible for developing and deploying new security cloud technologies and operationalizing alerts, metrics, scorecards, monitoring, and maintenance

- Participate in project teams providing consultation on cloud security DevOps initiatives

- Responsible for interconnecting various security event sources

    - Server logs, network, various security devices, threat feeds, antivirus, malware, vulnerability scanners, net flow, etc.

- Responsible for designing and operationalizing all aspects of the security infrastructure including cloud environments

- Familiarity with secure coding standards, e.g., NIST SP 800-53, ISO/IEC 27001, OWASP, PCI, HIPAA, NIST, CSA, and SEI CERT

- Experience with hybrid solutions mixing use of private datacenter and public cloud

You may often see the technologies listed that a specific corporation uses. Many customers have more than one cloud provider, so being able to apply cloud security to more than just Microsoft Azure is important in cloud security careers. If you have not created this type of line-of-business (LOB) engineering tool, you may want to use this list as a starting point for technologies:

- Apache Mesos, Kubernetes, Docker Swarm

- Docker, Rocket, Linux, Ubuntu, CoreOS

- Microsoft Azure, Amazon Web Services, Google Cloud Platform

- Puppet, Chef

- Software-defined networking, BGP, cloud load balancing, NGINX

- Hbase, Postgres, Cassandra, SQL, MySQL

- Java, Ruby, Python

Professional Education

For a cybersecurity career, an IT position provides a needed foundation, and it is necessary to help with the IT vocabulary. But you need to know how to best gain cybersecurity knowledge to build on the IT work. You can focus on understanding system security vulnerabilities and remediation techniques.

To understand remediation techniques, you first have to learn some of the professional options to strengthen your security knowledge and cybersecurity skills. If your company provides a reimbursement plan, you may want to consider one of the universities listed on the NSA web site, as shown in Figure B-1. The NSA lists the current academic programs in cyber-operations, the number years required for the designation, and the level of study that has met the criteria.

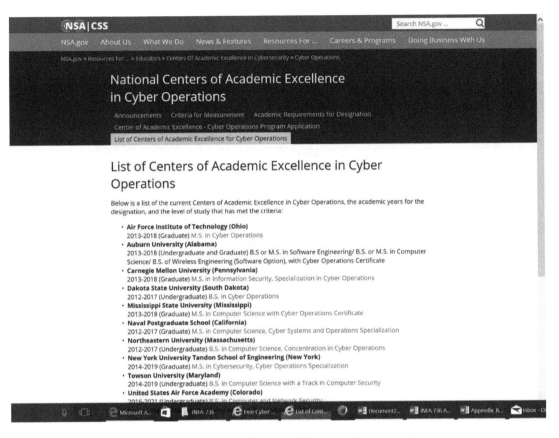

Figure B-1. *NSA's list of centers of academic excellence in cyber-operations*

These programs are multiyear and require a great deal of time after your "day job." The good news is many of the programs are available 100 percent online and include hands-on labs. As an example, Dakota State University in South Dakota provides undergraduate and graduate degree programs. There are specific requirements, in years, to complete a degree program that are supportive of working professionals.

■ **Security Tip**   You can find the NSA listing of universities, which closely follows the needed skill set of job postings by the NSA, at `https://www.nsa.gov/resources/educators/centers-academic-excellence/cyber-operations/centers.shtml`.

Additional classes for security-specific certification, such as CISSP or CEH, will help keep your skills up-to-date. You can also consider boot camps from professional training companies. There are many training options; none is inexpensive, but you should consider one.

The first one you can review is the InfoSec Institute, as shown in Figure B-2. It provides boot camp courses on security topics that last from three to six days.

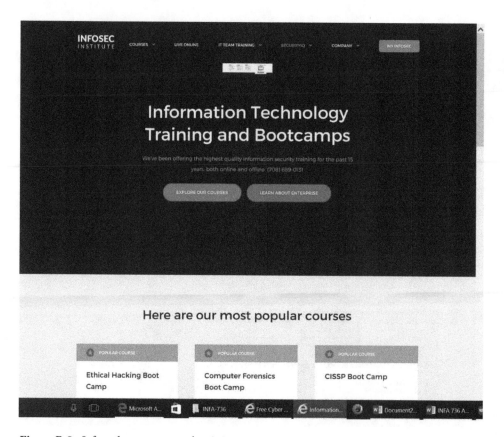

Figure B-2. *Infosec boot camps and training courses*

▨ **Security Tip**   Learn more about the Ethical Hacking Boot Camp at `https://www.infosecinstitute.com/`.

The Sans organization provides training across the United States, often several times each year in certain large cities. The classes are taught live, online, and on-demand with a structure of classes that cover novice, intermediate, and experienced cybersecurity experts. The computer security training and certification, shown in Figure B-3, is recognized as a security standard by nearly every business and government agency.

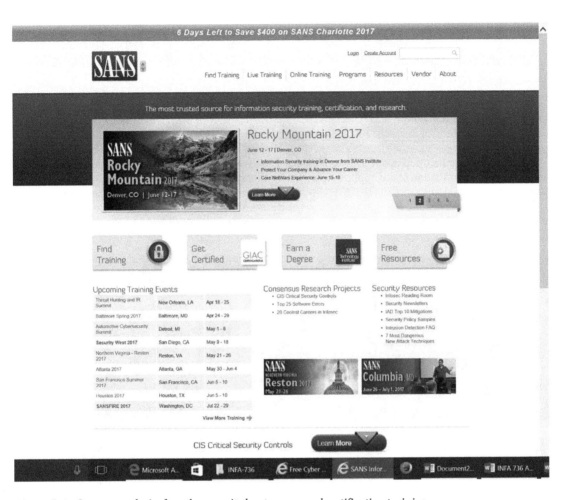

Figure B-3. *Sans.org web site for cybersecurity boot camps and certification training*

■ **Security Tip** You can find the Sans classes and schedules at `https://www.sans.org/`.

These are just a few training sites that provide a well-rounded cybersecurity education that builds on top of your current IT framework.

Security Risk Landscape

You need to know what your enemy knows; otherwise, you are always fighting cybersecurity attacks with a blindfold on. Some of the current cybersecurity tools you should learn are covered in the classes from universities and professional training companies, and you can download them for free.

▪ **Security Tip** The tools and utilities discussed should not be downloaded or installed on any corporate or public network. You should always use an isolated network for testing and training, with guidance from a certified professional cybersecurity trainer.

The agility and automation that cyber-attackers have can only be appreciated once you are professionally led through the tools. You will start to understand when you attend a professional training class or boot camp.

Metasploit, eventually acquired by Rapid 7, started out as a project to explore computer security and provide specific information about application and operating system security vulnerabilities. Metasploit's framework is a set of tools that can be used to automate and execute code against a remote machine. Metasploit Framework, shown in Figure B-4, now has a professional version and a free version, both of which include tools for developing and executing exploit codes.

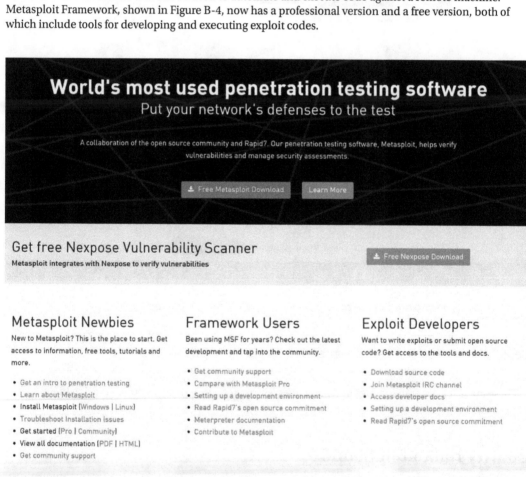

Figure B-4. Metasploit web page to learn about the framework

You should not attempt to download and install the framework in a corporate environment if you have no experience with this powerful exploitation tool. The Metasploit Framework community edition is a free, open source project that provides basic functionality through a command line. Metasploit Pro has more features for security programs with advanced penetration tests in small and enterprise security teams. Metasploit is used by professional testers who require advanced attack features for professional penetration testing on applications and networks.

■ **Security Tip** You can download Metasploit Pro or the free version at `https://www.metasploit.com/`. You can find more information about Rapid 7 at `https://www.rapid7.com/about/`.

Kali Linux is a Debian-based Linux distribution for conducting advanced penetration testing and security auditing. Kali contains several hundred tools for doing various information security tasks, such as penetration testing, security research, computer forensics, and reverse engineering.

Figure B-5 shows a view of the Kali Linux web site with links that guide you to become a certified professional who focuses on Kali.

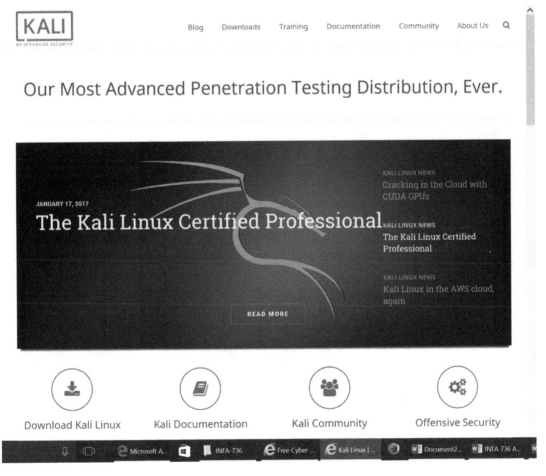

Figure B-5. Kali Linux web site with a certified professional training highlight

You may be asking why Kali is so dangerous. Your first introduction to Kali should be completed by a Kali-certified or well-trained cybersecurity professional. Kali can be used to exploit the weakness of your network, applications, and servers. The following quote on the Kali web site may help you realize why it is so popular and used by so many professionals:

> *Free (as in beer) and always will be: Kali Linux, like BackTrack, is completely free of charge and always will be. You will never, ever have to pay for Kali Linux.*

The original Linux distribution was a project titled BackTrack, and now Kali is the latest version used by professional trainers and internal and external security teams because it has several hundred pre-installed cyber-attack tools. Figure B-6 provides the first view of some of the hundreds of tools installed in the Kali OS.

KALI TOOLS

| | Home | Tools Listing | Metapackages | Q |

Information Gathering	Vulnerability Analysis	Wireless Attacks	Web Applications
• acccheck	• BBQSQL	• Aircrack-ng	• apache-users
• ace-voip	• BED	• Asleap	• Arachni
• Amap	• cisco-auditing-tool	• Bluelog	• BBQSQL
• Automater	• cisco-global-exploiter	• BlueMaho	• BlindElephant
• bing-ip2hosts	• cisco-ocs	• Bluepot	• Burp Suite
• braa	• cisco-torch	• BlueRanger	• CutyCapt
• CaseFile	• copy-router-config	• Bluesnarfer	• DAVTest
• CDPSnarf	• DBPwAudit	• Bully	• deblaze
• cisco-torch	• Doona	• coWPAtty	• DIRB
• Cookie Cadger	• DotDotPwn	• crackle	• DirBuster
• copy-router-config	• Greenbone Security Assistant	• eapmd5pass	• fimap
• DMitry	• GSD	• Fern Wifi Cracker	• FunkLoad
• dnmap	• HexorBase	• Ghost Phisher	• Gobuster
• dnsenum	• Inguma	• GISKismet	• Grabber
• dnsmap	• jSQL	• Gqrx	• jboss-autopwn
• DNSRecon	• Lynis	• gr-scan	• joomscan
• dnstracer	• Nmap	• hostapd-wpe	• jSQL
• dnswalk	• ohrwurm	• kalibrate-rtl	• Maltego Teeth
• DotDotPwn	• openvas-administrator	• KillerBee	• PadBuster
• enum4linux	• openvas-cli	• Kismet	• Paros
• enumIAX	• openvas-manager	• mdk3	• Parsero
• Faraday		• mfcuk	• plecost

Figure B-6. Kali pre-installed cyber-attack tools

Kali tools are divided into the following categories:

- Information gathering
- Vulnerability analysis
- Wireless attacks
- Web application (attacks)

The number of tools available for the Kali Linux distribution is less than the original 600 tools available in the BackTrack distribution (see Figure B-7). The predecessor, BackTrack, had a large number of tools installed by the project contributors that did not work or may have been duplicated tools.

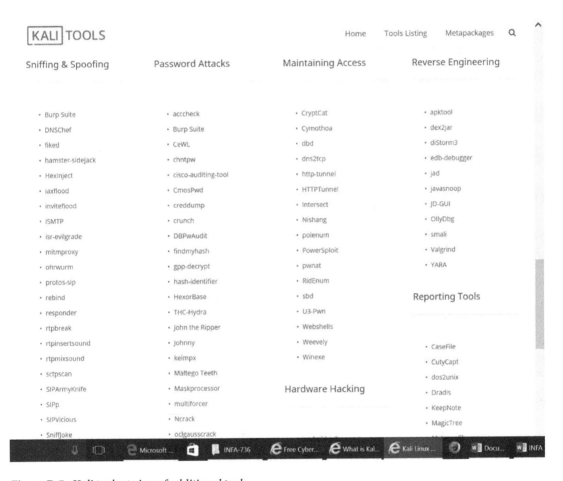

Figure B-7. Kali tool set view of additional tools

You may be looking at the information in Figure B-6 and Figure B-7 and realize your cyber-security enemy has this free tool and is ready to use it against your business. One of the hundreds of tools, provided by Kali distribution, is NMAP. To see the power of just a single tool, the following exercises are provided.

Understanding Cybersecurity Attack Details

Real-world data breaches and security incidents cause millions to billions of records to be exposed, depending on the reference document. The Verizon 2017 Data Breach Investigations Report provides data from incident collections by customers and from datasets from contributing security vendors.

As you have read throughout this book, security requires you to speak a common language and even a common dialect to truly understand the southern Austin, Texas, accent of security definitions, including security incidents, numbers of vulnerabilities, types of threats, customer verticals, and even what's included in the category of cybersecurity.

In Chapter 1 you saw examples of many security breach reports that are freely available to help you understand the scope of the challenges a global security team encounters daily. Reading as many different reports as you can is a best practice and necessary before you present "supportive" data to your executive team or the board of directors. There are many explanations to support the different definitions, regional exceptions, and conflicting numbers. As a best practice, you can start with the reports and downloads in Chapter 1 and then expand to other security companies like the following:

- Microsoft Security Incident Report

- Verizon 2017 Data Breach Investigations Report

- 2017 Thales Data Threat Report

- Ponemon Institute: 2016 Cost of Data Breach Study (IBM)

- 2017 Experian data breach industry forecast

Having the "correct" security metrics is an industry problem and involves more than simply counting breached records from one of the many reports, especially when you add in disparate definitions of *security incidents*, the numbers of vulnerabilities, and the framework used to enumerate accurate numbers. As an example, as discussed in Chapter 1, Verizon supports and encourages integration with a free framework called VERIS. The VERIS schema is available at https://github.com/vz-risk/veris. Another example, also discussed in Chapter 1, is in the public domain: NIST's National Vulnerability Database.

> *The Common Weakness Enumeration Specification (CWE) provides a common language of discourse for discussing, finding and dealing with the causes of software security vulnerabilities as they are found in code, design, or system architecture.*

The following are the two key components of the NVD support structure:

- The categorization of security is maintained at https://nvd.nist.gov/vuln/categories. Additionally, the MITRE Corporation with support from the National Cyber Security Division (DHS Department of Homeland Security) supports the

- The NVD uses the Common Vulnerability Scoring System (CVSS) version 2, which is an open standard for assigning vulnerability impacts that is used by a variety of organizations. The complete guide to use the free resource is at https://www.first.org/cvss/v2/guide.

Gaining and understanding how a report classifies and measures threats or even what's included as cybersecurity is different from organization to organization. The different terms, ways of accounting, and approaches make oranges-to-oranges comparisons difficult; however, you as a security architect needs to defend the security language when challenged.

Finally, you should read credible resources, such as Kreps on Security (`https://krebsonsecurity.com/`) and Mandiant (now part of FireEye).

> *The American private security firm Mandiant (in 2013) published a 60-page report that detailed about the notorious Chinese hacking group 'Unit 61398', suspected of waging cyber warfare against American companies, organizations and government agencies.*

These types of insight are released separately from the yearly security reports and provide greater details about other nations' cybersecurity armies. There are many types of reports, and some can be found at `https://www.fireeye.com/current-threats/threat-intelligence-reports.html`.

In the FireEye reports from just a few years ago, a Chinese cyber-army was linked to China's 2nd Bureau of the People's Liberation Army (PLA) General Staff Department (GSD) 3rd Department (Military Cover Designator 61398). Organized criminal groups continue to leverage ransomware to extort money from facilities rich with personally identifiable information (PII) like hospitals. PII refers to names, addresses, e-mails, home phone numbers, Social Security numbers, and more.

Now to the Why and How Cyber-Attacks Are Achieved

The Verizon 2017 Data Breach Investigation Report (DBIR) includes a starting point to understand the data from the year 2016 and what to plan for in the coming year. Figure B-8 shows the Verizon research team's perspective of the following:

- Attackers
- Tactics
- Victims
- Commonality

Figure B-8. *2017 Verizon DBIR executive summary*

Notice the correlation of 75 percent outsiders (not inside the company) and 51 percent of organized criminal groups with a view of tactics: 81 percent of the breaches are leveraged stolen or weak passwords. Victims were targeted, with 24 percent affecting financial organizations. The report shows that 73 percent of the attacks were financially motivated, and 66 percent of the malware was installed by malicious e-mail attachments (aka 66 percent successful phishing attempts).

As you continue to read the breach trends, several key areas help define attack details such as the type of attackers who use botnets (robot code) to steal passwords and breached point-of-sales (POS) systems. You need to be aware of the types of breaches and how web sites, specifically, can be breached, as identified by the Open Web Application Security Project (OWASP) Top Ten list. You can find the current 2017 Top Ten list candidates (not finalized for 2017) at `https://www.owasp.org/index.php/Category:OWASP_Top_Ten_Project#tab=OWASP_Top_10_for_2017_Release_Candidate`.

▪ **Security Tip**   As part of your cybersecurity training effort to educate users, you should include information about logging into social consumer web sites that support only single-factor authentication (username and password), but the user enters their name, address phone, and other data as part of the enrollment processes. Users should leverage sites that support two-factor authentication because not all web sites provide the necessary security to protect your PII data.

As you read through the data in the 2017 DBIR, the patterns of attacks are categorized by industries such as the following:

- Retail
- Public
- Manufacturing
- Information
- Healthcare
- Finance
- Education
- Accommodation

If your company clearly aligns with one of these sectors, then it would benefit you and the security team to read the attack details including patterns, actions, and assets that were specifically quantified for the attack based on the sector.

Appendix A defined a distributed denial-of-service (DDoS) attack and how it differs from a DoS, and often you may hear questions about a DDoS attack that targets a specific sector. Figure B-9 profiles the DDoS size by industry.

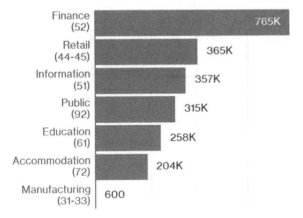

Figure B-9. *2017 Verizon DBIR industry median DDoS size (pps) by industry (n=2,133)*

The best way for you to learn the significance of a DDoS attack is to leverage the necessary background in the TCP/IP LAN communication, specifically for preparing conversations to explain to executives and members of the board of directors.

The normalization in 2017 and 2018 is to protect revenue-generating or publicly facing web applications and server infrastructures from DDoS attacks. A successful DDoS attack is a malicious attempt to take an online service offline or make it unavailable to users, typically by temporarily interrupting or suspending the web services. If you needed to summarize the type of DDoS attacks, it may be helpful to define the network flooding used by DDoS and categorize them into three significant types of flooding.

- Protocol based (ping of death, SYN flood)

- Application layer based (slow Apache or IIS web site response using HTTP GET/POST floods)

- Volume based (UDP, ICMP floods)

▪ **Security Tip**   Please refer to Appendix A for detailed defections and insight into some of the cybersecurity terms used. Also, you can gain insight into definition details using security vendor education sites like Sans.org or Imperva at `https://www.incapsula.com/ddos/ddos-attacks/`.

The large Internet network/wide area network (WAN) service providers have put in place DDoS identification services as well as DDoS protection services. The DDoS protection is architected to withstand a DDoS WAN attack in the magnitude of gigabits per second (Gb/sec). This is an important metric to understand because in the IT world the normal acronym is gigabytes per second (GB/sec). The small difference is a magnitude of 8:1 because 1 byte of data = 8 bits of data.

▪ **Security Tip**   Implementing protection again DDoS attacks is important, and one of the many security companies providing this service is Cloudflare. This company's products, like many others, have a free option for personal web sites or small business web sites. You can read the details at `https://www.cloudflare.com/`.

Refer to the 2017 Verizon DBIR things to consider list shown in Figure B-10 to start creating security best practices. This particular information is displayed for the accommodations and food services sector. The security risks are equally challenging for any company that provides methods of credit card payment services.

Things to consider:

Killing me softly with malware – The level of software installation occurring in this industry needs to decrease as this particular variety of integrity compromise represents 94% of breaches this year.

Remove this tab before use – Don't use default passwords as doing so makes criminals' lives much easier.

You can't get there from here – Filter remote access to your POS network. Only allow connections from whitelisted IP addresses.

Don't be outdated – Patch promptly and consistently and make certain all terminals and servers are running the most recent version of software.

Figure B-10. *2017 Verizon DBIR things to consider*

The Verizon 2017 DBIR report provides insight into industries such as financial, insurance, and healthcare. Detailed case incident insight about botnets and event chaining is provided. In addition, as shown in Figure B-11, time to discovery is identified as a continuing metric.

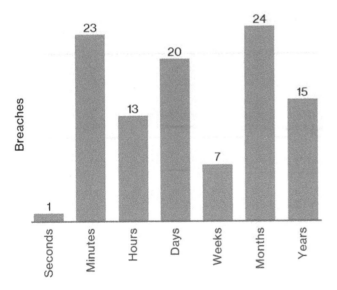

Figure B-11. *Verizon 2017 DBIR report showing time to discovery within healthcare industry breaches (n=103)*

Understanding the timelines for the breach of a network is an important metric, as is the time to discovery after the breach. The discovery processes are not easy and require correlation of all security log files with automated intelligence to alert on the breach attributes as a positive identification or a false alert. The normalization of TCP/IP traffic and normal alert data.

The example of the healthcare time to discovery is the first example of each sector identified in the Verizon 2017 DBIR report. Not all sectors identified have the same type of data graph, however. This report, like the others highlighted in Chapter 1, is important to read and use as a reference. You need to learn about the types of successful attacks such as ransomware, which often is a "weaponized" e-mail attachment that targets your end users. If you look at the details in Figure B-12, the rise of ransomware needs to be a concern.

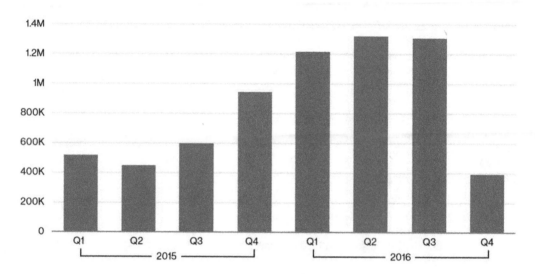

Figure B-12. *Verizon 2017 DBIR new ransomware samples per quarter (source: McAfee Labs)*

The ease of payment using bitcoins has made this cybersecurity attack popular and profitable for attackers. This example of ransomware highlights the family versions of attacks like Locky and CyptoWall, both variants of ransomware malware. This is a quote from the 2017 Verizon DBIR:

> *This big decline is mostly due to a reduction in generic ransomware detections, as well as a decrease in Locky and CryptoWall variants.*

You have come a long way on the cybersecurity journey and have gotten some insight into the types of attacks, financial motivation, and "ready to hack" tools at attackers' disposal that require little to no coding skills. The security breach reports are a great tool to use in security team awareness training and to gain insight into the measurement of attacks on a global basis. As cybersecurity attacks increase, you must leverage cloud security solutions such as Microsoft Azure Security Center to improve your cloud security posture, reduce security risks, and better enable your company's secure cloud.

APPENDIX C

■ ■ ■

Security Frameworks

Helpful Security Models

This appendix covers three security awareness models and three security strategies.

Security Awareness Models

This section discusses three security awareness models to help you understand the necessary frameworks used for designing and delivering an IT security awareness program. As you move into key positions in the IT security industry, it becomes important to understand and use specific frameworks.

This section compares these three security awareness models:

- NIST 800-50

- NIST 800-14

- European Model

NIST 800-50

This model, titled "Building an Information Technology Security Awareness and Training Program," is a good starting framework for you to understand. Many of the key areas in the framework support legal requirements such as these:

- Federal Information Security Management Act (FISMA) 2002

- Office of Management and Budget (OMB) Circular A-130

The model emphasizes that strong security awareness training is critical to keep customer security risks low. It provides the steps for designing an awareness program, including implementation and guidance on postimplementation steps.

This document includes a section for developing awareness and training material, but it is outdated. One of the shortfalls of this document, in the current version, is the fact that many new online components are available. Newer options are necessary to keep the attention of today's workforce, and using dated material can weaken the overall program.

This document does provide good guidance on delivering an awareness program, with three common approaches to support the business:

- Centralized policy, strategy, and implementation

- Centralized policy and strategy, distributed implementation

- Centralized policy, distributed strategy and implementation

These are different approaches to delivering an awareness program based on a distribution model that best supports the industry and users' locations.

There continues to be areas that aid in key deliverables for a successful program including establishing priorities, setting the bar on complexity, and funding the program (always challenging). Some of the document covers the topic of "partnership" with the delivery; however, the specifics of getting the message accepted by funding management is not addressed. This document clearly needs to be updated to support more current business cases and legislation.

NIST 800-14

"Generally Accepted Principles and Practices for Securing Information Technology Systems" is another NIST standard. This document is more supportive of overall security and not just a security awareness program, and it provides key guidance on policies and procedures.

This model is more focused on multinational businesses and internal business needs than the one previously covered. Areas of discussion include the size of a business; however, the security challenges are nearly identical in small vs. large businesses.

This document is for users focused on the management level and is more programmatic as a guide and not a framework. As with the previous NIST 800-50 document, the information and references are dated. It is not all out-of-date, but clearly using the Organization for Economic Co-operation and Development (OECD) guidelines from 1992 is not that relevant.

This guide needs to be updated to support the modern challenges of bring-your-own-device (BYOB) policies, tablets, mobile phones, and cloud technologies. There is great reference information for the following policies:

- Program policy

- Issue-specific policy

- System-specific policy

- Other policies

This document provides information found in other documents, such as risk management, risk assessment, and risk mitigation; however, there are topics described in great detail that should be considered in any awareness program or policy guide, such as uncertainty analysis and life-cycle planning.

Much of the document is focused on providing references for policy specifics such as the following:

- Personnel user issues

- User administration

- Preparing for contingencies and disasters

- Business plan

This document provides some details about the security awareness model but does not focus on this topic; it branches to other policy information.

European Model

"Implementation guide: How to make your organization aware of IT security" is similar to the NIST 800-50 guide, but a world of differences can be seen when compared to the NIST 800-14 guide. The opening pages provide a well-organized document and focus on the following:

- Perspective

- Getting started

- Four-phase approach

- Security awareness

The guide provides an overwhelming amount of information not covered in detail in the other two guides reviewed. Oftentimes documents introduce a topic and then move on; however, the European Model helps to identify the key role of the program manager. In addition to the role, attributes specific to the role are identified.

- Current roles and responsibilities

- Experience

- Skills

These are addressed in a table with relation information to make the feature meaningful and useful. Considerations of the resources needed are addressed, such as the following:

- Number of staff in the business

- Diversity of the staff

- Current security awareness level

One important area that is addressed in this document is diversity. The individual backgrounds and religions of employees are necessary to consider in today's business environment. Often the differences are felt around the holidays. For example, today most companies no longer have a "Christmas Party" but a "Winter Celebration Party" instead.

This guide uses a four-phase approach: scope, design, build, and execute. There are many graphs and tables to help deliver the message; this is different from the other two models, which are more text-based. Besides the numerous graphics with text interlaced, the document provides tips and warnings to help make each step more successful. The information is easy to follow and continues in the same manner through all four phases.

Summary

This section reviewed three security awareness models: NIST 800-50, NIST 800-14, and the European Model. The comparative analysis provides a clear frontrunner in completeness. The leading favorite is the European Model, "Implementation guide: How to make your organization aware of IT."

The information in NIST 800-16 is clearly a framework for more than just a security awareness program; however, to provide the breadth of data, the information is at a very high level. The information in the NIST 800-50 and the European Model are similar; however, the European Model provides information in a much more engaging manner. For a first-time user's guide, the European Model offers greater detail, better tables, and more guidance.

Analysis of Security Strategies and Frameworks

Businesses today must invest in the ever-changing requirements of security for their products, their intellectual property, their data, their computer networks, and their customers' privacy if the business wants to maintain public trust. It is often noted that if a business does not invest in profitability and in securing a future from threats (both physical threats and computer threats, as well as market competitors or cheap imitations), it is destined to go out of business in the future. This doesn't mean just store closings or consolidation or even Chapter 11 bankruptcy; a business simply cannot be in business without re-investing in its future. Security, including physical security and computer security, should be a high priority for every modern business today.

How do businesses, banks, hospitals, city governments, or schools choose to implement a framework that secures their computer network? What is the cost to implement and maintain a security infrastructure? What is the cost if they do not? What is the cost if the business, government, or hospital does not invest continuously in a security framework? Target Corporation may tell you it costs $3.6 billion (for more information, see https://www.pcisecuritystandards.org/). The estimates for liability from the security breach that Target "fell victim to" is one of the largest levied by the PCI Council that was formed by Visa, Mastercard, Discover, and American Express. The group defines how organizations manage cardholder data, and if retailers are found in violation of the standard, they can be fined anywhere from $50 to $90 per cardholder, as in the case of the Target security breach.

This discussion recognizes the business need to protect information and informational assets by promoting three architecture frameworks (security frameworks) to prevent a security breach like at Target. The goal is to review the three security frameworks so you are aware of their differences and can choose one to embrace and deploy for your organization. In addition, this appendix covers features that may be more applicable to specific types of security protection based on the nature of the security attributes or the business needs or both.

Zachman Framework

In the late 1980s and early 1990s, John Zachman continued to pioneer his work with business systems and refine an architecture framework to better model an enterprise design. This design concept, in its current version, is called the Zachman framework. Originally the presentations for this framework used buildings to best describe the concept of building blocks that could be rotated to fit a structure.

This framework helps an enterprise create a structure to clarify the relationships of the attributes that comprise the enterprise. The key component is a six-by-five matrix for classifying ideas into concrete operational levels. Zachman continued to evolve the solution by enabling better communication with six questions that comprise the columns on the x-axis of the framework, always presented in this order from left to right: why, how, what, who, where, and when. To complete the framework, the y-axis is as follows, from top to bottom: scope, business model, system model, technology model, detailed, and function enterprise. The intersection of the x- and y-axes creates a cell that has specific value to the interacting x- and y-components. Each cell's value is based on the cause and effect of the related variables. Six columns across multiplied by five rows down results in thirty-six cells that are equally important.

Once you have clearly defined the matrix for your enterprise, the next logical step would be for the framework to provide guidance for the deployment of your architecture. This is when the first controversies of the Zachman framework are realized, because its documentation does not cover how to manage or use the information described by the progression. In fact, many different interpretations of the framework have been used to organize and analyze data, schemes, and analytic models, and this framework does not specifically support a security framework in a business enterprise. One may ask, what good is it?

The Zachman framework has been successful in the management of enterprise models based on the connection it creates between the physical enterprise and the roles and responsibilities inside the enterprise. When deployed for information technology (and business or government agencies), it has been a successful model for building in an organized manner. However, be careful because the matrix is rigid and requires certain rules such as the following: columns are interchangeable but cannot be reduced or created, every column can have its own meta-model, each relationship is interdependent but unique, and so on. Another caution is certifying a successful deployment, which is achievable without certification but daunting.

A key feature that may help IT organizations decide to use this framework is that it was consciously defined to support independence and remove any need of other structures. This independence is key to IT infrastructure deployment; however, a negative feature is that the architecture teams are faced with 36 cells that have the same "weight" of importance to the enterprise. This even-handed distribution is not the best implementation for an IT organization; it would be better to assign an importance to each cell depending on a lower, average, or higher significance.

One final important strength of the Zachman framework is the explicit views that address the enterprise architecture; they provide an almost mandatory need to create documentation in the form of procedures. This allows IT organizations to concentrate on documentation as needed based on that the specified business implementation for knowledge management in car manufacturing is different from a government agency, for example. This is the first strategy, in the form of a framework, covered in this appendix; now I'll review two additional methods that provide different processes for creating a security framework.

Sherwood Applied Business Security Architecture (SABSA)

The primary characteristic of the Sherwood Applied Business Security Architecture is that it provides a narrower focus of operational security as the lines between business and IT disappear. SABSA is a framework, much like the Zachman framework previously discussed, where the structure provides a methodology for IT security enterprises. SABSA, like Zachman, was developed independently and has similarities that include but are not limited to structure. The SABSA model's driving factor is determining the criticality of a risk based on the specific business requirements or expansions, and the framework promotes two-way traceability. SABSA allows you to identify whether the business requirements have been met and the business justifications have been satisfied.

The Sherwood Applied Business Security Architecture is designed and implemented in the business life cycle to preserve the ongoing management and measurement of IT security. Some of the differences from the Zachman framework are in the matrix that you create when using the framework; specifically, each of the 36 cells has a different weighting. The original SABSA matrix includes AssetsWhat, MotivationWhy, ProcessHow, PeopleWho, LocationWhere, and Time/When. This matrix is designed to support the business and security models of IT and operational technology, and you can customize the matrix to meet your business needs.

A key similarity to the Zachman framework is that the attributes used when integrating or deploying the SABSA framework are similar; the attributes support any industry standards, sectors, and organizations. The framework can be used for development by architects to any scope or detail and is an open standard for models, methods, and processes. The Sherwood Applied Business Security Architecture requires no licensing for the organization, so its implementation may be more appealing for some.

The SABSA architecture accelerates the concept of the Zachman framework with the use of six specific views: business view, architecture view, designer view, builder view, tradesperson view, and service manager view. Specifically, for security implementation, the six views (layers) correlate this way: the business view is the "contextual" security architecture, the architect view is the "conceptual" security architecture, the designer view is the logical security architecture, the builder view is the physical security architecture, the tradesperson view is the component security architecture, and finally the services manager view is the security service management architecture. Unlike the Zachman framework, each layer, one on top of the other, creates the security service management architecture to support the four parts of the IT life cycle: strategy, design, implementation, and management and operations.

Some of the positive aspects are the security questions that the Sherwood Applied Business Security Architecture proposes so that they can be answered by the business. It includes questions about security goals to achieve, detailed functional descriptions, types of users (i.e., office, mobile, etc.), geographical infrastructure requirements, and usage times (i.e., 24/7, 8 hours/day, etc.). The SABSA matrix also asks about assets to be protected, motivation for security, processes needed for security, people vs. organization aspects, locations for security, and time-related aspects for security.

Additionally, the SABSA taxonomy for business attributes include the following: Users, Management, Operations, Risk Management, Legal/Regulatory, Technical Strategy, and Business Strategy. In short, it is an encompassing security framework with a well-defined matrix; in fact, it's more encompassing than the Zachman framework for the scope of the entire business. The use of SABSA as a framework is not specifically designed for small, isolated projects, however; a certain level of complexity is needed for SABSA.

SABSA and the Zachman framework attempt to answer who, what, when, where, why, and how for each layer in an organization. SABSA doesn't replace the Zachman framework but can enhance it by including security-focused directives that Zachman failed to realize. Using both strategies is a way of filling in the gaps in security that the Zachman framework does not address.

One other strategy examined in this discussion may address the need to implement two frameworks, examined next.

The Open Group Architectural Framework (TOGAF)

TOGAF was initiated in early 1990 and registered as the Open Group Architectural Framework in 2011 by the Open Group. It is clearly a different approach from the previous two frameworks discussed; it uses a less complex model that focuses on only four levels: business, application, data, and technology.

TOGAF has similar attributes as the SABSA and Zachman frameworks in the deliverables; it explains how to define an information system; shows how the "blocks" fit together; and supports a set of tools, standards, and a defined vocabulary.

A negative aspect of the Open Group Architectural Framework is that it does not follow the ANSI/ IEEE Standard 1471-2000 specification of architecture to the letter. The base is from the Architecture Development Method (ADM).

TOGAF is based on interrelated attributes titled *architecture domains* that create a foundation architecture and method for conducting enterprise information architecture planning and implementation. As mentioned, these domains include business architecture, application architecture, data architecture, and technical architecture. TOGAF is one of the Open Groups frameworks that is free to organizations for internal noncommercial purposes but controversially has a license associated with commercial deployment. The Open Group does not provide the TOGAF framework for "free," as in free beer.

One major difference between TOGAF and the Sherwood Applied Business Security Architecture is the wide adoption specifically for security and securing business requirements. The framework touches on virtually all the same subjects as the other two but from a different perspective and context. As revisions are made, disciplines are extended in scope and added to address shortcomings. The current TOFAF version is 9.1.

Similar to the Sherwood Applied Business Security Architecture framework, the Open Group Architectural Framework has endorsement by the large membership of the Open Group's Architecture Forum.

Summary

This appendix reviewed three different modeling frameworks that you can implement to support the security infrastructure of a business. The three strategies are the Zachman framework, the Sherwood Applied Business Security Architecture (SABSA), and the Open Group Architectural Framework (TOGFA). Each of them is excellent and equally flawed. As you learned, a great deal of overlap exists between enterprise, solutions, and business architectural frameworks.

It should be clear by now that deploying a security framework and then never revisiting it is no longer sufficient to support the security of the business, business products, or customers' data. A security framework enables the business and does not inhibit the business. However, the question remains, why do architectures sometimes fail?

One reason is that some organizations implement solutions with a technical goal, so the entire implementation is tactical for IT and does not focus on the business or shareholders. Like the need to keep bad guys out, a requirement is identified, and a single product is found, acquired, and deployed without the correct business model to review the broader implications. A project was started and completed without consideration to the entire security system plan.

Another reason architectures sometimes fail is that the cost of a specific security solution is sometimes disproportionate to the cost of deployment to mitigate the risk for protecting the business property or product. Yet another reason, and sadly often the truth for business, is that security is sometimes the last item to be considered when designing new business information systems. The problem then becomes even bigger, such as a specific security solution being isolated and not truly integrated. This approach of a "different hammer for each nail" leads to increased complexity, cost, and administration.

Target Corporation's record-breaking $3.6 billion in fines due to a data breach was just the tip of the iceberg; two class action lawsuits have been filed in the U.S. District Court in Minnesota on behalf of Target customers who were impacted (for more information, see `http://www.mercurynews.com/business/ci_24780851/targets-40-million-customer-data-breach-could-become`). Attorneys for the plaintiffs expect the class-action lawsuit to exceed $5 million. But what's $5 million more compared to the billions already levied?

If you are new to the security enterprise architect role, the question you must answer is how much would it cost the corporation if you did not implement a security framework that is integrated and supportive of every security aspect of the business?

Index

A

AAD. *See* Azure Active Directory (AAD)
Access control list (ACL), 152
Advanced Encryption Standard (AES), 176
Advanced persistent threat (APT), 175
Application vulnerability, 4
Asymmetric cryptography, 176
Attack method definitions, 177
    botnet arms, 178
    botnet DDoS attack, 178
    DNS amplification, 178
    DoS attack, 177
    HaaS platforms, 178
    HOIC, 178
    HTTP flood, 178
    LOIC, 178
    NTP amplification, 178
    ping flood, 178
    ping of death, 178
    smurf attack, 178
    SYN flood, 178
    UDP flood, 178
Availability, 176
Azure Active Directory (AAD), 45
Azure Resource Manager (ARM), 109, 165
Azure Security Center, 13
    accumulation, 57
    advanced detection capabilities, 57
    areas, 55
    challenges, cloud security, 56–57
    cloud deployment infrastructure, 55
    collection of data, 57
    configuration
        areas, 99
        Azure SQL servers and storage
          components, 102
        color coded, security health, 103
        Contoso.com, 75
        data collection, 77, 79, 82–83
        default dashboard, 96
        features, 98

        functions, operations team and
          security architect, 75
        infrastructure design (*see* Infrastructure
          design, Azure)
        Internet-facing endpoints, 100
        next-generation firewall, 104
        pricing tier, 83, 85
        SaaS, 75
        security health of Azure web
          applications, 103
        standard tier advantages (*see* Standard
          tier advantages)
        type of data the security team, 99
        virtual machines' resource security
          health, 97
        VM deployed, Azure subscription, 101
        vnets and virtual machines, 98
    Contoso.com, 73
    diagnostics, 165–167, 171–174
    evaluating, 105
    event management (SEIM) systems, 58
    functional perspectives, 57
    guidance, 105
    identification, security alerts, 58
    Internet addresses, 57
    intrusion detection and
        prevention, 55, 57
    on-premises security information, 58
    recommendations procedures, 109
        endpoint protection, 109–114
        NSG, 119–129
        prevention blade, 117–119
        remediate OS vulnerabilities, 115–116
    Security Center Placement (*see* Security
        Center placement)
    security control recommendations, 57
    security health monitoring, 106–108
    SOC generation capabilities, 58
    supscription (*see* Supscription, Azure
        Security Center)
    systems and networks, 57
    traditional log analysis, 58

© Marshall Copeland 2017
M. Copeland, *Cyber Security on Azure*, DOI 10.1007/978-1-4842-2740-4

Azure Security Center Cost Model. *See* Cost model,
    Azure Security Center
Azure virtual networking
    cloud administrators, 62
    Contoso, in chapter exercises, 63
    creation, 62
    fundamentals, 62
    on-premises network design, 62
    on-premises to Azure VPN connection, 63, 64
    TCP/IP communication, 62
    TCP/IP subnetting, 62

▓ B

Barracuda product trial, 151
Bitcoin, 175
Black hat, 175
Booters, 178
Botnet arms, 178
Botnet DDoS attacks, 178
BOT or botnet, 175
Brash cyber-attacks, 12
Breach, 175
Bring-your-own-device (BYOB), 196
Bring your own licenses (BYOL), 154
Brute-force dictionary attack, 24
Business
    cyber-attacks, 9
    loss of assets
        direct impact, 8
        indirect impact, 9
    unsecured solution, 11
    valuable assets, 8
Business continuity planning (BCP), 33

▓ C

Certified Ethical Hacker (CEH), 105
Certified expert penetration tester (CEPT), 48
Certified information systems security
    professional (CISSP), 48
Certified security analysis (CSA), 48
Certified security software lifecycle
    profession (CSSLP), 48
Chief executive officers (CEOs), 7
Chief information security officers (CISOs), 4
Cisco Annual Security Report, 23
Cloud architects, 11
Cloud computing, Navigating Microsoft Azure.
    See Navigating Microsoft Azure
Cloud security
    challenges, 56–57
    knowledge, 179
Cloud security professional (CCSP), 48
Command and control (C&C), 175

Common configuration enumeration ID
    (CCEID), 116
Common Platform Enumeration (CPE)
    dictionary, 28, 31
Common Vulnerabilities and Exposures (CVEs), 28
Common Vulnerability Scoring System (CVSS), 12
Common Weakness Enumeration
    Specification (CWE), 188
Confidential, 176
Confidentiality, integrity, availability (CIA), 176
Contoso.com network, 73, 106
Contoso Marketing Corporation, 10
Cost model, Azure Security Center
    AAD, 45
    Application Gateway, 46–47
    business-compliant reasons, 33
    cost of software, 33
    customers responsibility, 52
    data storage, 39
    enterprise, 49–50
    enterprise security architecture, 48
    firewall virtual applications, 47
    hybrid cloud infrastructure, 34
    intrusion detection systems, 33
    IPSs, 33
    license cost (*see* License cost of
        Security Center)
    on-premises datacenters, 34
    ransomware (*see* Ransomware)
    risk assessments and cost-benefit analysis
        annualized loss expectancy, 40
        annualized rate of occurrence, 40
        asset value, 40
        calculations, 41
        CISO, 40
        controls, 40
        exposure factor, 40
        flowchart, 41
        formula, security cost
            justification, 40
        maximum tolerable downtime, 44
        ransomeware, 42–44
        recovery point objective, 44
        recovery time objective, 44
        single loss expectancy, 40
        steps, 41–42
        types, 40
    shared cost model (*see* Shared cost model)
    support plans, 46
Cost-benefit analysis. *See* Cost model, Azure
    Security Center
Cross-site scripting (XSS), 145
Cryptographic hash file, 24
Cryptography, 176
Cyber-attacker, 6

Cyber-attacks, 105
    achieving, 189–192, 194
Cyber-crimes, 6
Cyber-reference, 174–175
Cybersecurity, 105, 179
    analysis, 11
    attack details, 188–189
    cloud architects, 11
    program, 61–62
    publications, 25

D

Data Breach Investigation
    Report (DBIR), 189
Data collection of Azure Security Center
    default "Security policy", 81
    default standard tier cost, 77
    options, 82
    Policy blade and Security policy blade
        journey, 80
    portal configuration changes, 83
    selection, 78
    welcome message, 79
Data Encryption Standard
    (DES), 176
Data storage, cost, 39
DDoS as a service, 178
Denial-of-service (DoS) attack, 117, 152, 177
Detection and security alerts, 133–137,
    139–140, 142
    anomaly and behavioral attack, 141
Dictionary attack, 24, 137
Digital certificate, 176
Digital security, 176
Digital Signature Algorithm (DSA), 176
Disaster recovery planning
    (DRP), 33
Distributed denial-of-service (DDoS)
    attack, 177, 191
DNS amplification, 178

E

Elliptical Cure Cryptography (ECC), 176
E-mail alerting in Security Center
    changes, notification policy, 91
    notification options, 90
    notification window message, 92
Encryption techniques, 177
Enterprise security architecture
    design solutions, 48
    generic, 48
    NIST, 49
    SAML, 48

    Sherwood applied business security
        architecture, 50
    Zachman framework, 49
Entropy, 24
European model, 197
Event-Logging service, 167
Executive
    capital expenditures, 4
    CISO, 4
    cyber-attacks, 6
    IT services, 7
    KPIs and KRIs, 4
    migrating cloud, 4
    NIST, 5
    NVD, 4–5, 28
    operational expenditures, 4
    reports, 5
    security analysts and architects, 5
    security breaches, 6
    security data, 4
    security resources, 5
    vulnerability, 6
Exfiltration, 17
Exploit, 175
Exploit kit, 12

F

Federal Information Security Management
    Act (FISMA) 195, 2002
File Transfer Protocol (FTP), 152
FireEye M-Trends 2017 Annual Security
    Report, 23

G

General Staff Department (GSD), 189
Georgia Tech Emerging Cyber
    Threats Report, 24
GitHub, 13
Graphics processing unit (GPU), 136
Gray hat, 175

H

HaaS platforms, 178
Hacker, 175
Hacking as a service (HaaS), 178
Hash function, 177
Hashing algorithm, 177
High Orbit Ion Cannon (HOIC), 178
HTTP flood, 178
Hypertext Markup Language, 152
Hypertext Transfer Protocol (HTTP), 145
    load balancing, 46

I, J

IBM-sponsored Ponemon Cost of Data
    Breach Study
    download, 22
    Global Analysis, 20
    importance, 22
    per-capita cost by industry classification, 22
    PII, 20
    records by country, 21
Information Systems Audit and Control
    Association (ISACA), 175
Infrastructure as a service (IaaS), 166
Infrastructure design, Azure
    administrator perspective, virtual
        machines, 77
    Contoso.com, 76
    network security processes, 76
    subnet deployment, POC designs, 76
Institute for Information Security and
    Privacy (IISP), 24
Integrity, 177
Intrusion detection systems (IDSs), 33
Intrusion prevention systems (IPSs), 33

K

Kali Linux, 185–187
Key performance indicators (KPIs), 4
Key risk indicators (KRIs), 4

L

License cost of Security Center
    cost analysis, 37
    free tier and standard tier pricing, 37
    node, 39
    selection, 38
    SLA, 39
    standard tier, 38
Line-of-business (LOB) engineering
    tool, 180
Linux system, 171
Local Security Authority Subsystem
    Service, 166
Low Orbit Ion Cannon (LOIC), 178

M

Malicious Software Removal Tool, 31
Malware, 175
Man-in-the-cloud attack, 14
Man-in-the-middle attack, 14
Mathematical algorithms (encryption), 177
Message digest, 177
Metasploit's framework, 184

Microsoft Azure
    management program, 27
    multifactor authentication, 26
    open authentication solutions, 26
    security certifications, 30
    services customers, 29
    vnets, 26
Microsoft Security Intelligence Report
    Azure Security Center, 13
    CVSS, 12
    download, 14
    Hackers breached networks, 12
    information, 13
    IT tool security teams, 12
    security-compliant system, 13
    SIR information, 13
    software vulnerabilities, 13

N

National Institution of Standards and
    Technology (NIST), 5, 25
Navigating Microsoft Azure
    cloud computing, 71
    creation, 71
    IT infrastructure, 71
    portal to start building Contoso.com test
        infrastructure, 72
    subscription, 71
Network security groups (NSG), 106,
    119, 131, 172
    architecting, 120
    best practices, 122, 129
    configuration, 76
    default inbound, 121
    default outbound, 121
    implementing, 119
    IP subnets restrictions, 120
    IP subnet to remove security
        risks, 122–128
    mid-tier and database IP subnets, 120
    perimeter network, 120
    rules, 119
Network Time Protocol (NTP) amplification, 178
Next-generation firewall (NGF), 131, 152–153
    adding, 153–156
Nonrepudiation, 177

O

Office of Management and Budget (OMB), 195
Offline attacks, 24
Online attacks, 24
Open Group Architectural Framework
    (TOGAF), 200
Open Systems Interconnection (OSI) model, 46

Open Web Application Security Project (OWASP), 26, 46, 59, 190
Operating system (OS), 166
Operational security assurance (OSA), 131
Organization for Economic Co-operation and Development (OECD), 196
Original equipment manufacturer (OEM), 131

P

Packet filter rules, 152
"Partner solutions" blade, 144
Pass-the-hash attack, 139
Password hash file, 24
Patching process, 144
People's Liberation Army (PLA), 189
Personally identifiable information (PII), 20
Ping flood, 178
Ping of death, 178
Platform as a service (PaaS) services, 165
Prevention blade, 117–119
Private key, 176
Process Explorer program, 171
Professional education, 180, 182–183
Public key, 176
Public key cryptography, 179
Public Key Infrastructure (PKI), 179

Q

Qualys vulnerability assessment, 163
Qualys vulnerability solution, 157
Quantitative risk assessments, Security Center cost model. *See* Cost model, Azure Security Center

R

Ransomware, 42–44, 176
    awareness, 52
    e-mail, 51
    forms, 50
    requirement, 52
    risk, 51
    spear phishing, 50
    Verizon DBIR report, 51
    whale phishing, 50
Red hat, 176
Reflector, 178
Remote Desktop Protocol (RDP), 122, 135
Rivest-Shamir-Adleman (RSA) algorithms, 176
Role-based administration access control (RBAC), 109

S

Secret-key cryptography, 177
Secure Sockets Layer (SSL), 179
    offloading, 46
Security as a service (SaaS), 105
Security awareness models, 195
    European model, 197
    NIST 196, 800–814
    NIST 195–196, 800–850
Security Center placement
    areas, 60
    Azure Security Center, 58
    cloud deployments, 59
    cybersecurity framework function and identifier categories, 59
    detection, 58
    development, cybersecurity program, 61–62
    financial resources, 58
    measures, controls and security protection, 58
    Microsoft's global cybersecurity knowledge, 58
    networking, 62–64
    NIST Cybersecurity Framework, 59
    OWASP, 59
    prevention, Azure Infrastructure Breach, 60
    security teams, 58
Security Center updates, 131, 133
Security-compliant system, 13
Security Content Automation Protocol (SCAP), 28
Security health monitoring, 106–108
Security incidents, 188
Security information and event management (SEIM), 39, 47
Security Operations Center (SOC), 58
Security recommendations procedures, 109, 142–145
    endpoint protection, 109–114
    NSG, 119
        architecting, 120
        best practices, 122, 129
        default inbound, 121
        default outbound, 121
        implementing, 119
        IP subnets restrictions, 120
        IP subnet to remove security risks, 122–128
        mid-tier and database IP subnets, 120
        perimeter network, 120
        rules, 119
    prevention blade, 117–119
    remediate OS vulnerabilities, 115–116
    web application firewall, 145–151
Security risk landscape, 183–187

Security strategies and frameworks, 198
    SABSA, 199–200
    TOGAF, 200
    Zachman framework, 198–199
Security strength, 176
Service level agreement (SLA), 39, 112
Shadow IT, 30
Shared cost model
    customer on-premises and Azure
        cloud hybrid security model, 35
    customers, 36
    hybrid infrastructure model, 34
    IaaS, PaaS and SaaS, 36
    IT security, 34
    Microsoft Azure, 35
    network security model, 37
    requirements, 36
    shared responsibility, 35
Sherwood Applied Business Security
       Architecture (SABSA), 199–200
Smurf attack, 178
Software-defined network (SDN), 76
Software development life
       cycle (SDLC), 26, 151
Spear-phishing attacks, 19
Standard tier advantages
    advanced threat detection, 85
    anomaly detection, 86
    behavioral analysis, 87
    "Choose your pricing tier", 89
    crash analysis, 86
    e-mail alerting, 90–93
    notification, 89
    policy changes
        changes, free tier to standard, 96
        prevention, 93
        save, 95–96
        subscription, 96
        vulnerability assessment, 94
    security features, 85
    selections, 87
    Standard-Free Trial option, 89
    standard tier change policy, 88
    subscription, 88
    threat intelligence, 86
Strength, definition, 177
Stressers, 178
Supscription, Azure Security Center
    Confirmation page and guidance, 70
    Credit card verification, 68
    free Azure trial, 66
    free trail, 66, 67
    Hotmail account creation, 67
    limits, 71
    navigation, 71–72

    options, 64
    purchase, 65
Support options, 46
Symmetric cryptography, 177
SYN flood, 178
Sysinternals, 168, 170–171
System Center Operations Manager
       (SCOM), 131–132
System security, knowledge, 179

■ T

Threat, 176
Transmission Control Protocol/Internet
       Protocol (TCP/IP), 174
TrendMicro, 112
Triple DES (3DES), 176
Troubleshooting, 165–167, 171–174

■ U

UDP flood, 178

■ V

Verizon 2016 Data Breach Investigations
       Report
    download, 20
    exfiltration, 17
    exploit details, 17–18
    features, 16, 19
    VERIS, 17
Verizon 2017 Data Breach Investigations Report
    download, 16
    executive briefing section, 15
    executive summary, 15–16
Virtual machines (VMs), 165
Virtual networks (vnets), 26
VM health blade, 108
Vocabulary for Event Recording and Incident
       Sharing (VERIS), 17, 188
Vulnerability, 176
Vulnerability assessment integration, 157
    adding, 158–163

■ W, X, Y

Weakness, 176
Web application firewall (WAF), 46, 131, 145–151
What hat, definition, 176

■ Z

Zachman framework, 198–199
Zero-day, 176

Get the eBook for only $5!

Why limit yourself?

With most of our titles available in both PDF and ePUB format, you can access your content wherever and however you wish—on your PC, phone, tablet, or reader.

Since you've purchased this print book, we are happy to offer you the eBook for just $5.

To learn more, go to http://www.apress.com/companion or contact support@apress.com.

Apress®

CPSIA information can be obtained
at www.ICGtesting.com
Printed in the USA
LVHW06s2309200418
574276LV00004B/30/P